The White Mountain Reader

THE
White Mountain
READER

Edited by
Mike Dickerman

Bondcliff Books · Littleton, New Hampshire

The White Mountain Reader

Copyright © 2000 by Mike Dickerman

Library of Congress Card Number: 00–190959

ISBN 0–9657475–8–1

Excerpts from *Shrouded Memories* appear courtesy of Floyd W. Ramsey.

"The Golden Age of the White Hills" and "Appalachian Mountain Club Trail System" appear courtesy of the Appalachian Mountain Club, 5 Joy Street, Boston, Mass., 02108.

Text composition by Passumpsic Publishing, St. Johnsbury, Vt.

Printed in the United States by Sherwin Dodge Printers, Littleton, N.H.

Additional copies of this book may be obtained directly from:
  Bondcliff Books
  P.O. Box 385
  Littleton, NH 03561

In memory of
GUY WATERMAN
Hiker, historian, friend

Contents

Introduction

I DON'T REMEMBER when it first started, this interest of mine in White Mountain history. It may have begun on Columbus Day weekend in 1982, when I made my first hiking trip up 6,288-foot Mount Washington, the highest peak in the Northeast. Just a few days after that hike, as I recall things now, I visited my hometown library in Lyndonville, Vt., and borrowed a copy of F. Allen Burt's *History of Mount Washington*, published in 1960. For some reason, I felt compelled to learn more about this mountain that I'd just climbed.

It might also have begun the following hiking season, when I took my first sojourn into the Pemigewasset Wilderness, walking along railroad grades once traversed by the logging trains of James E. Henry, the infamous White Mountain lumber baron of a century ago. Or it might have begun in May of 1984, when I started a summer job at the historic Mount Washington Hotel at Bretton Woods. As anyone who has worked at the hotel can relate, the place just oozes of history, and it's virtually impossible not to absorb at least some of that history during a full summer and fall of living and working at this relic of the Gilded Age.

At any rate, before I knew what had hit me I was transformed into a full-blown White Mountain history junkie, and as my collection of books, guides, maps, photographs and ephemera grew and grew, I realized there wasn't just a large amount of material in existence, but a large amount of *quality* material. These include Frederick Kilbourne's *Chronicles of the White Mountains*, Lucy Crawford's *History of the White Mountains*, Rev. Thomas Starr King's *The White Hills*, and John Spaulding's *Historical Relics of the White Mountains*, among others. Unfortunately, though, much of this material existed in books and newspapers either long out-of-print or at the very least not readily available to the average, modern-day reader. In effect, this left all but the most serious collectors out in the cold when it came to reading and enjoying aged material about the Whites. This just didn't seem right.

The idea of collecting into a single volume some of the more interesting pieces that I'd come across was something that I'd been thinking about for a long time, but it wasn't until just a few years ago that I figured out the proper format for such a collection. I have tried on the following pages to mesh all these selections into a new kind of pre-written history of the White Mountains, with the voices and writers of the past serving as the storytellers. Collectively, these pieces cover almost every aspect of the region's past, from the early days of exploring Mount Washington and the Presidential Range to the days when lumberjacks ruled in the forests, and from the time of pioneer settlers Ethan Allen Crawford and Hayes and Dolly Copp to the era of the grand resort hotels.

The 35 pieces collected herein represent a mere fraction of the White Mountain material to appear in print over the last 360 years (or since Darby Field first climbed Mount Washington in 1642). I would love to have included many more pieces, but only so many could be featured in a book of this size. Without a doubt, leaving certain selections on the cutting room floor was a most painful process. Perhaps these rejected selections, and other deserving pieces like them, can be included in a follow-up second volume at some point in the future.

As with *Mount Washington: Narratives and Perspectives*, the republished works appearing here are, for the most, in their original form, with their spelling, punctuation, and occasional factual errors virtually unchanged. Again, it is my intent, in keeping things as they were, to give readers a flavor of the times in which these words were first written.

Acknowledgments

RESEARCHING, then putting together this White Mountain anthology, has been nothing less than a labor of love for me. The process began in earnest two years ago, at about the same time that I was plotting my escape from the newspaper business, which I'd been involved with on a full-time basis for the previous 15 years. As with any writing project, there have been more than a few bumps encountered along the road to completion, not the least of which was the unplanned compiling of *Mount Washington: Narratives and Perspectives*, the companion anthology to this book that was published in 1999. That book resulted directly from my ongoing research for this book, and was a spin-off, if you will, of the book that you are now finally holding.

Throughout the process of compiling both anthologies, the number of people and organizations that have offered assistance in so many different ways has overwhelmed me. Without this support, what you see here is not necessarily what you would have gotten else wise. With that in mind, I'd like to take up a little space here thanking those whose contributions to this book have been so very much appreciated.

It's hard to know just where to begin, so I'll start right at home, sort of, with my wife, Jeanne, who also happens to be the Director of the Littleton Public Library (an invaluable source for many of the pieces collected in this book). Jeanne's unending enthusiasm for my various writing projects, plus her helpful comments and suggestions, convince me more and more every day that the two of us were always meant for each other.

As always, the staffs at Littleton Public Library, Bethlehem Public Library, and the State Library in Concord were exceptionally helpful throughout the course of this project. The same can be said for the staff at the Mount Washington Observatory's Weather Discovery Center in North Conway, and Peter Crane, in particular.

Contributing writers Floyd W. Ramsey and Buddy Newell need to be thanked for allowing me to use their fine pieces in this compilation. Ramsey and Newell also provided photographs which appear in the book, as did Robert Kozlow, Dave Govatski, David Sundman, the Littleton Area Historical Society, and the Mount Washington Observatory.

The Appalachian Mountain Club needs to be thanked for allowing me once again to reprint several extraordinarily important articles that originally appeared in their invaluable journal, *Appalachia*.

Thank yous also go out to John Dickerman, manager of Crawford Notch State Park, Art Tighe and the crew at Foto Factory in Littleton, booksellers Bob Cook of Titles & Tales in Bethlehem and Steve Smith of The Mountain Wanderer in Lincoln, Trish Ilacqua, Scott Cahoon, and Tim Leavitt, Nancy Collins, Roger Doucette, and Doug Garfield Jr. at Sherwin Dodge Printers.

None of this would have been possible without each and every one of you.

Littleton, N.H.   *Mike Dickerman*

The White Mountain Reader

The Scenic Mountains

1874

The White
Mountain Area

Charles H. Hitchcock

From *Geology of New Hampshire* (Vol. 1)

Early in the summer of 1868, the New Hampshire legislature authorized the governor of the state to appoint a new state geologist. Named to the post on September 8 of that year was Charles Henry Hitchcock (1836–1919), the son of former Amherst (Mass.) College president Edward Hitchcock, a well-known geologist himself. As the second state geologist in New Hampshire history, Charles Hitchcock was placed in charge of a monumental geological survey of the Granite State that would ultimately include the first thorough exploration of the White Mountains region. In the course of the three-year-long survey (1869–71), many first ascents of White Mountain region summits were recorded by participating survey members. The project culminated in the 1874 publishing of the massive three-volume Geology of New Hampshire, *from which the following chapter is excerpted. It was no wonder that Governor Walter Harriman named Hitchcock to the state post. In previous years, Hitchcock participated in similar state surveys in both Maine and Vermont, and for a time held the position of State Geologist of Maine. For some 40 years, beginning also in 1868, Charles Hitchcock also served as professor of geology and mineralogy at Dartmouth College in Hanover, N.H.*

THE WHITE MOUNTAINS of New Hampshire cover an area of 1,270 square miles, bounded by the state line on the east, the Androscoggin river and the Grand Trunk Railway on the north-east and north, the Connecticut river valley, or an irregular line from Northumberland to Warren, on the west, the less elevated region of Baker's river on the south-west, the

Pemigewasset river and the lake district on the south. The Pemigewasset valley makes a prominent notch in it in Thornton and Woodstock. The Saco river cuts the White Mountains into nearly equal parts; — and it may be convenient sometimes to speak of what lies on the east and west sides of this stream.

The mountains may be grouped in ten sub-divisions. 1. Mt. Starr King group. 2. Mt. Carter group. 3. Mt. Washington range, with a Jackson branch. 4. Cherry Mountain district. 5. Mt. Willey range. 6. Mts. Carrigain and Osceola group. 7. Mt. Passaconaway range. 8. Mts. Twin and Lafayette group. 9. Mts. Moosilauke and Profile division. 10. Mt. Pequawket area. Divisions 2 and 3 may be termed "Waumbek" for convenience, and divisions 5, 6, and 8 may receive the name of "Pemigewasset."

Considered as a whole, the main range would commence with Pine mountain in Gorham, follow the Mt. Washington ridge, cross the Saco below Mt. Webster, and continue south-westerly by Nancy mountain, Mt. Carrigain, Mt. Osceola, and terminate in Welch mountain in Waterville. Another considerable range may be said to commence with the Sugar Loaves in Carroll and Bethlehem, and continue westerly by the Twin mountains, Lafayette, Profile, Kinsman, and Moosilauke. A third of some consequence might embrace the Carter range, with Iron mountain in Bartlett. These mountain groups differ much in geological character, age, and marked topographical features.

1. *Mt. Starr King group.* This has not been explored very extensively, and it is not so much frequented by visitors as most of the other districts. It is embraced in the remote portions of the towns of Gorham, Randolph, Jefferson, Lancaster, Stark, Milan, Berlin, and the whole of Kilkenny. It may be bounded by the Upper Ammonoosuc and Androscoggin rivers on the north and east, by Moose and Israel's rivers on the south, and the Connecticut slope on the west. From the extreme outlying foot hill on the west line of Stark to Gorham, the longest diameter of this group, the distance is sixteen miles. The greatest width is thirteen miles, or from Jefferson hill to Milan water-station. The shape of the area, as mapped, is oval-elliptical, being more pointed at the north than the south. The area may comprise 150 square miles.

The Upper Ammmonoosuc river flows in a broad valley in Randolph and Berlin, and thereby divides the group into two parts. The source, called the Pond of Safety, is nearly 900 feet above Milan water-station, and there is a depression in the ridge in the south towards Jefferson. For geological reasons, we understand that the northern portion of the Starr King region was once an immense plateau, and the numerous valleys in it now are the result of atmospheric erosion. Not less than seven streams have notched in the edge of this plateau,—the three most prominent erosions being from Berlin, Stark (Mill brook), and Lancaster. There is a central ridge through Kilkenny, the Pilot mountain range, connected by a valley with Mt. Starr King in Jefferson. A branch diverges from this range to Pilot mountain in Stark, formerly ascended by a foot-path from Lost Nation. Green's ledge and Black mountain are spurs to the east from the Pilot range.

From Starr King to Berlin Falls there runs an irregularly curved range. It is composed of Pliny, Randolph, and Crescent mountains, and Mt. Forest. Section X passes through the center of this district from Berlin Falls to Lancaster, from which the reader may learn the irregularities of the surface-profile. Mts. Starr King, Pilot, and Randolph are the culminating points, being 3,800, 3,640, and 3,043 feet respectively.

2. *Mt. Carter group.* This lies in Shelburne, Bean's Purchase, Chatham, and Jackson, and is the least known of all the mountain districts. I do not find any explorer of it anxious to continue his investigations therein. The mountains, however, are like all other elevated tracts of land far away from habitations. There seems to be a heavy range from Gorham to Jackson, quite near the Peabody and Ellis valleys, while on the east the slope towards the Androscoggin is quite gradual. Mt. Moriah is one of the more northern peaks of this chain. Wild River occupies a broad valley in Bean's Purchase, trending north-easterly. The highest part of the Carter range lies next the Peabody river; and the western slope is much steeper than the eastern. A view of Mt. Carter, from a point south of Gorham, is quite impressive. Imp Mountain lies between Moriah and Carter. There is a very deep notch between Height's and Carter's mountains, in the edge of Jackson. The east branch of Ellis river flows from it south-easterly; and the range courses easterly so as to form the entire westerly and southerly rim of the Wild river basin. Several tributaries flow to Wild river on the north; and others to Saco on the south of this easterly range. It curves more northerly near the Maine line, so far as New Hampshire is concerned, in Mt. Royce, directly on the border.

The Carter mountain group sends five spurs into Jackson and Chatham. The first is the continuation of Height's mountain, adjoining the Pinkham road, to Spruce and Eagle mountains, near Jackson village. The second comes down from Carter mountain, to include Black and Tin mountains. The third spur takes in Doublehead mountain, and is bordered easterly by the east branch of the Saco and Wildcat Branch. Near the line of Bean's Purchase and Chatham lies Baldface mountain, 3,600 feet high, from which run the fourth and fifth spurs. The fourth comprises Sable mountain, in Jackson, and its foot hills. The fifth is composed of Mts. Eastman and Slope, in Chatham, which run into the Pequawket area.

3. *Mt. Washington Range.*   The main range of Mt. Washington extends from Gorham to Bartlett, about twenty-two miles. The culminating point is central, with a deep gulf towards Gorham, a slope on the north, formed partially by the westerly Mt. Deception range, which also produces the broad Ammonoosuc valley on the west, in connection with the axial line of summits. On the south there are two principal valleys, the more westerly occupying the depression of Dry or Mt. Washington river, and the easterly passing down the slope of Rocky branch, which travels easterly near its termination, so as to be parallel with the Saco in Bartlett. Starting with the Androscoggin valley, the range commences in the low Pine mountain. In the south-east corner of Gorham, this is intersected by the pass of the Pinkham road between Randolph and the Glen house. Next, the land rises rapidly to the top of Mt. Madison, 5,400 feet. The range now curves westerly, passing over the summits of Adams, Jefferson, and Clay. The gap between Clay and Washington is the best place to behold the deep abyss in which the west branch of Peabody river takes its rise. From Washington, one can easily discern the east rim of the Great Gulf, for upon it is located the carriage-road to the Glen house. From the Lake of the Clouds, and the eminence south of Tuckerman's ravine to Madison, it is easy to imagine the area an elevated plateau,—of which Bigelow's lawn is a portion,—out of which Washington may rise 800 feet. On the east of Washington, two deep ravines have been excavated,—Tuckerman's and Huntington's. The first runs easterly, and holds the head waters of Ellis river; the second commences at the southernmost angle of the carriage-road, at the fifth mile post, and runs toward the first.

Past Mt. Washington the main range descends to the pass of the Lake of the Clouds,—the source of the Ammonoosuc river,—5,000 feet high. The first mountain is Monroe—a double, ragged peak scarcely ever visited, and the road passing around it. Next follow in order Mts. Franklin, Pleasant, Clinton, Jackson, and Webster. The gaps between all these are small. Mt. Pleasant may be recognized by its dome shape. Mt. Webster is a long mountain with precipitous flank on the side towards the Saco. It is directly opposite the Willey house. It is one of the main features of the notch.

The east flank of the mountains, from Monroe to Webster, is washed by the powerful Mt. Washington river, which forms the central line of Cutt's grant, heading in Oakes's gulf. It is the proper continuation of the

Saco valley, its source being several miles farther away than the small pond at Crawford's. In dry seasons the water may be low, which fact, in connection with a broad, gravelly expanse of decomposed granite near the lower end of the valley, gave rise to the early appellation of "Dry river." Dr. Bemis proposed that it receive the name of Mt. Washington river.

From the east side of Oakes's gulf, or the continuation of Bigelow's lawn, two ranges course southerly. The western follows the Saco to just opposite Sawyer's rock, having, in the lower part of its course, Giant's stairs, Mt. Resolution, Mt. Crawford, Mt. Hope, and "Hart's ledge," of Boardman's map.

The more easterly range is elevated but is not conspicuous, and consequently is not named. It is flanked by Rocky Branch on the west and by Ellis river on the east. Near Jackson village it curves easterly, and terminates in the granitic Iron mountain. Between Sawyer's rock and the mouth of Rocky Branch there is a range running easterly, with a spur towards Mt. Crawford, separated by Razor brook from the Mt. Hope ridge. It lies between the southern termini of the two divergent ranges pointing southerly from Bigelow's lawn.

Mount Monroe (5,384 ft.) and the Lakes of the Clouds
as they appeared in the latter days of the 19th century.

4. *Cherry Mountain District.* The Mt. Deception range consists of four peaks,—Mt. Mitten, Mt. Dartmouth, Mt. Deception, and Cherry mountain, formerly called Pondicherry. It is separated by a considerable valley from Mt. Jefferson, and its gentler slope lies on the northern flank toward Israel's river. The road from Fabyan's to Jefferson passes between Cherry and Deception. The range runs nearly at right angles to the main mountain axis. Cherry mountain has a northerly spur of large dimension, called Owl's Head. The northern part of the range seems to be the highest.

5. *Mt. Willey Range.* This starts from near the White Mountain house in Carroll, and terminates in Mt. Willey. Its northern terminus is low, and the highest peak is at the southern end of the range. Six granitic summits may be counted before reaching the high summit of Mt. Tom, just behind the Crawford house. This peak is high and imposing, as seen from the vicinity of the Crawford house. The stream forming Beecher's cascade passes between Tom and the next summit north.

This latter peak has been named Mt. Lincoln, in honor of the late President Abraham Lincoln, by some unknown person. This title has been applied to stereoscopic views of it: but if we apply to the naming of mountains the canons of nomenclature required for scientific terms, it will be impossible to retain the name of Lincoln, because it has been preoccupied at Franconia. It is doubtful whether Mr. Fifield proposed to call the nameless peak Lincoln in advance of photographic usage at Crawford's; but the fact of its prior publication in a map is sufficient reason for adopting the name in Franconia, and hence to reject the appellation in the other case. I propose, therefore, the name of *Mt. Field* for the eminence near the Crawford house, in honor of the worthy gentleman (Darby Field) who first ascended Mt. Washington in 1642, and will use it upon the map and in the descriptions of this report.

From Mt. Field to Mt. Willey the high land is continuous, reaching an elevation of 4,300 feet. It then drops off abruptly, and terminates, while the water-shed continues into the Carrigain district. Ethan's pond is situated a little to the south-west of the base of the precipice. This is the extreme head of the waters flowing into Merrimack river. The Field-Willey range is directly opposite to Mt. Webster; and the intervening valley is the most striking part of the White Mountain notch. The head of the notch is formed by Mt. Willard, only about 550 feet above the Crawford plain. It is covered by trees on the north side; and the south is precipitous, looking down the valley of the Saco.

6. *Carrigain and Osceola Group.* Across from Mt. Webster the Mt. Washington range is continued in the mountains culminating in Carri-

The snow-capped peaks of Mounts Washington
(left of center), Adams and Madison.

gain, 4,678 feet high. This is a lofty, conical summit, occupying the most
conspicuous position in the horizon when seen from Mts. Washington,
Crawford, Pequawket, Moosilauke, and Lafayette. Two summits in this
line, north of Carrigain, have names, viz., Mts. Nancy and Lowell,—the
latter after Abner Lowell, of Portland, and known heretofore as Brick-
house mountain. There is an interesting gap between Lowell and Carrigain. The depth and impressiveness of the notch remind one of the great
gap between Willey and Webster. It would be a good route for a carriage-
road from Bartlett over to the east branch of the Pemigewasset. Nearly
west from Carrigain is Mt. Hancock (Pemigewasset of Guyot). It is nearly
as high as Carrigain (4,420 feet), and falls off gradually to the forks of the
East Branch on the east line of Lincoln. The space between Carrigain and
Osceola abounds in granite mountains, often with precipitous sides. Tripyramid may represent a spur (if not an isolated group) from them, running towards Whiteface. Between Tripyramid and Osceola there is a deep
gap, in which the Greeley ponds are situated. Osceola, or "Mad River
peak" of Guyot, is a double mountain with a deep excavation on the south
side for one of the tributary streams of Mad river. The range is continuous into Tecumseh, Fisher's, and Welch mountains in Waterville.

Cone mountain succeeds Welch, but this is not so conspicuous an eminence as appears upon some of the maps. North-westerly from Osceola the high granitic range continues as far as the East Branch, the last summits being Black and Loon Pond mountains. This very interesting region is unknown to most tourists. The only mountain accessible by a path is Osceola, from which most of the others can be seen to advantage.

7. *Passaconaway Range.*   This has an easterly course, and bounds the White Mountain area upon the south. The most massive of the series is Black mountain, or "Sandwich Dome" of Guyot, on the line between Sandwich and Waterville, over 4,000 feet high. A path leads to this summit, where one can see advantageously the Waterville basin as flanked by Tripyramid and the Osceola range. A high plateau extends from Black to Tripyramid and Whiteface. The latter is double, and the southern part has been recently occupied by the U. S. Coast Survey as a signal station. From here Passaconaway looms up majestically. It is a sharp dome, covered by trees to the very summit, and rises far above the surrounding peaks. Our most recent calculations place this summit in the east edge of Waterville. Passaconaway lies a little north of the main ridge. The space between this and Chocorua is occupied by low, ragged mountains.

Chocorua is the sharpest of all the New Hampshire summits, and can be the most easily recognized and located on this account. The cone is composed of an uncommon variety of granite. To the eastward the mountains gradually fall off till the plains of Conway are reached. The country south of the mountain range is low and undulating.

Albany Mountains.   Swift river divides the Albany mountains into two parts, rising on the long easterly slopes of the Carrigain-Osceola range and Green's cliff. Those just described form the southern rim of this basin. Those upon the north side are the Mote mountains, adjacent to Conway. and mostly unnamed peaks along the south bank of the Saco in Bartlett, joining on to Tremont in a wild tract of forest. The Mote mountains have been burnt over, so that they appear unusually barren when seen from a distance. They are the newest of the White Mountains, while the foundations of the Passaconaway range are the oldest. With a different arrangement of description, the *Albany basin* may be said to have very gentle slopes upon the inside, but on the Saco valley range and Chocorua group the hills dip abruptly in opposite directions. This basin may also be termed a projection eastwardly from the Carrigain range.

8. *Mts. Lafayette and Twin.*   This area is bounded on the north by the Ammonoosuc, on the east by the New Zealand river and the east branch of the Pemigewasset,—which curves so as to make it the south line, also,

—on the west by the north branch of the Pemigewasset. It contains two prominent ranges,—first, the western one, from Haystack to the junction of the two branch streams; and the other, from the Twin mountains to the mouth of the Franconia branch. The Haystack, a conical peak, is separated by a series of small gaps from Lafayette. The Lafayette mountains are peculiar in form. The range is quite elevated, extremely narrow, and consisting of seven summits. Lafayette, 5,290 feet, is the second from the north. Then follow Mt. Lincoln of Fifield, 5,101 feet, two nameless peaks, Mts. Liberty and Flume, each 4,500 feet, the latter to the south-east of the usual course of the ridge. This elevated ridge is composed of dark felsite. The peaks south of Mt. Flume are coarsely granitic, being Big and Little Coolidge, Potash, mountain, and others.

The Twin mountain range occupies the middle line between the Saco and Pemigewasset rivers. The two most prominent peaks are a mile apart, eight miles south of the Twin Mountain house, and are 5,000 feet high. Scarcely any mountains are more difficult to reach than these, on account of the stunted growth near their tops. The ridge is broad, and keeps at almost the same level for two or three miles south of the summit. On the west of this range there is an isolated ridge of great dimensions; and, on the north-east, a mass of mountains has been separated from the main summits by the erosive action of Little river. The highest of these separated peaks is sometimes confounded with the Twin mountains, because only one of the Twins is seen from the hotel named after them. The double character is seen from either Washington or Lafayette, and not from the Twin Mountain house. That the early distinctions may not be forgotten, and for the sake of fixing the position of a noble mountain, I venture to name the highest of the unnamed peaks north-east of Little river *Mt. Hale*, after Rev. E. E. Hale, of Boston, editor of *Old and New*, who assisted Dr. Jackson in exploring the White Mountains, and has done much to make them famous by his writings.

To the north of Mt. Hale are three granitic lumps, which, for convenience, I have called the Three Sugar Loaves. On the north-east side of Twin Mountain is a curious nubble or small conical summit 150 feet high, which is observable from several places along the Ammonoosuc valley. It is probably an enormous vein of very coarse granite.

There is a deep and broad valley between Mt. Tom and the Twin range. The divide between the New Zealand waters flowing to the north, and of the East Branch rivulets descending southerly, is quite low. It has all been excavated by atmospheric agencies,—since, from geological reasons, it is clear that Mts. Twin and Tom were once continuous.

9. *Moosilauke and Profile.*   A narrow gap, 2,000 feet above the ocean, separates the Lafayette from the Profile range, at the site of the famed "Old Man of the Mountains." On the north is Eagle Cliff, too precipitous to be scaled; while the Profile or Cannon mountain on the southwest is nearly as steep, and it is absolutely perpendicular a mile southerly.

The north end of the range consists of a pile of granite hummocks, attaining the height of 3,850 feet. A terribly rough valley separates it from the long range of Mt. Kinsman, which extends to the extreme south-east corner of Landaff. It is ascended from the village of Landaff, and the trip is easily made. The relations between the Profile and Lafayette range may be seen in a view of them from Thornton. Lafayette is the highest peak on the right, and Mt. Flume appears a little lower down. The deep valley of the Pemigewasset lies in the center, and Profile on the left. The precipitous character of Profile does not show advantageously. Only the lower summit of this mountain is generally visited, the apex being still covered by trees.

Moosilauke is the most south-westerly spur of the White Mountains. The summit is in the eastern part of Benton; but Woodstock and Warren own parts of its expanse. The water-shed continues from it into Carr's mountain in Warren and Wentworth; but the saddle between them is a low one over which a road to the Pemigewasset valley has been contemplated. Two ranges of foot hills border Moosilauke on the west, — first, the familiar name of "Black mountain;" second, five peaks, called respectively, —proceeding northerly from the railroad,—Owl's Head, Blueberry, Hog's Back, Sugar Loaf, and Black mountains.* The map shows a long range, called Blue ridge, on the east flank of Moosilauke, in Woodstock. The name of Moosilauke is said to signify a bald place. This is one of the finest of the White Mountains to visit for scenery, and it is easily ascended over the recently constructed turnpike road.

10. *Pequawket.*   This is the smallest of all the areas described. The predominant mountain is conical in shape, 3,300 feet above the sea. A house upon the summit can be seen from every point of the compass. On the north this peak passes into the north-easterly spur coming down from the Carter district. On the south a connection is made with the Green hills, which are elevated granitic piles in the east part of Conway.

---

*This makes two Black mountains in the same town.

1870

The Mountains

Rev. Benjamin G. Willey

From *History of the White Mountains*

Though he is best known as the brother of Samuel Willey—who perished along with his family in the disastrous Crawford Notch landslide of August 1826— Benjamin J. Willey (1796–1867) was a well-known White Mountain figure in his own right. In 1855, the Conway native authored one of the earliest histories of the region, Incidents in White Mountain History. *This book is listed among the "classics" in Allen H. Bent's* A Bibliography of the White Mountains, *published in 1911.* Incidents *was first published in 1856, then revised and reissued in 1870 under the title,* History of the White Mountains. *From 1824–1832, Benjamin Willey served as pastor of the First Church of Christ in Conway. He died in East Sumner, Maine in 1867.*

"Mount Washington, I have come a long distance, have toiled hard to arrive at your summit, and now you seem to give me a cold reception."
DANIEL WEBSTER.

THE WHITE MOUNTAINS embrace the whole group of mountains in northern New Hampshire, extending forty miles from north to south, and about the same distance from east to west. The term has sometimes been applied exclusively to the central cluster, including the six or seven highest peaks, and very properly, though in its comprehensive sense we think it should embrace the extended group. Mount Blanc and Mount Jura constitute not the whole of the Alps; neither do Washington or Monroe, the White Mountains. Clustering around their central height, like children of one large family, no merely arbitrary division should ever separate them.

These mountains are the highest land east of the Mississippi river, "and, in clear weather, are described before any other land by vessels approaching our eastern coast; but, by reason of their white appearance, are frequently mistaken for clouds. They are visible on the land at the distance of eighty miles, on the south and south-east sides. They appear higher when viewed from the north-east, and it is said they are seen from the neighborhood of Chamblee and Quebec."

The Indian name of these mountains, according to Belknap, is Agiocochook. President Alden states that they were known to some of the more eastern tribes of Indians by the name Waumbekketmethna; Waumbekket, signifying white, and methna, mountains. And still other tribes gave them the appellation Kan Ran Vugarty, the continued likeness of the Gull. All these names, we see, have the same general meaning, and refer to the white appearance of the mountains.

"During the period of nine or ten months the mountains exhibit more or less of that bright appearance, from which they are denominated white. In the spring, when the snow is partly dissolved, they appear of a pale blue, streaked with white; and after it is wholly gone, at the distance of sixty miles, they are altogether of the same pale blue, nearly approaching a sky color; while, at the same time, viewed at the distance of eight miles or less, they appear of the proper color of the rock. Light fleecy clouds, floating about their summits, give them the same whitish hue as snow.

"These vast and irregular heights, being copiously replenished with water, exhibit a great variety of beautiful cascades; some of which fall in a perpendicular sheet or spout; others are winding and sloping; others spread, and form a basin in the rock, and then gush in a cataract over its edge. A poetic fancy may find full gratification amidst these wild and rugged scenes, if its ardor be not checked by the fatigue of the approach. Almost everything in nature, which can be supposed capable of inspiring ideas of the sublime and beautiful, is here realized. Old mountains, stupendous elevations, rolling clouds, impending rocks, verdant woods, crystal streams, the gentle rill, and the roaring torrent, all conspire to amaze, to soothe, and to enrapture."

These mountains were first visited in 1632, by one Darby Field, whose glowing account of the riches he had discovered on his return, caused others immediately to make the same exploration. The visit of a Mr. Vines and Gorges is thus described by Winthrop: "The report brought by Darby Field, of shining stones, &c., caused divers others to travel thither; but they found nothing worth their pains. Mr. Gorges and Mr. Vines, two of the magistrates of Sir F. Gorges' province, went thither about the end of this month (August). They set out, probably, a few days after the return of Field, dazzled by visions of diamonds and other precious minerals, with which the fancy of this man had garnished his story.

"They went up Saco river in birch canoes, and that way they found it ninety miles to Pegwagget, an Indian town; but by land it is but sixty. Upon Saco river they found many thousand acres of rich meadow; but there are ten falls which hinder boats, &c. From the Indian town they went up hill (for the most part), about thirty miles, in woody lands. Then they went about seven or eight miles upon shattered rocks, without tree or grass, very steep all the way. At the top is a plain, about three or four miles over, all shattered stones; and upon that is another rock or spire, about a mile in height, and about an acre of ground at the top. At the top of the plain arise four great rivers; each of them so much water at the first issue as would drive a mill: Connecticut river from two heads at the N. W., and S. W., which joined in one about sixty miles off; Saco river on the S. E.; Amascoggin, which runs into Casco bay, at the N. E.; and the Kennebec at the N. by E. The mountains run east and west, thirty or forty miles; but the peak is above all the rest. They went and returned in fifteen days."

Josselyn, who visited them still later, has thus curiously described them: "Four score miles (upon a direct line), to the N. W. of Scarborow, a ridge of mountains runs N. W. and N. E., an hundred leagues, known by the name of the White Mountains, upon which lieth snow all the year, and is a landmark twenty miles off the sea. It is a rising ground from the sea-shore to these hills; and they are inaccessible, but by the gullies which the dissolved snow hath made. In these gullies grow saven bushes, which, being taken hold of, are a good help to the climbing discoverer. Upon the top of the highest of these mountains is a large level, or plain, of a day's journey over, whereon nothing grows but moss. At the further end of this plain is another hill, called the sugarloaf—to outward appearance a rude heap of mossie stones, piled one upon another—and you may, as you ascend, step from one stone to another, as if you were going up a pair of stairs, but winding still about the hill, till you come to the top, which will require half a day's time; and yet it is not above a mile, where there is also a level of about an acre of ground, with a pond of clear water in the midst of it, which you may hear run down; but how it ascends is a mystery. From this rocky hill you may see the whole country round about. It is far above the lower clouds; and from hence we behold a vapor (like a great pillar), drawn up by the sunbeams out of a great lake, or pond, into the air, where it was formed into a cloud. The country beyond these hills, northward is daunting terrible; being full of rocky hills, as thick as mole-hills in a meadow, and clothed with infinite thick woods."

The mountains which have more particularly attracted the attention of the tourists and writers, are near the northern boundary of the group, extending from the "Notch," a distance of fourteen miles in a north-easterly direction. The different peaks of this cluster gradually increase in height from the outside to the centre, where towers Mount Washington high above all. The lower and surrounding mountains are beautifully wooded to their very tops; while the bold Alpine summits of the central ones rise up far above the limits of vegetation, amid the clouds.

The heights of the different summits, as given by Professor Bond, of Cambridge, are, perhaps, the most accurate. Commencing at the "Notch," and giving the heights of each peak as it stands in the range,—Mount Webster is 4,000 feet above the level of the sea; Jackson, 4,100; Clinton, 4,200; Pleasant, 4,800; Franklin, 4,900; Monroe, 5,300; Washington, 6,500; Clay 5,400; Adams, 5,700; Jefferson, 5,800; Madison, 5,400.

Approaching the central cluster from the south-east, the mountains gradually close upon you, until they come together at the gate of the "Notch." This gate, or chasm, is formed by two rocks standing perpendicular at the distance of twenty-two feet from each other. Here, by great labor, a road has been constructed on the side of a little brook, whose rugged bed was formerly the only opening in the mountains. The entrance on each side is guarded by high overhanging cliffs, and the walls adjoining the road rise up perpendicularly fifty feet. This defile was known to the Indians, who formerly led their captives through it to Canada; but it had been forgotten or neglected, till the year 1771, when two hunters (Nash and Sawyer) discovered and passed through it.

The Notch itself is a narrow pass, about three miles in length, running in a north-westerly direction, turning to the right a little at the northern extremity. The mountains here are abruptly torn apart, forming a very narrow valley, through which flows the Saco. "The sublime and awful grandeur of the North baffles all description. Geometry may settle the heights of the mountains, and numerical figures may record the measure; but no words can tell the emotions of the soul, as it looks upward and views the almost perpendicular precipices which line the narrow spaces between them; while the senses ache with terror and astonishment, as one sees himself hedged in from all the world beside. He may cast his eye forward and backward, or to either side—he can see only upward, and then the diminutive circle of his vision is cribbed and confined by the battlements of nature's cloud-capt towers, which seem as if they wanted only the breathing of a zephyr, or the wafting of a straw against them, to displace them, and crush the prisoner in their fall."

Facing the north, on either hand, rise up steep perpendicular walls, two thousand feet above the road at their base, regular and equal, for a great part of the way. On the left is Mount Willey, gloomy and grand; its sides torn and furrowed by the slides, and here and there abrupt ledges, over whose topmost edge the gathering mass of rocks and earth leaped into the depths below.

On the right is Mount Webster. "This vast and regular mass rises abruptly, from the plain below, to the height of about two thousand feet. Its shape is that of a high fort, with deep scarred sides; its immense front apparently wholly inaccessible. Its top, nearly horizontal and rough with precipitous crags, juts over with heavy and frowning brows; so mighty a mountain wall, so high, so wide, so vast, and so near the spectator, that all its gigantic proportions and parts are seen with the utmost distinctness. It fills at once the eye and the mind with awe, admiration, and delight. In a bright day, when its outline at the top is seen sharp and distinct against the blue sky, its gray granite cliffs and ledges colored with iron-brown or stained with darker shades, its sides seamed with long gullied slides of brown gravel, its wide beds of great loose rocks, black with lichens, contrasted with the summer greens, or varied autumnal colors of the trees, make it as beautiful and interesting in its varied hues and parts, as it is great and sublime in its total impression."

Passing through the gate of the Notch, we come to the valley of the Ammonoosuc; and after a distance of four miles, generally through a thick wood, which prevents all views of the surrounding mountains, we come out suddenly into a wide cleared opening, where the whole mountain cluster bursts upon our view. Standing upon an isolated eminence, about sixty feet in height, known as the Giant's grave, the whole range of mountains is in sight.

You stand in the centre of a broad amphitheatre of mountains; the lofty pyramid of Washington, with its basin-shaped top, resembling the crater of a volcano, and its bare gray rock sides marked by long gullies, and lower down by broad slides, directly before you, while, far away on the right and left, Mounts Webster and Madison stand at the extremities of he range.

The tops of the mountains are covered with snow from the last of October to the end of May. Occasionally, during the months of July and August, they are almost white with a new-fallen snow or sleet. As the snow melts away, on most of the rocks may be seen mosses and lichens of various hues; while here and there, in the spaces sheltered by high rocks, beautiful and

Mount Webster provides the dramatic backdrop
to the narrow Gateway to Crawford Notch.

brilliant flowers, tiny alpine plants, spring up, mixed with the coarse
mountain grass.

"The base and sides of the mountains are clothed with a dense and luxurious forest of the trees of the country; and the ground beneath their
shade is ornamented with the beautiful flowers of the northern woods, and
deeply covered with a rich carpet of mosses. Below is the sugar-maple,
with its broad angular leaves, changing early in autumn, when every leaf
is a flower, scarlet or crimson, or variegated with green, yellow, and brown;
the yellow birch, of great size, with its ragged bark, and wide-spreading
arms; the beech, with its round trunk, its smooth bark, marbled, clouded,
and embroidered with many-colored lichens; its stiff slender branches, and

its glossy leaves; the white birch, with its smooth and white bark—most abundant in the districts formerly burnt—showing, after its changed yellow leaves have fallen, its slender, wand-like white trunks ranged closely and regularly on the hill sides. With these are mixed a frequent, but generally less abundant growth of black spruces and balsam firs,—the tall spruce, with its stiff and ragged outline, and horizontal branches, the fir, with its beautiful spires, regularly tapering from its base to its tip, and its dark rich foliage, often, as it grows old, hoary with the long, hanging, entangled tufts of the beard-moss, which here so abundantly covers its dying branches. Of the many other trees, smaller or less frequent, we will only mention the striped maple, the mountain ash, the aspen poplars, the hemlock, and the white pine. Higher up, the spruce and fir become the prevailing growth, with the yellow and white birch, gradually growing smaller as they ascend, until the dwarf firs, closely interwoven together, and only a few feet high, form a dense and almost impenetrable hedge, many rods wide, above which project, in fantastic forms, like the horns of a deer, the bare, bleached tops and branches of the dead trees. The dwarf trees are so closely crowded and interwoven together that it is as easy to walk on their tops as to struggle through them on the ground; and the road is made by removing them with their roots. Above this hedge of dwarf trees, which is about four thousand feet above the level of the sea, the scattered fir and spruce bushes, shrinking from the cold mountain wind, and clinging to the ground in sheltered hollows by the side of the rocks, with a few similar bushes of white and yellow birch, reach almost a thousand feet higher. Above are only alpine plants, mosses, and lichens."

Over the mountains are scattered a variety of berries, such as cranberries, whortleberries, and several other kinds. They grow high up the mountains, and some of them far above any other vegetable, except grass and moss. Their flower is, however, very different from those of the plain. Even the whortleberry, which grows on these hills, has, in its ripest state, considerable acidity.

The vicissitudes of sunshine and shade are here very frequent, not exactly like the shadows flying over the plains; for here the individual is actually enveloped in the cloud, while there it only passes over him. The cloud is discovered at a considerable distance, rolling along on the surface of the mountain; it approaches you rapidly; in an instant it encircles you, and as soon passes away, to be followed by others in endless succession. These phenomena are presented only when the clouds are light and scattered. When they are surcharged with rain, even at mid-day, all is darkness and gloom.

Although the waters of these hills apparently give life to no animal or insect, yet, in the heat of summer, the black fly, a little, tormenting insect, is very troublesome. At the same time, the grasshopper is here as gay as on the finely-cultivated field. The swallow, too, appears to hold his flight as high over these mountains as over the plain. It is, however, a place of extreme solitude. The eye often wanders in vain to catch something that has life and animation; yet a bear has been known to rise up, even in this solitude, to excite and to terrify the traveller.

Says a correspondent of the New York Express, writing from the top of Mount Washington: "I have seen but few birds here, and they do not tarry long after getting here; the ground-sparrow and plover are the only species I have noticed. Insects are quite plenty, and of various kinds. The honey-bee and humble-bee occasionally find the way up here, but are not plenty. There are scarcely any of the common house-fly here, but a large blue fly, and another of a bright gold color, are exceedingly plenty in warm days, but the first fog that arises scatters them, and they are not seen again for several days."

The dead trees, slightly referred to by Oakes, are deserving of more notice. From different persons these trees have received different names. Some call them buck's horns, and others bleached bones. The winds and weather have rendered them perfectly white; and, as neither the stem nor branches take any definite direction, they are of all the diversified forms which nature, in her freaks, can create. The cold seasons, which prevailed from 1812 to the end of 1816, probably occasioned the death of these trees; and their constant exposure to the fierce winds which prevail on the mountains has, aided by other causes, rendered them white. It can hardly be doubted that, during the whole of the year 1816, these trees continued frozen; and frost, like fire, is capable of extinguishing life, even in the vegetable kingdom. Fire could not have caused the death of these trees; for fire will not spread here, in consequence of the humidity of the whole region at this elevation.

The mountains, seen, with their well-defined outlines and shapes, in a clear day, present not the only aspect in which to behold them. Clouds sailing up their long ranges, now floating along their sides, severing their summits from their base, now settling down and capping their peaks, now drooping down still lower, till rock, and moss, and flower, and luxuriantly wooded base, are all hid in the dun, thick pall; then, bursting and fleeing with a wind-like speed, as the storm clears up, and the mountains come out, their wet sides glistening, in the returning rays of the sun, like huge piles of burnished silver, give to the rugged heights an aspect of beauty unsurpassed. The mountains are seldom seen free from clouds. Light, fleecy vapors are almost continually hovering about the different peaks.

By moonlight, in those clear, autumnal evenings, when the full, round moon looks so calmly down, throwing the shadows of the mighty giants broadly over the valleys, peopling each hidden nook and lurking ravine with grotesque forms and superstitious fancies, gazing on those majestic heights, one almost involuntarily repeats the matchless lines of Coleridge:—

> "Thou, most awful form,
> Risest from forth thy silent sea of pines,
> How silently! Around thee and above
> Deep is the air, and dark, substantial black,
> An ebon mass; methinks thou piercest it
> As with a wedge! But when I look again,
> It is their own calm home, thy crystal shrine,
> Thy habitation from eternity!
> O, dread and silent mount! I gaze upon thee,
> Till thou, still present to the bodily sense,
> Didst vanish from my thought; entranced in prayer
> I worshipped the invisible alone."

Nor in winter are they destitute of beauty. Their white summits standing out so distinctly from the deep blue depth of sky in the background, the trees around their sides and base loaded with ice, glistening in the dazzling rays of the sun like the enchanted diamond and jewelled halls of Eastern story, the reflecting and glittering of the moonbeams upon the frozen crust, all give to them a bewildering splendor indescribable.

The slides now seen at the White Mountains are mostly those which took place in the year 1826. At the Notch they present the appearance of deep gullies a few rods wide. On Mount Washington and the high peaks many of the slides are a quarter or a half a mile in width. The amount of material torn in that one night of dreadful storm from the mountains, and hurled into the valleys below, is incalculable. Thousands of acres of rocks, and earth, and trees, slipped from their fastening, and were thrown into the valleys. As seen from a distance of twenty or thirty miles, they look like long roads, winding up the mountains in all directions.

From the summit of Mount Washington the eye commands the circumference of the entire group of mountains. You stand in the centre, looking down upon a multitudinous sea of ridges and peaks, here extending out in long ranges, enclosing broad valleys, through which wind rivers,

glittering amid the forest and settlement like polished metal, now towering up like insulated cones, now grouped together like loving friends.

"In the west, through the blue haze, are seen in the distance the ranges
of the Green Mountains; the remarkable outlines of the summits of Camel's
Hump and Mansfield Mountain being easily distinguished when the atmosphere is clear. To the north-west, under your feet, are the clearings and
settlement of Jefferson, and the waters of Cherry Pond; and, further distant, the village of Lancaster, with the waters of Israel's river. The Connecticut is barely visible, and often its appearance for miles is counterfeited
by the fog rising from its surface. To the north and north-east, only a few
miles distant, rise up boldly the great north-eastern peaks of the White

Mount Washington and the Presidential Range as they appeared from present-
ay Bretton Woods in July 1873. Note the Ammonoosuc River on the right and
rude dirt road winding its way toward the western base of the mountain.

Mountain range,—Jefferson, Adams, and Madison—with their ragged tops of loose, dark rocks. A little further to the east are seen the numerous and distant summits of the mountains of Maine. On the south-east, close at hand, are the dark and crowded ridges of the mountains of Jackson; and, beyond the conical summit of Kearsarge, standing by itself, on the outskirts of the mountains, and, further over the low country of Maine, Sebago Pond, near Portland. Still further, it is said, the ocean itself has sometimes been distinctly visible.

"The White Mountains are often seen from the sea, even at thirty miles distance from the shore, and nothing can prevent the sea from being seen from the mountains, but the difficulty of distinguishing its appearance from that of the sky near the horizon.

"Further to the south are the intervales of the Saco, and the settlements of Bartlett and Conway, the sister ponds of Lovell in Fryeburg, and, still further, the remarkable four-toothed summit of the Chocorua, the peak to the right being much the largest, and sharply pyramidical. Almost exactly south are the shining waters of the beautiful Winnipisogee, seen with the greatest distinctness in a favorable day. To the south-west, near at hand, are the peaks of the southwestern range of the White Mountains; Monroe, with its two little alpine ponds sleeping under its rocky and pointed summit; the flat surface of Franklin, and the rounded top of Pleasant, with their ridges and spurs. Beyond these, the Willey Mountain, with its high, ridged summit; and, beyond that, several parallel ranges of high wooded mountains. Further west, and over all, is seen the high, bare summit of Mount Lafayette in Franconia."

The appearances of the mountains and the surrounding country at sunrise is worth the journey and toil from any part of the country to witness. In the language of the eloquent Brydone, "The whole eastern horizon is gradually lighted up. The sun's first golden ray, as he emerges from the ocean, strikes the eye, and sheds a glimmering but uncertain light; but soon his broad disc diffuses light and beauty, first on the hills, and soon on the region eastward. The sides of the mountains fronting him appear like a solid mass of gold dazzling by its brightness. While this process is going on to the eastward, the whole country to the westward is shrouded with darkness and gloom. The eye turns away from this comfortless scene, to the gay and varied one to the eastward. If this prospect is beheld immediately after a rain, the tops of a thousand hills rise above the fogs, appearing like so many islands in the midst of a mighty ocean. As these mists clear away, the houses, the villages, and the verdant fields within the circle of vision, arise to view. At the moment of the sun's rising, the noble vale of the Connecticut, which stretches along from the north till it is lost among the hills at the south-west, appears like an inland sea. This is occasioned by the vapors which had ascended from the river during the night. As the sun advances in his course, these vapors are chased away by his rays, and the farms in Jefferson, Bethlehem, and Lancaster, with its village, appears as if rising by magic from what but a little time before seemed nothing but water. The various hills, in the mean time, which surround the mountains, appear to be arranged in many concentric circles; and the circle the furthest removed seems the highest and most distinct, giving the whole an air of order and grandeur beyond the power of description."

From this lofty summit the Indians had a tradition that Passaconaway, a powerful chief, famed to hold a conference with the spirits above, once passed to a council in heaven.

> "A wondrous wight! For o'er 'Siogee's ice,
> With brindled wolves, all harnessed three and three,
> High seated on a sledge, made in a trice,
> On Mount Ogiocochook, of hickory,
> He lashed and reeled, and sung right jollily;
> And once upon a car of flaming fire,
> The dreadful Indian shook with fear to see
> The king of Penacook, his chief, his sire,
> Ride flaming up towards heaven, than any mountain higher."

Franconia Notch

Thomas Starr King

From *The White Hills: Their Legends, Landscape and Poetry*

Unitarian minister Rev. Thomas Starr King (1824–1864) was a frequent visitor to the White Mountains during his short but distinguished life. A collection of written dispatches about his mountain explorations—many of which appeared first in the Boston Evening Transcript *newspaper—was published in 1859, and this work,* The White Hills, Their Legends, Landscape, and Poetry, *was responsible for attracting thousands of first-time visitors to the region. Two prominent White Mountain landmarks still bear Rev. Starr King's name. They are King Ravine, the massive ravine just north Mount Adams in the Presidential Range, and Mount Starr King (3,913 ft.) in the Pliny Range just north of the village of Jefferson.*

METHINKS ye take luxurious pleasure
In your novel western leisure;
So cool your brows and freshly blue,
As Time had nought for ye to do:
While we enjoy a lingering ray,
Ye still o'ertop the western day,
Reposing yonder on God's croft,
Like solid stacks of hay;
So bold a line ne'er was writ
On any page by human wit;
The forest glows as if
An enemy's camp-fire shone
Along the horizon.

Or the day's funeral pyre
Were lighted there;
Edged with silver and with gold,
The clouds hang o'er in damask fold,
And with such depth of amber light
The west is dight,
Where still a few rays slant,
That even heaven seems extravagant.

The Franconia Notch, to which the lines just quoted furnish an appropriate introduction, is a pass about five miles in extent between one of the western walls of Lafayette and Mount Cannon. The valley is about half a mile wide; and the narrow district thus enclosed contains more objects of interest to the mass of travellers, than any other region of equal extent within the compass of the usual White Mountain tour. In the way of rock sculpture and waterfalls, it is a huge museum of curiosities. There is no spot usually visited in any of the valleys, where the senses are at once impressed so strongly and so pleasantly with the wildness and the freshness which a stranger instinctively associates with mountain scenery in New Hampshire. There is no other spot where the visitor is domesticated amid the most savage and startling forms in which cliffs and forest are combined. And yet there is beauty enough intermixed with the sublimity and the wildness to make the scenery permanently attractive, as well as grand and exciting.

The mountains are not nearly as high, or so noble in form, around the Franconia Pass as around the Glen; but the walls are much closer and more precipitous. The place where the Profile House is situated would be much more properly called a glen, than the opening which now bears that name by the Peabody River, at the base of Mount Washington. There is no wild and frowning rock scenery either visible or easily accessible from the Glen House. In the White Mountain Notch there is no hotel at which travellers stay. The Crawford House is situated just outside of it. And if there were a hotel so placed within it as to command its vast walls and its most powerful lines, the scene would be too terrific and desolate to win travellers to a visit of many days. The sides of the White Mountain Notch are many hundred feet higher than the highest cliff of Franconia. But they are torn with landslides and torrents; there is very little forest growth upon them; and their bare sand and gravel, and their scarred, grim ledges, overpower and awe sufficiently to overshadow the scene of pleasure and refreshment which one wants to feel in the scenery which he chooses to dwell in for

The first Profile House in Franconia Notch was built in 1852–53 and,
after a series of expansions, could accommodate as many as 600 guests.
This building was razed in 1905 and replaced with a more
modern facility, called the New Profile House.

several weeks or days. That which makes the White Mountain Notch the
most astonishing spectacle, at the first visit, or on any short visit, which
the whole region has to show, makes it the less welcome as a place to stay in.

The Franconia Pass is not oppressive. Large portions of the wall opposite the Profile House are even more sheer than the Willey Mountain, or
Mount Webster, in the great Notch; but it bends in a more graceful curve;
the purple tinge of the rocks is always grateful to the eye; and instead of
the sandy desolation over and around the Willey House, the forest foliage
that clambers up the sharp acclivities, fastening its roots in the crevices and
resisting the torrents and the gale, relieves the sombreness of the bending
battlement by its color, and soften its sublimity with grace. Every one who
has been driven into Franconia from Bethlehem or from Littleton, and
who has had the privilege of an outside seat on the stage, must have been
struck with the gentle crescent line of the vast outworks of Lafayette, suggesting the sweep of a tremendous amphitheatre, whose walls are alive
with the ascending orders of the wilderness.

One of the most interesting portions of the steep easterly rampart of
the Notch is the Eagle Cliff, immediately in front of the Profile House,
which shoots up some fifteen hundred feet above the road. It derives its

name from the fact that a pair of winged "Arabs of the air" have kept far up on the cliff their "chamber near the sun." It is a charming object to study. Except in some of the great ravines of the Mount Washington range, which its costs great toil to reach, there is no such exhibition of precipitous rock to be found. And how gracefully it is festooned with the climbing birches, maples, spruces, and vines! There are those to whom the sight of such a crag, sharply set at the angle of a mountain wall, is one of the most enjoyable and memorable privileges of a tour among the hills. Such will find the best points for appreciating the height and majesty of the Eagle Cliff, by ascending a few hundred feet on the Cannon Mountain opposite, or by walking to the borders of Profile Lake only a moderate distance from the hotel. If there were a pleasant boat on this small sheet of water, visitors would find it a most delightful use of the hour before sunset, to see from the further shore the ebbing of the ruddy light from the base of the cliff, till fainter contrasts of purple and green are left again in the evening shadow. In thinking of that view as it was given, towards sunset, while seated under the shadow of the dark firs that hem the western edge of Profile Lake, the music of the good old abbot's evening meditation, in Longfellow's "Golden Legend," floats into our memory:—

Slowly, slowly up the wall
Steals the sunshine, steals the shade;
Evening damps begin to fall,
Evening shadows are display'd.
Round me, o'er me, everywhere,
All the sky is grand with clouds,
And athwart the evening air
Wheel the swallows home in crowds.
Shafts of sunshine from the west
Paint the dusky windows red;
Darker shadows, deeper rest,
Underneath and overhead.
Darker, darker, and more wan
In my breast the shadows fall,
Upward steals the life of man
As the sunshine from the wall.
From the wall into the sky,
From the roof along the spire;
Ah, the souls of those that die
Are but sunbeams lifted higher.

This cliff, and the whole wall with which it is connected, shows its height more impressively in some of the misty dogdays, when fogs play their tricks along its breastworks. Sometimes they break away above, and let the pinnacles of rock be seen disconnected from the base. Then we can hardly believe that Lafayette himself has not moved a little nearer, and pushed aside the curtains to look down at the Profile House. Sometimes they tear themselves into horizontal stripes, through whose lines of gray the green and purple of the trees and rocks give peculiar pleasure to the eye. Sometimes they thicken below and break above, to show a dash or a long line of delicate amber light upon the edge of the wall. At last the whole texture gets mysteriously loosened, and the broad curtain begins at once to rise and melt. The sunshine pours unobstructed over the Notch, and only here and there a shred of the morning fog is left to loiter upwards. Watch it, and think of Bryant's poem:

> Earth's children cleave to the Earth—her frail
>   Decaying children and dread decay.
> You wreath of mist that leaves the vale;
>   And lessens in the morning ray:
> Look how, by mountain rivulet,
>   It lingers as it upward creeps,
> And clings to fern and copsewood set
>   Along the green and dewy steeps;
> Clings to the fragrant kalmia, clings
>   To precipices fringed with grass,
> Dark maples where the wood-thrush sings,
>   And bowers of fragrant sassafras.
> Yet all in vain—it passes still
>   From hold to hold, it cannot stay,
> And in the very beams that fill
>   The world with glory, wastes away,
> Till, parting from the mountain's brow,
>   It vanishes from human eye,
> And that which sprung of earth is now
>   A portion of the glorious sky.

The most attractive advertisement of the Franconia Notch to the traveling public is the rumor of the "Great Stone Face," that hangs upon one of its greatest cliffs. If its inclosing walls were less grand, and its water gems less lovely, travellers would be still, perhaps, as strongly attracted to the spot, that they might see a mountain which breaks into human expression,

—a piece of sculpture older than the Sphynx,—an intimation of the human countenance, which is the crown of all beauty, that was pushed out from the coarse strata of New England thousands of years before Adam.

The marvel of this countenance, outlined so distinctly against the sky at an elevation of nearly fifteen hundred feet above the road, is greatly increased by the fact that it is composed of three masses of rock which are not in perpendicular line with each other. On the brow of the mountain itself, standing on the visor of the helmet that covers the face, or directly underneath it on the shore of the little lake, there is no intimation of any human features in the lawless rocks. Remove but a few rods either way from the guide-board on the road, where you are advised to look up, and the charm is dissolved. Mrs. Browning has connected a law of historical and social insight with a passage and a fancy, that many of our readers will be glad to associate with their visit to the spot where the granite Profile is revealed to them:—

> Every age,
> Through being beheld too close, is ill-discerned
> By those who have not lived past it. We'll suppose
> Mount Athos carved, as Persian Xerxes schemed,
> To some colossal statue of a man;
> The peasants, gathering brushwood in his ear,
> Had guess'd as little of any human form
> Up there, as would a flock of browsing goats.
> They'd have, in fact, to travel ten miles off
> Or ere the giant image broke on them,
> Full human profile, nose and chin distinct,
> Mouth, muttering rhythms of silence up the sky,
> And fed at evening with the blood of suns;
> Grand torso,—hand, that flung perpetually
> The largesse of a silver river down
> To all the country pastures. 'Tis even thus
> With times we live in,—evermore too great
> To be apprehended near.

One of Mr. Hawthorne's admirable "Twice-told Tales" has woven a charming legend and moral about this mighty Profile; and in his description of the face the writer tells us: "It seemed as if an enormous giant, or Titan, had sculptured his own likeness on the precipice. There was the broad arch of the forehead, a hundred feet in height; the nose, with its long bridge; and the vast lips, which, if they could have spoken, would have

The Old Man of the Mountain, high above Franconia Notch, remains
one of New Hampshire's most recognizable natural features.

rolled their thunder accents from one end of the valley to the other." We
must reduce the scale of the charming story-teller's description. The whole
profile is about eighty feet in length; and of the three separate masses of
rock which are combined in its composition, one forms the forehead, another the nose and upper lip, and the third the chin. The best time to see
the Profile is about four in the afternoon of a summer day. Then, standing

by the little lake at the base and looking up, one fulfills the appeal of our great transcendental poet in a literal sense in looking at the jutting rocks, and,

> through their granite seeming
> Sees the smile of reason beaming.

The expression is really noble, with a suggestion partly of fatigue and melancholy. He seems to be waiting for some visitor or message. On the front of the cliff there is a pretty plain picture of a man with a pack on his back, who seems to be endeavoring to go up the valley. Perhaps it is the arrival of this arrested messenger that the old stone visage has been expecting for ages. The upper portion of the mouth looks a little weak, as though the front teeth had decayed, and the granite lip had consequently fallen in. Those who can see it with a thundercloud behind, and the salty scud driving thin across it, will carry away the grandest impression which it ever makes on the beholder's mind. But when, after an August shower, late in the afternoon, the mists that rise from the forest below congregate around it, and, smitten with sunshine, break as they drift against its nervous outline, and hiding the mass of the mountain which it overhangs, isolate it with a thin halo, the countenance, awful but benignant, is "as if a mighty angel were sitting among the hills, and enrobing himself in a cloud vesture of gold and purple."

The whole mountain from which the Profile starts is one of the noblest specimens of majestic rock that can be seen in New Hampshire. One may tire of the craggy countenance sooner than of the sublime front and vigorous slopes of Mount Cannon itself—especially as it is seen, with its great patches of tawny color, in driving up from the lower part of the Notch to the Profile House. Yet the interest of the mountain to visitors has been so concentrated in the Profile, that very few have studied and enjoyed the nobler grandeur on which that countenance is only a fantastic freak. And many, doubtless, have looked up with awe to the Great Stone Face, with a feeling that a grander expression of the Infinite power and art is suggested in it than in any mortal countenance. "Is not this a place," we have heard it said, "to feel the insignificance of man?" Yes, before God, perhaps, but not before matter. The rude volcanic force that puffed the molten rocks into bubbles, has lifted nothing so marvellous in structure as a human skeleton. The earthquakes and the frosts that have shaken and gnawed the granite of Mount Cannon into the rough semblance of an intelligent physiognomy, are not to be compared for wonder to the slow action of the chemistries that groove, chasten, and tint the bones and tissues of a human head into correspondence with the soul that animates it, as it grows in wisdom and moral beauty. The life that veins and girdles the noblest mountain on the earth, is shallow to the play of vital energies within a human frame.

> No mountain can
> Measure with a perfect man.

The round globe itself is only the background upon which the human face is chiselled. Each one of us wears more of the Infinite art,—is housed in more of the Infinite beneficence, than is woven into the whole material vesture of New Hampshire. And the mind that can sap the mountain, untwist its structure, and digest the truth it hides,—the taste that enjoys its forms and draperies,—the soul whose solemn joy, stirred at first by the spring of its peaks, and the strength of its buttresses, mounts to Him who "toucheth the hills and they smoke,"—these are the voyagers for which the Creator built

> this round sky-clearing boat
> Which never strains its rocky beams;
> Whose timbers, as they float,
> Alps and Caucasus uprear,
> And the long Alleghanies here,
> And all town-sprinkled lands that be,
> Sailing through starts with all their history.

1890

The Heart
of the Wilderness

Julius Ward

From *The White Mountains: A Guide to Their Interpretation*

Much like his literary predecessor Thomas Starr King, Rev. Julius Ward (1837–1897) frequently shared his experiences in the White Mountains with readers of a popular Boston newspaper. Ward, an editorial writer with the Boston Sunday Herald, *saw a collection of these essays put into book form in 1890, when* The White Mountains: A Guide to Their Interpretation, *was published by D. Appleton and Company of New York. In 1893, as widespread logging threatened to destroy the mountain country that he so loved, Ward penned the article, "White Mountain Forest in Peril" in the widely read* Atlantic Monthly *magazine. In this piece, he termed the lumbering practices of the day "barbarous" and insisted that preserving the White Mountains for future generations was not just a regional, but a national issue.*

IT WAS SAID of Agassiz that if you gave him the bone of a fish he could reconstruct its physical system from his knowledge of where that bone belonged. The same laws of construction do not hold in the formations of outward Nature that are found in organic life. It is not possible to predict from a single peak the configuration of the valleys and hills and water courses, except in a general way. The grand outlines are nearly always the same, but the details of any system of hills or mountains are never quite alike. On seeing one mountain in a system or group you are not sure that you have caught the "stream of tendency" that prevails among them. It is difficult for the uninitiated to gain a proper idea, on Mount Washington, of the structure of the distant peaks. The configuration of the Presidential range is easily traced, but that of the Franconias is not easily followed, and that of the Sandwich range is not indicated. From Mount Kearsarge you see the eastern range at a special advantage; from Moosilauke you observe the general structure of the whole system; the mountains group themselves so that they henceforth arrange themselves in a natural order; from Mount Lafayette you survey the Pemigewasset, as from the summit of Mount Washington you trace the sources of the Ammonoosuc and Saco rivers, but at no one of these points do you see the mountains as from a centre of unity.

It is the distinguishing character of Mount Carrigain that it is in the centre of the White Mountain system and holds the key to the entire country. It is a bold and massive peak, wooded nearly to the summit, not desolate like Chocorua, not rifted with the fury of the gods like Mount Washington, but unique in its beauty as seen from a distance, and presenting a wonderful panorama of the wilderness when you have climbed its summit and from its cairn look out at all points of the compass upon an uninhabited world. I have stood on the brow of the cliff that hangs over Kineo Bay at Moosehead Lake and strained the eye in every direction over the untrodden forest; I have surveyed the Adirondacks from the nose of Mount Mansfield and swept the field of vision through the lower Canadas; I have felt, as others have felt who have climbed these peaks, that there was something about the view from them and something in the silence that reigns upon them which appeals strongly to the conception of universal Nature; but I think that the sense of utter separation from humanity, the sense of entire lostness in the wilderness, the sense of the complete abandonment of the soul to Nature was never realized as it was during my stay of a few hours on the topmost peak of Mount Carrigain. I separated myself from my companions after the ascent so that I might feel this aloneness in all its intensity. I put my thought and feeling into the structure of Nature and tried to measure my heart-beats by the rhythm of the life of the mountains, to surrender myself to the spirit that ruled the scene.

It was pure imagination to be touched by emotions at such a view, and yet I remember, when the hermit of Mount Mansfield took me to his favorite point on the Chin, where the lightnings had torn up the solid rock in their fury, that he confessed to this same power of identifying himself with Nature in her wildest and grandest forms, and that his eyes shone as if lit by divine fire, as he recounted what he had seen and felt on that spot in storm and calm. There is something about one's thoughts on these desolate peaks that can not be spoken, just as there is something that one

Mount Carrigain (left) and Carrigain Notch
as viewed from the summit of Mount Tremont.

never tells about his religious life. Are there not special confidences that with Nature on the part of the open soul? Do not the great elevation and the absence of human environment lift one into the higher mood of unspoken communion with God? Where else does the lone spirit so brave itself go forth to the Alone? Coleridge's Hymn to Mont Blanc, through a translation into which the translator breathed a larger meaning, still fails to express all that one feels on a spot like this, where the accidents of life are removed, and pure spirit and pure Nature meet together on equal terms. To many this scene of unbroken forest, reaching to the horizon in every direction, would be what the primrose was to Peter Bell; but to one who could hear, as Wordsworth heard, the whispers of the forests on the mountains as clearly as he could catch the voices of the shepherds watching their flock upon their sides, the wooded world was all alive with countless ministrations addressed to Nature and to the sensitive soul of man.

The view from Mount Carrigain is as if one knew only the mountain world. The dark peaks crowd up into the sky and dominate the horizon. It seems like the country of the giants. You are oppressed with the largeness of nature. Emerson made Monadnock, which was his nearest mountain, the symbol of all mountains. It was to him both Alps and Himalaya.

This is well when you have a single mountain as a near neighbor. It is like living with a bit of genuine sea or a glimpse of a distant hill from your window, but when one looks out in every direction upon a wilderness (and it is a gigantic wilderness), the virgin forest, the wilderness where the axe of the woodman has never resounded through the defiles, where the reign of Nature has been undisputed since the opening of the world, where life and death have wrought with the same regularity in nature that life and death have wrought in the country village, where man is the stranger and intruder into a world with which he has nothing to do—he feels as if there were other worlds than ours, and that this mountain region, which is opened to his astonished vision from the summit of Mount Carrigain, is one of them.

To look at Mount Carrigain from Mount Washington, or from any one of the adjacent peaks, it would seem to be difficult of access. It is in the centre of the mountain system. For ten or twenty miles in any direction there is nothing but the unbroken forest before you. One's heart faints within him at the idea of making his way for this distance through the undergrowth and over fallen trees, and if he selects a water course, the passage through the wilderness, if safer, is not much more rapid. Happily for the few who wish to climb Mount Carrigain, the lumber company who have made their way up Sawyer's River, and own the town of Livermore, which lies at its base, have constructed a railroad of their own, which reaches from the Portland and Ogdensburg track to the Livermore Mills, and makes travel for the first miles as easy as it is anywhere in the country. Then begins the difficult part of the climb. The road to the base of the mountain is at first a fairly good path, which is used for taking logs out of the woods in winter, and all through this section, which is perhaps four miles in length between the hills, the big trees are seldom to be found. It is only when you are on the cone of Carrigain and are ascending apparently at a pitch of thirty degrees, seemingly climbing straight into the sky, that you reach a point where the woodman's axe has not been used and Nature is in a primitive condition. The climb is by a blazed path through the forest, where you secure your footing by uncertain efforts, and are happy if you do not lose it. Nothing tests a person's wind like a steep pitch of this sort. The only advantage is that where the ascent is so sharp it is correspondingly rapid, and yet even then it is not a quick climb; it takes experts more than two hours to make the ascent from the base, and when the bare ridge is reached there is still half an hour's walk by another blazed path before you stand by the cairn and have command of the wilderness.

The first thought on reaching the tiptop is that Carrigain is not half so high as it seems to be when you are deep down in the ravine and looking up at its summit. Heights, like other distances, are only relative, and when Carrigain is but one among brethren its peak is nothing more than the top of a pretty large hill, Yet the view is extensive, and if great mountains seem, when you are with them, nothing more than big hills at rest among their fellows, it is simply because you make your standard of measurement when you are in the midst of them correspond with their size. One of the first impulses on reaching the top of a central mountain like Carrigain is to look around and try to identify the different peaks. You look down upon them or glance across to them and lose both the feeling of size and the sense of distance. You have for the first time in the White Mountains the idea of relativeness.

When on Mount Washington, every other peak is dwarfed. You look across to Mount Adams and feel as if it were not more than half a mile from the Great Gulf to its summit, or you look over Tuckerman's Ravine to Boott Spur and feel that it is not much of a climb, but if you attempt to walk in either direction the illusion is directly lost. So if you take a more distant range, the same deception is repeated to the eye. Moosilauke and Lafayette, though over on the extreme verge of the Pemigewasset Valley, seem nothing more than big hills with a number of little hills crowded in between. In a similar way Mount Washington seems robbed of its glory when seen from the peak of Carrigain. It is simply a little higher ridge on the edge of the horizon. The Presidential range is seen for a good part of its length to great advantage. The ridges stand out in all their rugged in-tensity. You feel as if you could reach out and rub your hands all over them. The huge fissures are shorn of their awfulness in the distance. You feel a certain familiarity with the different peaks; Carter Dome is just visible beyond Mount Washington; the Giant's Stairs are so near to the eye that you feel as if you could step across the intervale and climb them without difficulty; Doublehead is like a couple of neatly stacked haystacks against the sky; Mount Kearsarge is a wonderfully symmetrical peak all by itself, an eastern sentinel; the Moats lie out on the southeast against the sky like a great tableland, on which you could lie down without rolling off; and just below stands the beautiful Chocorua, like a huge icicle piercing the sky.

There is constant refreshment to the eye in the survey of these succes-sive peaks, and there is a certain majesty in their magnificent repose. South-ward from Chocorua and westward to Moosilauke, the mountain wall is continuous; there is no notch like that between Wildcat and Carter Dome; the curtain is held up against the sky at all points; the peak of Passacona-way is like a sugar-loaf trimmed with evergreens, and there is a certain largeness of base to Tripyramid which reminds one of the buttress of an immense castle; Lake Winnipesaukee is over beyond, but no hint of it is given in the view from Mount Carrigain. To the southwest there is nothing grand, but the peaks rise in succession like the ranks of a regiment all ready for action; you note a certain symmetry in their form and order, reminding you of the houses on a street; each peak is wooded to the summit; it is tufted off and finished according to the plan of Nature; Tecumseh is the farthest off, and nearer in the same line of view are, first, Osceola, then Kancamagus, then Black and Huntington, then Hitchcock, and finally Hancock crouches at your feet.

Then you shift your place to a more favorable quarter, to the west and northwest. Beneath your feet, as if a sheet had been let down by the four corners, lies the Pemigewasset wilderness, the course of its stream faintly marked among the forest trees, and the whole stretch of intervale colored only by the darkened foliage. To the northward and far away lies Cherry Mountain, and beyond it is Starr King, and still beyond are the dusky ranges that blend their lines with the blue ether above. The country seems open, and yet it is effectually shut in. Right beyond the intervale and to the northwest are the mountains called Bond and Guyot, and higher still are the North and South Twins, and just to the west is Garfield; and then the eye rests on the only near peak that approaches Mount Washington in its isolation or grandeur, Mount Lafayette. Here the strength of the western system is found.

The wall from north to south, which takes in the entire Franconia range, is wonderfully impregnable; the wooded slopes please the eye, but do not conceal the massiveness of their structure; and far away Moosilauke looms up like a ship in a distance at sea, keeping watch in the west, and holding the chain as securely at one end as Mount Washington holds it at the other. The eye here has its feast, and there is nothing on which it can rest but the grand and the vast in Nature. Near by are small mountains, spurs, ledges, peaks, and half-peaks, but what are these among so many? After you have seen the king and his titled companions, what is there to admire in a common man?

The mind is so touched with imaginative life by a few hours' stay on this watch-tower among the hills that it is not easy to return to the small details of a rapid descent by the Appalachian path to the world below, but the impression of such a view, if it has been quietly received and seen by the mind's eye, becomes forever a part of the conscious property of an educated and refined mind. The picture, as a whole or in sections, is like Keats's description of beauty, "a joy forever."

1916

Passaconaway's Pyramid

Charles Edward Beals, Jr.

From *Passaconaway in the White Mountains*

Charles E. Beals Jr. was just 20 years of age when he penned Passaconaway in the White Mountains *in 1916. Not a whole lot is known about Beals, the son of the Rev. Charles Edward Beals, who for many years summered in the Albany Intervale north of Mount Passaconaway. According to the elder Beals, who wrote the introduction to his son's book, "The young man who wrote this book commenced his explorations of Passaconaway-land when four years old." His love for the mountains undoubtedly grew in intensity after the Rev. Beals purchased a small parcel of land in the Intervale and built a summer cottage— "Score-o'-Peaks,"—where the Beals family returned year after year.*

Miss Lucy Larcom bestowed the name of the great Bashaba upon the loftiest, wildest, yet most symmetrical, most awe-inspiring mountain of the Sandwich Range. She also gave Indian names to other peaks of this southmost range of the Crystal Hills, namely, Paugus, Wonalancet, and the Wahwah Hills. But head and shoulders above these, old Passaconaway lifts its head, monarch of all.[1] As in life he loomed in pre-eminence high above his tribesmen, so now, nearly two and a half centuries after his translation, his mountain lifts its head in solemn pride.

With its smoothly sloping and in places almost perpendicular sides, it tapers up to a lofty, often cloud-wreathed, dome,[2] gracefully holding itself in proud aloofness from its inferior comrades. Chocorua is picturesque—

1. Osgood: White Mountains, 337.
2. Same.

40

many consider it the most picturesque mountain in New Hampshire—but Passaconaway is grand, awe-inspiring, a huge monarch and leader of this southern herd of blue elephants; the challenging trumpeter of the herd.[3]

To this sovereign do the storm demons seem to look for orders, and to old Passaconaway's countenance do the natives of the valley turn for their weather forecasts. For, not until this huge sentinel, guarding us from the southern tempests, has covered his face, will he let the storm wreak its fury on our valley. No matter how dark and threatening the sky, the southern storms do not dare touch us until Passaconaway veils his face in cloud. "Uncle Jim" Shackford, for years the proprietor of the Passaconaway House, used to say, when his opinion was asked on a threatening day, "Waal, I gorry, I dunno; it may rain and it may not, but when old Passaconaway puts on his night-cap, it's time to run for shelter."

This massive peak, with face far up among the clouds, is, from the southern side, almost a perfect cone with a somewhat blunted and rounded apex. Often have I wondered how vegetation and huge trees could cling to such precipitous sides. A thick, black, almost impenetrable growth of tall spruces and pines completely covers this gigantic pile of rock. Because of its great height and heavily wooded, well-rounded dome, it may easily be distinguished from distant points in all directions. The top of Passaconaway is 4,200 feet (according to A.M.C. Guide, p. 326, 84 feet less) above sea level. From summit to field Passaconaway is over three thousand feet in altitude;[4] on its southern side it falls almost perpendicularly for seventeen hundred feet; while on the northwestern slope the steep drop is only about seven hundred.[5]

As already said, the view of the mountain from its southern side presents only one rounded peak; while three distinct promontories are visible from our northeastern, or Swift River, side. The central of these, the true summit, is a lofty, wood-covered knob, only a few feet higher than the other two.

Lying at the eastern base, the groveling Paugus reposes far below, and through the pass between the two runs the "Old Mast Road." A very unique spur of this monarch of the range is found here. From the Mast Road trail which leads from the town road in Albany Intervale through the valley to the hamlet of Wonalancet, a towering cliff, known as Square

---

3. Compare Bolles: At the North of Bearcamp Water, 271.
4. See Bolles: At the North of Bearcamp Water, 155.
5. Chas. E. Fay in Appalachia, vol. VI.

Ledge, may be seen. Square Ledge is a gigantic scarred face of perpendicular ledge. There is a long, low ridge, artistically dipping and gently rising at its eastern end, until, at this spur, it drops perpendicularly. Square Ledge appears to have been cleft off, sharply and squarely, as if some Indian Deity or some giant had sawn vertically downwards until the ridge had been sawed off, as if endeavoring to get a cross-section of this hill, and, being satisfied, had carried off the eastern half. Such a sight well repays one for the two-mile walk through the once beautiful woods. This great "jump-off" is clearly seen from the town road at Mrs. Colbath's, or, better still, from a point a few rods west, where the railroad crossed the town road.

Passaconaway appears at its best from our little valley at the extreme west end of the "Great Intervale." The three peaks are set regularly apart, and the middle one rises just enough above the others to give the mountain the appearance of a darkly draped head and shoulders. Then, too, there is the long graceful slide, showing white and shiny from beneath the dark coat. This is the laundered shirt-bosom of the great Bashaba's dress suit. Especially is this noticeable when, on a moonlight evening, one sees the inky black form, with overcoat carelessly thrown over the shoulders, the clear-cut outlines of the monarch standing out against the star-studded sky, and the pale moon shining upon the now glistening white granite slide as upon a smooth and jeweled shirt-front. This is very striking in winter, too, when the slide is coated with spotless snow and edged with dark spruces. In the case of this mountain, instead of being a horrible, ugly scar, the great slide seems to add contrast, beauty and fineness of line to what otherwise might be a vast unbroken stretch of dark bluish green forest.

Still gazing upon the mountain from the north, Passaconaway appears surrounded by a band of loyal retainers, Potash, Whiteface, and Hedgehog. These peaks give it a more haughty and grand appearance than perhaps from any other viewpoint. On the northmost promontory, and on the path up from our valley, several precipitous ledges are seen. These afford to climbers famous lookouts.

There are three different ways of climbing Passaconaway: from Birch Intervale, or Wonalancet; from Whiteface, by the lofty ridge; and from our Passaconaway or Swift River Valley, by way of the slide. At best they are all "up-hill sidewalks." Hence none but the strong should attempt the climb.[6] Let us ascend from Passaconaway. A cool and charming little walk

6. See Osgood: White Mts., 337.

Mount Passaconaway rises
in the distance behind the
snow-covered Sandwich
Range summit of neigh-
boring Mount Hedgehog.

of perhaps two miles up the musical Downes Brook will take us to the foot
of the slide. On our way, about half a mile from the town road, is a deserted
lumber camp. In the winter of 1914–1915 this camp was in full swing, but
now it lies half tumbled down, for the lumber-jacks have gone.

Here, only last summer (1915), while leisurely strolling down the lumber road, we made the acquaintance of a big Canadian lynx. First, his be-
whiskered nose appeared on the left side of the path; next his long tasselled
ears came into sight; and presently he was standing, face on, directly in the
road ahead, in full view. Not wishing in any way to irritate his pussyship,
and yet hoping that he would make his decision promptly—lest we should
be forced to assume the responsibility of deciding—we slowed down our
pace almost to a standstill. Much to our relief, after sizing us up as too sour,
green, bony or tough to waste his time on, the great cat crossed the road
and disappeared behind a log. The old rascal probably thought that, with
the log between us, he would be hidden from our sight; but not so, for we
could see his tasselled ears, his powerful tawny shoulders, and once in a

while his back and bob-tail, as he leisurely climbed up the little embank-ment. A moment later our new acquaintance had vanished.

We cross on our trail several old, beautiful, little corduroy bridges. Over one of these a thickly leaved tree hangs, artistically screening the opposite bank from our gaze. The winding path reveals innumerable spots of beauty to the aesthetic climber. At length some broad white ledges, over which a tiny rill plays, are seen shining through the leafy partition. Looking up the mountainside through the trees, we see, in some places, the brook spread-ing out and, in a broad sheet of water, flowing over a ledge; in others, narrowing to a mere shining ribbon; and, at still others, tumbling over or eddying round boulders, here lying in a silent little pool, there rushing through a rocky channel. Pressing through the thin curtain of foliage, we look up over the foot of the slide, which came to a standstill in the bed of the Downes, and see a series of rocky ledges gradually rising one above another. While approaching the foot of the slide, we notice how rocky the brook-bed is. In some places large boulders have been rolled over and over, until finally brought to rest half a mile or more below the junction of the slide with Downes Brook. It is very noticeable for quite a distance before the slide is reached. The natives say that for a mile the rocks and boulders rolled with thunderous booming down the tiny brook-bed on that fateful November night in the early 1890's.

Running parallel with the lower half of the slide, up as far as the turn in the slide, is a tote-road, only a few rods to the west. Even by this road the climb is arduous enough, but nothing as compared with what the trip used to be when the trail was the ledgy brook-bed. The road rises at an angle of from twenty to thirty-five degrees, and is gullied by scores of tiny brook-beds and washouts, making the walking difficult in some places. Still this way of walking half the distance from the hotel on a lumber road is far easier than the former way of leaping from stone to stone up a cou-ple of miles of brook-bed. Well do I recall when, a four-year-old boy, I was taken on this trip by my parents. A strong, fatherly hand every now and then grasped the suspenders of my little overalls and I was swung across from rock to rock over rapids too wide for me to jump. How tickled I was if only, upon landing on a rock, my foot would slip off into the cool water!

After reaching the "turn of the slide," we see the slippery ledges of its upper half waiting to be scaled. Half an hour later, having reached the inverted V-shaped top of the slide, where, on the wind-swept shoulder of Passaconaway, the angry tempest in the nineties tore up the trees which, crashing down, loosened dirt and stone until the whole mountain-side seemed to be slipping down, we find a narrow little path leading to the summit. Above this there is a stretch of firs and spruces, through which we journey onward and upward. Presently we reach the ledges of a northerly lookout. Instead of the huge broad-shouldered monarch, the mountain now appears an almost perpendicular, tree-fringed shaft, rapidly tapering to this lofty eagle-nest of a cliff.

The slide is lined with bushes and scrub-trees; in spots there are piles and lanes of "slide salad"—finely chipped rock, splintered and ground up timber, and sand all stirred together. Gorgeous views may be had in retrospect all the way up the upper half of the slide, and, of course, the higher up we go the better and broader the view. Nearly all the Sandwich Range peaks, the blue northern mountains and our miniature valley are spread out before us.

When the path reaches the crest of the northern spur it becomes dark, damp, and mossy. The real "Crag Barons," the deer and wild-cat and bear, reign supreme here, and here also the sun rarely penetrates the thickly branched and needled spruces. Occasionally beech trees also are found. So wet is the moss underfoot that from a handful considerable water may be wrung. As we pass through this damp wood, involuntarily we shiver from the chilliness of the atmosphere and the loneliness of the great mountain wilderness.

All at once a welcome rift appears just ahead. We hurry on and are shortly rewarded by coming out upon a deliciously warm, sun-kissed ledge. This is the northwestern outlook. We rest here long enough to drink in the view of the Franconia system and the mountains lying between us and that region, for from the main outlook we shall not have a view of this section. Tripyramid bulks large from here. And just across a gently dipping valley to the west and southwest, seemingly only at arm's length, lies Mount Whiteface, to which a good trail leads from our very feet. We shall not need to look at the northern sky-line from here, for we shall have a better view from the top.

Hastily we cover the easy quarter mile of comparatively level trail leading to the final goal. And now our feet rest on the ledge which constitutes the actual summit of Passaconaway. What a view is ours! To the northward the mountains of the Presidential Range lift their blue peaks into the clear sky. Eastward the sharp teeth of Moat and Chocorua chew jagged holes in the azure of the heavens. Far over into Maine we can see. Southeasterly lie Portland and the Atlantic Ocean. Over between Madison and Eaton a tiny thread of smoky steam catches our eye, and through our glasses we see a microscopic work slowly crawling northward. This is a train from Boston, laden with its hundreds of passengers on their way to seek rest and health in the ozone of God's Mountain Country. To me the best of the view is the herd of blue elephants, humping and rolling to the northward —the Presidential Range, the handiwork of a Maker more powerful than the architects of locomotive-works or the tiny builders of human ant-hills —our modern cities. Your trains, your hotels, your automobiles no doubt "may be all right for some," as the old guide, "Jack" Allen used to say, but give me a wild, craggy mountain, far away from the noise and dirt and confusion of towns. Here, for a time, at least, let me be a refugee from civilization."[7]

Here, on the very ridgepole of the Sandwich and Albany country, let us eat our luncheon, meanwhile drinking in the skyline. And now, having satisfied the ravenous hunger of a mountaineer, we unscrew the cover of that metallic cylinder which the Appalachians have placed in a little cairn here on the summit. In it we find a long list of names of persons who have climbed the mountain before us. We add our names to the list.

Although Passaconaway is nearly seven hundred feet higher than Chocorua, because of its rounded and wooded top, it does not afford a panoramic view of the entire sky-line. Now that we are rested, let us make our way a few rods to the southwest, through the woods, for we must not go down until we have had a glimpse of Winnepesaukee and the Lake Country. 'Twill cost but a few additional steps, for which we shall be repaid a thousandfold. No wonder the Indians loved the "Smiling Waters" (Winnepesaukee) and Squam Lake! Far off in the dim blue we can make out the Uncanoonucs, Monadnock and Wachusett.

Would that we might "build tabernacles" here in which to stay forever! But the noon-day sun is now making its way westward and we must think of descending to that little white speck in the Albany Intervale which we call "Score-o'-Peaks" and "home."

Passaconaway is the ideal haunt for bears. In the cylinder in which we registered are brief records of trampers seeing Ursa Major and Ursa Minor. What could be more fitting than that the little "Teddy Bears" of to-day, when chased by savage hunters, should flee of old Passaconaway, for was not Passaconaway, the chieftain, the "Son of the Bear"? Truly, one would naturally expect that Passaconaway's name-bearing mountain would offer shelter to the bear papooses in their fear and danger.

Many summers ago, while we were peacefully sleeping early one night, a blood-curdling scream aroused us. Again and again it was repeated. It

7. Paul Elmer More: Shelburne Essays, First Series, 24.

came from a bear in the Downes Brook valley, at the foot of Passaconaway, probably calling to his mate.

One morning, about nine o'clock, a young lumberman came speeding down the road. When opposite our cottage he was asked by some one why he was hurrying so; whereupon, with pallid features, he replied that just inside the edge of the woods, on the Passaconaway road, a shaggy old bear had introduced himself, with evident intentions of becoming better acquainted. The Frenchman at once remembered an urgent engagement requiring his presence at the lumber-store. Therefore the haste!

A couple, planning to climb Passaconaway from the Wonalancet side, had notified the Shackfords of their intention of coming over the mountain, and had reserved a room for the night. Evening approached, and at length the stars appeared. Just as the proprietors were beginning to worry about the belated pedestrians, a message arrived from the other side of the range, saying that, after almost gaining the summit, the people had decided to retrace their steps. Later, the reason for this change of plan was explained in detail. When they approached the summit, a huge black bear stuck his muzzle out from behind a ledge at the side of the path and sniffed at the bold trespassers. After a short pause, in which the said trespassers perceived no sign of retreat on the part of Mr. Bear, and not wishing to disturb the transquillity of the ursine mind, they—unarmed—quietly and (need I add?) speedily retraced their steps.

Returning from the ascent of Passaconaway one day, two of our inti mate friends, just at dark, met a huge bear in the path.

Years ago, in a pouring rain, a pair of wet, tired, and bedraggled trampers descended from the mountain. The man was leading his wife, who was blind. Eight years later my parents met the same couple in Switzerland. The gentleman was reading passages from guidebooks and telling his wife about the scenery. They had traveled for years in this way, having ridden up Pike's Peak, among other mountains. Amid the wonders and grandeur of the Alps these New Englanders chatted together once more, agreeing that the beauties of the Rhone Valley were strikingly similar to the glories of the Albany Intervale in the White Mountains.

1904

On Bald Mountain

Bradford Torrey

From *Nature's Invitation*

Turn-of-the-century naturalist Bradford Torrey (1843–1912) loved to visit the White Mountains, where he spent much of his time observing the flowers, trees and birds of the area. Torrey, the author of several other books besides Nature's Invitation, *was especially fond of the Franconia Notch region. His excursions around this spectacular area of the White Mountains were written up in such books as* Footing it in Franconia, Birds in the Bush *and* The Foot-Path Way.

"FOUR INCHES OF SNOW at the Profile House:" such was the word brought to us at the breakfast table, the driver of the "stage" having communicated the intelligence as he passed the hotel an hour or two earlier. We were not surprised. It rained in Franconia night before last, and yesterday, when the clouds now and then lifted a little, the sides of the mountains were seen to be white. This morning (October 7), although even the lower slopes were veiled, the day promised well, and at the first minute I set out for the Notch.

It was evident almost immediately that at some time within the last forty-eight hours there had been a great influx of migrating birds. Song sparrows, white-throated sparrows, snowbirds, bluebirds, and myrtle warblers were in extraordinary force. Soon I began to hear the wrennish calls of ruby-crowned kinglets,—which have been very scarce hitherto,—and presently more than one was heard rehearsing its pretty song. What with bluebird voices, song sparrows' warblings (no set tune, but "continuous melody"), the cackle of robins, and the croaking of rusty blackbirds, the air was loud. To these travelers, as to me, the weather seemed to be changing for the better, though the sun did not yet show itself, and finding themselves in so delectable a valley, they were in exuberant spirits.

Just above the Profile House farm the road took me into a flock of birds that proved to be the better part of half a mile in length. The wayside hedges were literally in a flutter, snowbirds being the most abundant, I think, with white-throats and myrtle warblers not far behind. Hermit thrushes, winter wrens, chipping sparrows, song sparrows, and ruby-crowns were continually in sight, and an unseen purple finch was practicing niggardly, disconnected, vireo-like phrases, as the manner of his kind is in the autumnal season.

Then, when the older forest was reached, there came an interval of silence, broken at last by the distant, or distant-seeming, voice of a red-breasted nuthatch and the cheerful notes of chickadees. Soon two hermits showed themselves, facing me on a low perch, and lifting their tails solemnly in response to my chirping; and not far away were a winter wren or two, and a flock of white-throats and snowbirds. I had never seen the dear old road birdier, even in May, though of course I had often seen the number of species very much larger.

At the height of land I came upon the first snow, a ragged fringe left on the shady side of the way. I made a snowball, for the sake of doing it (or, as I said to myself, suiting the boyish act with a boyish word, "for greens"), and decided to at once not to go down into the Notch, but up to the top of Bald Mountain. From that point, if the sky cleared, as I felt hopeful it would, there would be sights worth remembering.

The mountain is only a little one, but it is steep enough — the upper half, at all events — to give the eager pedestrian a puff for his money. For myself, I had time to spare, and, fortunately or unfortunately, had been over the path too often to be subject to the state of mind (I know it well) which we may characterize as climber's impatience. Unless something unforeseen should happen, the summit would wait for me. Halfway up, also, a flock of blue jays, five or six at least, who were holding a long and mysterious confabulation close by the path, afforded me a comfortable breathing spell. For a moment I suspected the presence of an owl, against whom the rascals were plotting mischief; but their voices were much of the time too soft, too intimate-sounding, too lacking in belligerency. Some of the birds might even have been communing with themselves. Their whole behavior had an air of preternatural gravity and cunning, and their remarks, whatever the purport of them, were in the highest degree varied. One fellow was a masterly performer upon the bones (jay scholars will understand what I mean, and I should despair of explaining myself in a few words to

The view of Echo Lake and Mount Lafayette from Artist's Bluff,
at the east end of the Bald Mountain ridge.

any one else), while another furnished me with a genuine surprise by
whistling again and again in the manner of a red-tailed hawk.

Well, the conspirators dispersed, the solitary climber pocketed his curiosity, and in a few minutes longer his feet were at the top. The rocky cone
of Lafayette was still densely capped, but under the fringed edges of the
cloud there was plenty of snow in sight. All the upper slopes of Kinsman,
Cannon, and Lafayette were covered with it, except that the deciduous
trees (broad patches of yellow) stood bare. Apparently the snow had stuck
only upon the evergreens, and the effect at this distance was very striking,
the white over the green producing a beautiful gray. I could never have
imagined it. The hotel and its cottages, nestled between the mountains, all
had white roofs, but the landscape as a whole was anything but wintry.
Everywhere below me the great forest still showed an abundance of bright
hues,—red, yellow, and russet,—a piece of glorious pageantry, though
many shades less brilliant than I had seen it two days before.

So I am saying to myself when suddenly I look upward, and behold, the
cap is lifted from Lafayette, and the mountain-top is clear white, shining
in the sunlight against the blue sky; a vision, it seems; something not of
this world; splendor immaculate, unearthly, unspeakable. I feel like shouting, or tell myself that I do; but for some reason I keep silence. Clouds still

hang about the mountains, their shapes altering from glory to glory with every minute. Now a band lies clean across Lafayette, immediately below the cone, detaching the white mass from everything underneath, and leaving it, as it were, floating in the air.

A sharp-shinned hawk sails past me, nuthatches call from the valley woods, a snowbird perches on a dwarf spruce at my elbow, a red squirrel breaks into sudden spluttering, and then, with hands uplifted, sits silent and motionless. I mention these details, but they are nothing. What I really see and feel is the world I am living in: the sunshine, the stillness, the temperate airs, the bright encircling forest, in which my little hilltop is cradled, and the white peak yonder in the sky. The snow lends it lightness, airiness, buoyancy. As I said just now, it seems almost to float in the ether.

I remained with this beauty for an hour, divided at the last between the luminous, snowy peak above me and the soft—ineffably soft—world of leafy tree-tops below. Then, as I had done only day before yesterday, I bade the place good-by. Probably I should not come this way again till next summer, at the soonest. Good-by, old mountain. Good-by, old woods. No doubt you have many worthier lovers, but let me be counted as one of the faithful.

I was still on the cone, making my way downward, when a grouse drummed and in a minute or two repeated himself. The sound struck me as curiously wanting in resonance, as if the log were water soaked (though I do not believe he was striking one), or his breast not fully inflated. Perhaps he was a young fellow, a new hand with the drumsticks, and so excusable. Certainly the difficulty lay not in the matter of distance, for between two of the performances I turned a sharp corner, effectively triangulating the bird, and it was impossible that he should be more than a few yards away. On all sides the little nuthatches were calling to each other in their quaint childish treble. I love to hear them, and the goldcrests also; but here, as on the heights above, the birds were less than the forest. I was in a susceptible mood, I suppose. The mere sight of the tall, straight trunks, with the lights and shadows on them, gave me a pleasure indescribable. Though the friend who had been my walking companion for a week past (and no man could wish a better one) is sure to read this column, I cannot refrain from saying that solitariness has its merciful alleviations. I was no longer tempted to babble, and the wise old trees took their turn at talking. If I could only repeat what they said!

Historical Perspectives

1874

First Visits
to Mount Washington

Warren Upham

From *Geology of New Hampshire* (Vol. 1)

Warren Upham (1850–1934) of Nashua was an undergraduate student at Dart-mouth College when Prof. Charles Hitchcock was conducting his intensive geo-logical survey of the state in 1869–1871. During the summer of 1871, Upham was a member of Hitchcock's team, and during a month-long summer sojourn into the unexplored corners of the White Mountains, Upham and another student partic-ipant probably became the first persons to reach the remote peaks of Mounts Bond and Guyot in the Pemigewasset Wilderness. Several years after graduating from Dartmouth, Upham also became quite active in the newly formed Appalachian Mountain Club.

THE EARLY HISTORY of the White Mountains may well be of inter-est to all who feel a pride in the beautiful scenery or in the material pros-perity of this portion of our state. It is only a meagre record, however, that we are able to present. Even the name of the first adventurer who ascended these mountains was for some time uncertain. It was stated by Dr. Bel-knap, in the early editions of this history of New Hampshire, that Walter and Robert Neal were the first to climb the highest summit of the White Mountains, in 1631. This appears to be incorrect; and the error was noticed by the author in the edition of 1812. It is now considered settled that this credit is to be assigned to Darby Field, of Pascataquack (Portsmouth), who made the ascent, accompanied by two Indians, in June, 1642. An account of this has been preserved by Winthrop, from which it now appears that "within 12 miles of the top was neither tree nor grass, but low savins, which they went upon the top of sometimes, but a continual ascent upon rocks, on a ridge between two valleys filled with snow, out of which came two branches of Saco river, which met at the foot of the hill, where was an Indian town of some 200 people. By the way, among the rocks, there were two ponds,—one a blackish water, the other a reddish. The top of all was plain, about 60 feet square. On the north side was such a precipice as they could scarce discern to the bottom. They had neither cloud nor wind on the top, and moderate heat. About a month after he went again, with five or six in his company." The appearance of the mountains is thus seen to have been the same two hundred years ago as now; but besides this description, Field brought back a glowing account of precious stones, &c., and even sheets of "Muscovy glass," or mica, forty feet long! The enumeration of these wonders was probably employed to collect the party for his second expedition.

This inducement, also, says the historian, "caused divers others to travel thither, but they found nothing worth their pains." Of these are particularly mentioned Thomas Gorges and Mr. Vines, two magistrates of the province of Sir Ferdinando Gorges, who went about the end of August of the same year. "They went up Saco River in birch canoes, and that way they found it 90 miles to Pegwaggett, an Indian town; but by land it is but 60. Upon Saco River they found many thousand acres of rich meadow; but there are 10 falls, which hinder boats, &c. From the Indian town they went up hill (for the most part) about 30 miles in woody lands. They then went 7 or 8 miles upon shattered rocks, without tree or grass, very steep all the way. At the top is a plain 3 or 4 miles over, all shattered stones; and upon that is another rock or spire, about a mile in height, and about an acre of ground at the top. At the top of the plain arise four great rivers; each of them so much water at the first issue as would drive a mill; Connecticut River from two heads at the N. W. and S. W., which join in one about 60 miles off; Saco River on the S. E.; Amascoggin, which runs into Casco Bay, at the N. E.; and Kennebeck, at the N. by E. The mountain runs E. and W. thirty miles, but the peak is above all the rest. They went and returned in 15 days."

The route taken by Field, and probably by the other explorers also, lay from the Saco up Ellis river nearly to its source, and thence up the great ridge south-east of Mt. Washington, known as Boott's Spur. Tuckerman's ravine and Oakes's gulf, on either hand, are recognized as the "two valleys filled with snow." The summit of this spur brought them to the broadest portion of the comparatively level tract at the southern base of Mt. Washington, the south-eastern part of which is the grassy expanse of some forty acres, known as Bigelow's Lawn. Between this and the summit they encountered the Lake of the Clouds, and smaller ponds, which no doubt furnished Gorges with a part of the sources of his rivers; and no one who has looked into the abyss somewhat absurdly denominated the "Gulf of Mexico," will wonder at its notice in the brief account of the first explorer. E. Tuckerman, in 1843, endeavored to trace the path of these earliest ascents, and was surprised with a view of Mt. Washington as a somewhat regular pyramid rising from an apparent plain, which is the way it was described by Gorges, and afterwards by Josselyn. Davis's bridle-path, opened in 1845, traversed the bold part of this ridge, and afforded the same view while it was in use.

The first mention of the White Mountains in print occurs in John Josselyn's "New England Rarities Discovered," which was published in 1672, containing the earliest notice of the botany of the country. The materials for this and a subsequent work were collected by the author during two visits to New England, coming first in 1638 and remaining fifteen months, and again in 1663, remaining eight years. In his account of the mountains, he describes a pond upon the highest summit,—either from a defect of memory, or because he was satisfied with seeing them at a distance, without making the ascent, and mistook its position, as described by explorers. "Four-score miles," says Josselyn, "to the North-west of *Scarborow*, a Ridge of Mountains runs North-west and North-east an hundred leagues, known by the name of the *White Mountains*, upon which lieth snow all the year, and is a Landmark twenty miles off at Sea. It is rising ground from the seashore to these Hills, and they are inaccessible except by the Gullies which the dissolved Snow hath made. In these Gullies grow *Saven* bushes, which, being taken hold of, are a good help to the climbing discoverer. Upon the top of the highest of these Mountains is a large Level or Plain, of a day's journey over, whereon nothing grows but Moss. At the farther end of this Plain is another Hill called the *Sugarloaf*, to outward appearances a rude heap of massie stones piled one upon another; and you may, as you ascend, step from one stone to another as if you were going up a pair of stairs, but winding still about the Hill till you come to the top, which will require half a day's time,—and yet it is not above a Mile,—where there is also a Level of about an Acre of ground, with a pond of clear water in the midst of it, which you may hear run down, but how it ascends is a mystery. From this rocky Hill you may see the whole country round about. It is far above the lower clouds; and from hence we behold a Vapour (like a great Pillar) drawn up by the Sun Beams out of a great Lake or Pond into the air, where it was formed into a Cloud. The Country below these Hills Northward is daunting terrible, being full of rocky Hills as thick as Mole-hills in a Meadow, and cloathed with infinite thick Woods." In his "Voyages," published a year or two later, Josselyn corrects what he says of the snow's lying the whole year upon the mountains, by excepting the month of August.

The "Voyages" contain an account of the Indian traditions which clustered about our highest mountains. "Ask them," says Josselyn, "whither they go when they dye, they will tell you, pointing with their finger to Heaven, beyond the White Mountains; and do hint at Noah's Floud, as may be conceived by a story they have received from Father to Son, time out of mind, that a great while agon their Countrey was drowned, and all the people and other Creatures in it, only one *Powaw* and his *Webb*, foreseeing the Floud, fled to the White Mountains, carrying a hare along with them, and so escaped. After a while, the Powaw sent the Hare away, who not returning, emboldened thereby, they descended, and lived many years after and had many children, from whom the Countrie was again filled with Indians." None of the traditions of the native tribes appear to have been so widespread as that of a flood; and many notices might be cited similar to this of the White Mountains. Caitlin describes a ceremony referring to this which he witnessed among the Mandans, on the upper Missouri river, where the only survivor was represented as white.

The next mention of explorations among the White Mountains is on April 29, 1725, when "a ranging company ascended the highest mountain on the N. W. part,"—probably the first ascent from this side. As was to be expected, they found the snow deep and the Alpine ponds frozen. Another ranging party being "in the neighborhood of the White Mountains, on a warm day in the Month of March, in 1746, were alarmed with a repeated noise, which they supposed to be the firing of guns. On further search, they found it to be caused by rocks falling from the south side of a steep mountain." This is the first notice we find of the mighty force that has left its furrows and scars all through the mountains, and which caused to be written the saddest page in their history.

Discovery of the White Mountain Notch

It is supposed that the Indians were aware of the central pass through the White Mountains, and took their captives through it to Canada; but its existence was unknown to the English at the time of the first settlement of the Coös county. The value of these lands was thus very diminished on account of the wide circuit which must be made either to east or west to communicate with the seaboard, so that it became a matter of inquiry to the authorities of the state how a way should be opened through this almost impassable chain. Its discovery was made in 1771 by one Timothy Nash, a pioneer hunter who had established himself in this solitary region. Climbing a tree on Cherry mountain in search of a moose, he discovered, as he thought, the wished-for pass. Steering for the opening, he soon struck the Saco river, a mere brook, and following down, stopped at what is now known as the gate of the notch. Here the sharp rocks came so near together as to prevent his following the stream; but, seeing that by a reasonable expenditure a road could be opened at the point, he scaled the cliffs and continued on to Portsmouth. Here he made known his discovery to Governor Wentworth. The wary governor, to test the practicability of the pass, informed Nash that if he would bring him a horse down through the gorge from Lancaster, he would grant him the tract of land now known as Nash and Sawyer's Location. To accomplish this, Nash admitted a fellow hunter, Benjamin Sawyer, to share in his trade. By means of ropes they succeeded in getting the horse over the projecting cliff and down the rugged pathway of the mountain torrent, and brought him to the governor. When they saw the horse safely lowered on the south side of the last projection, it is said that Sawyer, draining the last drop of rum from his junk bottle, and breaking it on the rock, called it Sawyer's rock, by which name it has ever since been known. A road was soon opened by the proprietors of land in the upper Coos, and settlers began to make their way into the immediate vicinity of the mountains. Jefferson, Whitefield, Littleton, and Franconia were first settled within two or three years after this date. A road was also commenced through the eastern, or Pinkham notch, in 1774, and Shelburne, which included Gorham, received its first inhabitants in the following year.

The earliest articles of commerce taken through the notch have not escaped mention. They appear to have been a barrel of tobacco, raised at Lancaster, which was carried to Portsmouth, and a barrel of rum which a company in Portland offered to any one who should succeed in taking it through the pass. This was done by Captain Rosebrook, with some assistance, though it was nearly empty, we are informed, "through the politeness of those who helped manage the affair." The difficulty of communication was often the occasion of more serious want, and it was no rare thing to suffer from scarcity of provisions. In 1800, the inhabitants of Bethlehem were obliged to leave their occupations, go into the woods, and cut and burn timber enough for a load of potash, with which to procure provisions after a journey of one hundred seventy miles. The original cost of the road was forty thousand dollars, and the expense of repairs was large; but it proved a profitable investment. Strings of teams of a half a mile in length were sometimes seen winding through Conway on their route to Portland, the great market at that time for all northern New Hampshire.

Visits of Scientific Parties

Mt. Washington was ascended in July, 1784, "with a view to make particular observations on the several phenomena which might occur," the party consisting of the Rev. Manasseh Cutler, of Ipswich, Mass., a zealous member of the American Academy of Arts and Sciences, the Rev. Daniel Little, of Kennebunk, Me., also a member of the Academy, and Col. John Whipple, of Jefferson (then Dartmouth), together with others to the number of seven in all. They are said to have been "the subject of much speculation" as they passed through Eaton and Conway. Dr. Belknap, the early historian of the state, and Dr. Fisher, of Beverly, Mass., were of this party, but neither of them succeeded in reaching the summit. Dr. Fisher remained at the notch "to collect birds, and other animal and vegetable productions." The objects of the expedition were but partially attained. It happened unfortunately that thick clouds covered the mountains nearly the whole time, so that the instruments, which they had carried up with much labor, were rendered useless. They made some unsatisfactory barometrical observations, but were unable to test them in an attempted geometrical measurement from the base. The barometer had suffered so much agitation that an allowance was necessary, and the altitude was computed in round numbers at 5,500 feet above the meadow in the valley below, and nearly 10,000 feet above the level of the sea. This was no greater altitude than appears to have been generally assigned to these mountains. Dr. Belknap, in 1792, gave his opinion that these figures were too small, predicting "that whenever the mountain can be measured with the requisite precision, it will be found to exceed ten thousand feet, of perpendicular altitude, above the level of the ocean."

The plants of the upper region were now described for the first time, but only in a general way. The following extract from a manuscript of Dr. Cutler, which is quoted by Belknap, points out the more prominent botanical features, as seen by the first scientific party: "There is evidently the appearance of three zones,—1. the woods; 2, the bald, mossy part; 3, the part above vegetation. The same appearance has been observed on the Alps and all other high mountains. I recollect no grass on the plain. The spaces between the rocks in the second zone and on the plain are filled with spruce and fir, which perhaps have been growing ever since the creation, and yet many of them have not attained a greater height than three or four inches; but their spreading tops are so thick and strong as to support the weight of a man without yielding in the smallest degree;—the snows and winds keeping the surface even with the general surface of the rocks. In many places on the sides we could get glades of this growth some rods in extent, when we could, by sitting down on our feet, slide the whole length. The tops of the growth of wood were so thick and firm as to bear us currently a considerable distance before we arrived at the utmost boundaries, which were almost as well defined as the water on the shore of the pond. The tops of the wood had the appearance of having been shorn off, exhibiting a smooth surface from their upper limits for a great distance down the mountain." "On the uppermost rock" the letters "N. H." were engraved; and a plate of lead bearing the names of the party was deposited under a stone.

The route by which Cutler and his party reached the mountain is probably indicated by the stream which bears his name in Bigelow's narrative. "In less than half a mile southward from this fountain,"—that is, of Ellis river, at the height of land between the Saco and Androscoggin, in Pinkham woods,—"a large stream, which runs down the highest of the White Mountains, falls into Ellis river; and, in about the same distance from this, another falls from the same mountain. The former of these streams is Cutler's river, the latter New river. " The name is said to have applied to the stream at Dr. Cutler's express wish.

A "Second Scientific Visit" was made in 1804 by Dr. Cutler, who was accompanied by W. D. Peck, afterwards professor of natural history at Cambridge, Mass. Barometrical observations made on this occasion, and computed by Mr. Bowditch, gave to Mt. Washington an elevation of 7,055 feet above the sea. A collection of the alpine plants was made by Dr. Peck, and was afterwards seen by Mr. Pursh, in whose "Flora of North America," printed in 1814, many of the most interesting species were described. Naturalists soon began to give special attention to the peculiar Arctic flora and fauna of these mountains. A quite complete enumeration and description of the phaenogamous plants, together with a statement of much concerning their mineralogy and zoology appeared in Dr. Bigelow's "Account of the White Mountains of New Hampshire," published in 1816, from explorations made during the same season. Dr. Francis Boott, Mr. Francis C. Gray, and the venerable Chief Justice Shaw were members of this party. The barometrical observations which they obtained gave

6,225 feet above the sea. This visit was made in June; and Dr. Boott made a second visit the succeeding month, adding a considerable number of species to the botanical collections. The ascent was from the eastern pass, following Cutler's river. In 1819, Abel Crawford opened a footway to Mt. Washington following the south-western ridge. This and the new road made two years later by Ethan Allen Crawford along the Ammonoosuc, subsequently became the more common ways of ascending the mountains. Botanists were gainers by this change, especially those whose work enabled them to examine the finest localities for Alpine plants while on their way to the summit. An account of the expedition of 1816 appeared in the *New England Journal of Medicine and Surgery* for November of the same year.

Maps, Surveys, and Names

The first and only map of New Hampshire issued under the direction of the state authorities, was that of Philip Carrigain, published in 1816. The author's name is still preserved at the White Mountains, as that of the noblest of the peaks upon the east branch of the Pemigewasset,—too distant, however, from settlements to be often visited by tourists. This map notices that recent barometrical calculations give 7,162 feet above the sea as the height of the White Mountains; and states that, being below the line of perpetual congelation, which must be 7,200 feet lower than in Europe on the same parallel, they cannot exceed 7,800 feet. The author then somewhat incorrectly adds,—"After every abridgment of the heretofore exaggerated estimates of their altitude, it will be found doubly to exceed that of any mountain in the United States other than those of New Hampshire." The Franconia and Mt. Washington ranges, with intervening ranges and peaks, are laid down on this map; but no names are applied to individual summits throughout this central area of the White Mountains, with the exception of Lafayette, which is called "Great Haystack." The prominent mountains which stand on guard just outside this area, however, were already distinguished by the same names as now. We find "Pigwacket Mt., formerly Kiarsarge;" "Corway Peak Mt." (Chocorua); also "Corway" pond and river; and, on the west, Kinsman's Mt. and "Moosehillock" Mt. The latter is in the town of "Coventry," changed to Benton in 1840. Albany, Woodstock, Carroll, Randolph, and Jackson are designated by the names *Burton, Peeling, Breton Woods, Durand, and Adams*. The name of "Merrimack River, or Pemigewasset Br.," is applied to that stream above Franklin; while the East Branch is marked "Merrimack R." The names

Hancock Br. and *Moosehillock Br.,* and the old form *Ammariscoggin,* are also found on this map. In his short notice of the productions and natural features of the state, the author remarks, referring to its lake and mountain scenery, "It may be called the Switzerland of America,"—a term which has been generally adopted in descriptions of New Hampshire.

The first carefully prepared map of the White Mountains was published by Prof. G. P. Bond, of Cambridge, Mass., in 1853, from original triangulation. The history of the efforts of the geological survey to secure more perfect maps of this region, with the result of these labors, is given in another part of this work.

Considerable interest appears to have been awakened as to the altitude of these mountains, on account of the conflicting results of barometrical measurements; and we find that in July, 1820, a party of engineers and others from Lancaster visited the whole range between the notch and Mt. Madison, and, on a second visit, measured the altitudes with a spirit level. The first party consisted of Adino N. Brackett, John W. Weeks, Gen. John Wilson, Charles J. Stuart, Noyes S. Dennison, and Samuel A Pearson, of Lancaster, with Philip Carrigain and E. A. Crawford, the latter acting as pilot and baggage-carrier. This party gave names to Mts. Pleasant, Franklin, Monroe, Jefferson, Adams, and Madison. They called the Lake of the Clouds "Blue pond," and the locality since named after Bigelow was by them called "Carrigain's lawn." The dead, gnarled trees, which are especially conspicuous on Moosilauke and common on all the mountains, received special notice. They were called by some members of the party *buck's horns,* and by others *bleached bones.* The cause of the death of these trees they supposed to have been the cold seasons which prevailed from 1812 to 1816, saying,—"It can hardly be doubted that during the whole year 1816 these trees continued frozen." This was the year long remembered as the "year without a summer." About a month after this visit, Weeks, Stuart, and Brackett, accompanied by Richard Eastman, spent seven days in levelling to the tops of all these mountains from Lancaster, encamping on them four nights;—that of August 31st on the summit of Mt. Washington. They must have been the first party who ever spent the night upon the summit. They made Mt. Washington 6,428 feet above the sea, or 5,850 feet above the river at Lancaster. An interesting account of these visits is found in the "New Hampshire Historical Collections" for 1823. During the year following these visits, Capt. Partridge again computed the height of Mt. Washington from barometrical observations, giving 6,234 feet. The observations by Dr. C. T. Jackson, in 1840, were quite accurate for the difference in height between Mt. Washington and the notch. Correcting the error for the height of the notch, his figures would stand 6,303, instead of 6,228, only ten feet in excess of the correct height. Prof. Arnold Guyot, in 1851, from barometrical observations, gives the figure of 6,291 feet. In his memoir of the "Appalachian Mountain System," published in 1861, he has altered these figures to 6,388. In 1853, Capt. T. J. Cram levelled to the summit of Mt. Washington, under the direction of the United States Coast Survey, and reported its height to be 6,293 feet, which may be assumed to be the true altitude.

The Indians are said to have been restrained by awe and fear from climbing to the summits of these mountains. Their traditions represented that here was the residence of the Great Spirit, who, with a motion of the hand, could raise a storm and destroy the daring adventurer who presumed to approach his abode. They never felt, amid the sublimity and awfulness of the mountains, that sense of ownership and appropriation which was inspired by rivers and lakes, with their calmer beauty and life-sustaining productiveness. Thus, while solitary mountains throughout the state, like nearly all the rivers, still preserve the names of their ancient baptism, always the last memorial of a departed race, the central portion of the White Mountains is wholly English in name and associations. We do know that the Indians distinguished them by any other than a collective name. This, according to Dr. Belknap, was *Agiocochook* in one dialect, and in another *Waumbekket-Methna*, signifying *Mountains with snowy foreheads*. The English name *White Mountains* we meet in the earliest account of them that was published. It is not probable that this name was applied to them while as yet they were only known to adventurous mariners in their exploring voyages along the coast.

It is possible to ascertain who first proposed to call the highest of these summits Mt. Washington. Dr. Belknap, in 1792, says of it, — "it has lately been distinguished by the name of Mt. Washington." He quotes from the manuscript of Dr. Cutler, in another place, the account of the zones of vegetation, where mention is made of "Mount Washington." as if it were well known. As his visit was made in 1784, it is not unlikely that the name was proposed soon after the close of the revolutionary war, probably by Dr. Cutler's party. Of other prominent peaks, besides those named by the party of 1820, Mt. Clinton received its name from some undiscoverable source, certainly before 1837. Mts. Clay and Jackson were named by Mr. Oakes. This gentleman was with Prof. Tuckerman and sent up his guide, Amasa Allen, to build a fire on the top of the south spur of Clinton; and thus, with a fiery baptism, the mountain was christened Jackson. Mt. Willard was named from Mr. Sidney Willard, of Boston; and it is probable that the name of Mt. Webster was proposed by Mr. Willard for the peak known to earlier visitors as Notch mountain. Lower down the Saco, Mts. Crawford and Resolution, as well as the Giant's stairs, received names from Dr. S. A. Bemis. The names of Tuckerman's ravine, Oake's gulf, and Bigelow's lawn were given, in honor of three eminent botanists who had particularly distinguished themselves in the study of the White Mountain flora, to three fine localities as well as marked topographical features. It is difficult to ascertain the origin of many of the names of natural objects about the mountains. Dr. Bemis has perhaps applied more appellations than any other person to these features. Other names have been given by chance visitors, and preserved by usage among guides.

No Indian legends remain about the mountains, and but few localities have a particular history. There is one cascade, however, about a quarter of a mile from the former residence of old Abel Crawford, which is more distinguished by the sad story associated with it, than by the picturesqueness of the crags through which it hurries for the last mile of its descent. It is called "Nancy's Brook." Here, late in the autumn of 1788, a young woman, who had lived with a family in Jefferson, was found frozen to death. She was engaged to be married to a man who was employed in the same family where she served, and had entrusted to him all her earnings, with the understanding that in a few days they should leave for Portsmouth to be married there. During her temporary absence at Lancaster, nine miles distant, the man started with his employer for Portsmouth, leaving no explanation or message for her. She learned the fact of her desertion on the same day, and at once walked back to Jefferson, tied up a small bundle of clothing, and, in spite of all warnings and entreaties, set out on foot to overtake them. The distance to the notch was thirty miles, with no settlement on the way, the only road being a hunter's path marked by spotted trees. It had been snowing, but she pressed on over this road through the night, in hope of overtaking her lover at the camp in the notch before the party should start in the morning. She reached it soon after the party had left, and it appeared to those who, alarmed for her safety, had followed on from Jefferson to overtake her, that she had tried in vain to rekindle the fire in the lonely camp. Failing in this, she had hurried on, climbing the wild pass of the notch, and following the track of the Saco towards Conway. Several miles of the roughest part of the way she travelled thus, often fording the river. But her strength was spent by two or three hours of such toil; and she was found by the party in pursuit of her, chilled and stiff in the snow, at the foot of an aged tree near "Nancy's Bridge," not many hours after she had ceased to breathe.

January 1899

Some Old Tales and Traditions of the White Mountains

T. C. Gibson

From *The Granite Monthly*

First published in 1877, The Granite Monthly *was New Hampshire's premier statewide magazine for a period lasting more than 50 years (1877–1931). Published in Concord, the monthly periodical was devoted almost entirely to the "history, biography, literature and state progress" of New Hampshire. The magazine's frequent "historical sketches" of communities across the state make for exceptionally interesting reading today, more than a century after many of these pieces first appeared in print.*

IT IS PECULIARLY characteristic of the mountainous countries that they have nearly always a romantic and interesting history, and that their hills and valleys are usually associated with strange traditions and weird legends. This is strikingly exemplified in such European countries as Scotland, Spain, Switzerland, the Tyrol, the mountainous parts of Germany, Norway, and other mountainous countries, all of which have a fascinating history, and are rich in traditional folk-lore. Who has not been enchanted by legends of the Vikings, or thrilled by tales of Sir William Wallace, or of William Tell? Who, during the past few months, has not been deeply interested in the romantic story of Cuba, amongst whose beautiful mountains has been carried on for so long that patriotic struggle for freedom which is now by aid of the American arms, about to be brought to a successful issue?

But it is not necessary to go so far afield as Europe or Cuba to find a mountainous country of romantic interest. Nay, indeed, it is not necessary to go further away than New England, for in the beautiful White Mountains of New Hampshire there is to be found a wealth of material awaiting the pen of the romanticist, that seems to have been strangely neglected up till the present.

The White Mountain region was once the home of powerful Indian tribes, and these entertained some strange beliefs regarding the mountains. Their theory of the origin of the White Mountains is as interesting as it is singular: "Cold storms were in the northern wilderness, and a lone red hunter wandered without food, chilled by the frozen wind. He lost his strength and could find no game; and the dark cloud that covered his life-path made him weary of wandering. He fell down upon the snow and a dream carried him to a wide, happy valley, filled with musical streams, where singing birds and game were plenty. His spirit cried aloud for joy, and the 'Great Master of Life' waked him from his sleep and gave him a dry coal and a flint-pointed spear, telling him that by the shore of the lake he might live, and find fish with his spear and fire from his dry coal. One night he had lain down his coal, and seen a warm fire spring therefrom with a blinding smoke. And a great noise like thunder filled the air, and there rose up a vast pile of broken rocks. Out of the cloud resting upon the top came numerous streams, dancing down, foaming cold; and the voice spake to the astonished red hunter, saying: 'Here the Great Spirit will dwell and watch over his favorite children.'"

The Indians held the mountains in great fear and veneration. A curious superstition peopled the higher peaks with superior beings, invisible to the human eye, who had complete control of the tempests. These mountains they never dared to ascend; and when the first white explorers came, the Indians not only assured them that to make the ascent of those mountains was impossible, but earnestly entreated them not to make the attempt, lest the spirits that ruled the tempests might be offended and utterly destroy them. Once, indeed, tradition says that a famous Indian chief named Passaconaway, who held a conference with the spirits above, ascended

> "To those mountains white and cold
> Of which the Indian trapper told,
> Upon whose summit never yet,
> Was mortal foot in safety set;"

and from thence passed to a council in heaven. Another Indian tradition told of a great flood once having taken place when all the world was drowned save the White Mountains. To these one single powwow and his squaw retreated and found safety from the waters, and thus preserved the race from extinction.

Perhaps the most interesting Indian tradition is that which is associated with Mount Chocorua, a peculiarly shaped peak to the north [actually south] of the Presidential range. Chocorua was once a powerful chief, who, after the rest of his tribe had left the country, remained behind amidst his native hills and valleys over which he had once held sway. There seems to be more than one version of the tradition relating to his death and his curse. The one given by Drake in his "History of the North American Indians" is usually regarded as correct and is to the following effect: Pursued by a miserable white hunter Chocorua had retreated to the mountain which now bears his name. He had climbed to the highest point where his further flight was barred by a great precipice, where he stood unarmed, while below stood his pursuer within gunshot. Chocorua besought the hunter to spare his life. He pleaded his friendliness to the whites, and the harmless, scattered condition of his few followers. But the hardened hunter was unmoved; the price of his scalp was too tempting; gold pleaded stronger than the poor Indian. Seeing that he should avail nothing, the noble chieftain, raising himself up, stretched forth his arms, and called upon the Gods of his fathers to curse the land. Then, casting a defiant glance at his pursuer, he leaped from the brink of the precipice to the rocks below. "And to this day, say the inhabitants, a malignant disease has carried off the cattle that they have attempted rearing around this mountain." In an old volume which the writer has had the privilege of examining there is another story given in connection with Chocorua's curse, the truth of which, however, is not vouched for. It is a sad, though a beautiful story and we regret that it is not possible to give it in full, but an outline must suffice. Cornelius Campbell had been a follower of Cromwell, and a bitter enemy of the House of Stuart; and on the restoration of Charles II he had been compelled to flee to America, where he and his beautiful and noble-hearted wife found a home amongst the New Hampshire hills. Campbell is described as a man possessed of great intellectual powers and a gigantic frame, and passionately devoted to his wife and family. To their house came the son of Chocorua, a boy of nine or ten years, to whom Mrs. Campbell showed much kindness. One day this boy accidentally drank some poison while paying one of his usual visits to the Campbells, and shortly afterwards died. From that time Chocorua meditated revenge, and one day Cornelius Campbell returned home to find his wife and children murdered, and that so cruelly that there could be no doubt as to who was the perpetrator of the foul deed. For a time Campbell's frenzy amounted to madness, but at last he set out with a party in pursuit of the Indian, who had retreated to the mountain which now bears his name. Here he was found by Campbell at the edge of the precipice already mentioned. With an Indian's calmness Chocorua faced his terrible adversary, saying that the "Great Spirit" had given life to Chocorua and that he would not yield it to the white man! "Then," said Campbell, "hear the Great Spirit speak in the white man's thunder," and raising his gun, deliberately took aim and fired. Chocorua, with his dying woods, prayed that a curse might rest on the land. It is a somewhat curious coincidence that for long it was found impossible for cattle to live in the neighborhood of the mountain. Scientists eventually discovered that the trouble was in the water, but for long the superstitious believed that Chocorua's curse lay on the district.

The power of the White Mountain Indians was completely broken in the fight known as the battle of Saco Pond. The expedition which terminated in this fight was organized by Captain Lovewell, and the object was to put a stop to Indian depredations which had for long kept settlements in the vicinity of the mountains in a state of perpetual fear and terror. The most dreaded tribe was the Pequawkets, and Lovewell determined to attack them at their home on the Saco. His band at first numbered forty-six volunteers, but on the march that number was reduced by sickness to thirty-three. This intrepid band fell into an ambush at Saco pond and a desperate fight ensued which lasted from ten in the morning "till the going down of the sun." Among the first to fall mortally wounded was the brave Captain Lovewell; and when night fell only nine of his heroic followers remained unwounded, and of the Indians only twenty left the field uninjured. Their brave chief was among the slain and although the advantage lay with them at the close of the fight their power was so broken as never again to be rallied. The story of the retreat of the whites is full of pathetic interest and noble self-sacrifice.

The settlement of the White Mountains is of comparatively recent date. Not more than a century ago the first settlers were struggling to overcome difficulties that seemed all but insurmountable, and braving dangers from which the boldest might shrink, with a fortitude and heroism to which justice has never been done. Slowly, inch by inch almost, had they to clear their way through a forest of remarkable density, through which prowled many fierce animals, such as the wolf, bear, and most dreaded of all, the terrible lynx or gray-cat. But even when a clearing had been made and fenced off from the attacks of the wild beasts there still remained to be removed a vast quantity of rocks and great boulders, and this was often a more difficult undertaking than the clearing of the forest.

The pass through the White Mountain Notch was only discovered as recently as 1779, and this way he set down as the real starting point in the history of the settlement of the White Mountains. This important discovery was made quite accidentally by a hunter named Nash while on a hunting expedition on Cherry mountain. This pass gave direct communication with the lower towns, and the seaboard. Hitherto a long detour had to be made around the mountains in order to get to any of the lower settlements. The first article of merchandise to be brought up through the Notch was a barrel of rum, which, it is recorded, was, when delivered at its destination, nearly empty "through the kindness of those who helped bring it up." Many years elapsed, however, before a road was made through the Notch, and many hardships had to be endured before roads and railways were known amongst the mountains.

One of the first settlers was Captain Rosebrook, whose cabin it is said was thirty miles from any other human habitation and the way to it was only marked by "spotted trees." Captain Rosebrook was a man strong and athletic, and inured to hardship. During the Revolutionary War his services had proved of great value to the American forces in the Indian warfares they were often obliged to carry on. Of his connection with the mountains many stories are told. It is said on one occasion the want of salt compelled the Captain to go on foot to Haverhill, a distance of 80 miles through a trackless wilderness, following the Connecticut river as his guide, to obtain a supply of this humble commodity. There he obtained one bushel which he shouldered and trudged home over the same rude path.

The town of Bethlehem is now one of the most popular summer resorts in America. Its situation, commanding a most magnificent prospect of mountain and valley, is unequaled. Occupying an elevated plateau from which, in the background, rises Mount Agassiz, Bethlehem annually attracts thousands of health and pleasure seekers from all parts of this country and even from beyond the seas. Its magnificent street, extending along the base of the mountain for two miles, is lined with palatial hotels, boarding houses, and summer residences, where every luxury abounds in plenty. New York and all the principal New England towns are within a few hours' journey. But let us look at Bethlehem as it was in 1799 — not quite a hundred years ago. We see then a backwoods settlement, far removed from any populous district, surrounded by the great primeval forest through which prowl many fierce beasts and where still lurk a few miserable Indians, remnants of the once powerful tribes that had formerly held sway in this region. Often in the night would the settlers be startled by the howling of packs of hungry wolves; or on arising in the morning would find that during the night bears had broken in on their flocks, killing and devouring them. But, worst of all, there comes a famine.

Provisions have run short. The nearest towns, where fresh supplies can be got, are far away; and besides they have not the means to purchase provisions. But these people have all their lives been accustomed to hardships; and have faced difficulties and dangers only to overcome them. On this occasion, therefore, their expedient is to go into the forest where they burn wood sufficient to make a load of potash for a team of oxen, which they dispatch to Concord a distance of one hundred and seventy miles. But four weary and anxious weeks must elapse ere the teamster can return with provisions and during that time the people keep themselves alive by eating green chocolate roots and such other plants, to be found in the forest around, as will yield them any nourishment. Such is a picture we have of Bethlehem a hundred years ago. The town of Littleton, which is now the principal business centre in northern New Hampshire, within the memory of some still living, consisted of three small houses built of logs.

There have been, happily, few tragedies connected with the history of the White Mountains, and these have already been often told. The best known is probably that connected with Nancy's brook. Nancy, a servant-girl, was engaged to a man in the employ of Colonel Whipple, and it was arranged that they should accompany the Colonel to Portsmouth to be married. Having entrusted all her savings to her lover, Nancy went to Lancaster to make some purchases necessary for the journey, and on her return found that Colonel Whipple and her lover had already departed. Though it was late at night and midwinter at the time, Nancy started out in the hope of overtaking them, and her body was found by the brook which now bears her name, cold and frozen, with her head leaning on her staff. A few years afterwards her recreant lover died a raving maniac.

All who are acquainted with the White Mountains are familiar with the story of the terrible disaster which caused the destruction of the Willey family in the night of the great slide in 1826. Houses of entertainment were at that time not very plentiful in the mountains, and the one kept by Samuel Willey at the White Mountain Notch was much frequented by farmers as a stop-over place on their way to and from market. A long spell of drought was followed by a terrific storm which in one single night is said to have dislodged a greater quantity of trees, rocks and soil than the slides of the previous hundred years had done. A tremendous slide took place on the mountain behind the Willey house. The house itself escaped

Nancy Brook in Crawford
Notch, near the spot where
Nancy Barton was found
frozen to death in 1778.

as if by a miracle, a great rock behind the house dividing it to the right and
left of the house. But the whole family, consisting of nine persons, perished. In seeking to escape they had been overtaken by the terrible avalanche. Six of the bodies were afterwards taken from beneath the debris,
some of them terribly mutilated, but three bodies still lie buried beneath
the awful mass of rocks and earth that overwhelmed them on that night
of terrors. The writer has been told by one who can recollect of that awful
storm, that the appalling noise made by the slides that night could be distinctly heard in Bethlehem fifteen or twenty miles distant.

It has often been deplored that the White Mountains are almost destitute of interesting traditions and associations, and it has been said that if
they were only in Europe instead of America that there would be a story
or a legend connected with every rock and crag, and that every mountain
and glen would be wrapped in an air of mystery and romance. It must
be remembered, however, that the White Mountains were practically
unknown a hundred years ago, and compared with those of European

countries that is but as yesterday. It must necessarily follow, therefore, that the romance of the White Mountains must always be essentially different from that which the legends and traditions of remote ages have associated with the mountainous countries of Europe. But it does not, therefore, follow that there is nothing of poetry or romance to be found in the New England mountains. We think there is much of both to be found in the life of the pioneers and settlers, in their struggles and sacrifices, their patient toiling, their bravery and heroism, and their great hardihood and perseverance. The romance of the White Mountains has still to be written. Surely such grand scenes are worthy of the pen of a Scott or a Byron; and it may be that there will one day arise another "Wizard of the North" whose pen shall weave around the old mountain dwellings, where, far away in the shades of the almost trackless forest the travelers of a century ago were wont to find rest and shelter, stories of romance; who shall make a Trossachs of this beautiful region, or make classic the Saco or Ammonnosuc; and who shall throw around the White Mountains of New England a bright halo of romance that time shall not dim.

February 1926

The Golden Age
of the White Hills

Frederick Tuckerman

From *Appalachia*

Since 1876, Appalachia *has served as the official journal of the Boston-based Appalachian Mountain Club. The idea of establishing a club journal was conceived by Samuel H. Scudder, AMC's second president. With the exception of just a couple of years, the journal has been published twice a year for the last 124 years. White Mountain history buffs will find early issues of* Appalachia *particularly interesting as these frequently contained accounts of ventures into unexplored reaches of the White Hills.*

MUCH HAS BEEN WRITTEN respecting the White Mountains of New Hampshire, but no other period in their history, of equal length, it seems to me, is so rich in associations, in variety of wealth of interests, and so fertile in literary and scientific production and achievement as the years between 1840 and 1860. The writings of the preceding half century were chiefly narrative or of a scientific nature. The journals of Cutler, Belknap, Little, and Bigelow are exceedingly valuable. President Dwight's description of the scenery, and of the first settlers of Nash and Sawyer's and Hart's Locations, for its particularity and appreciativeness, has rarely been surpassed. And since Winthrop's account in 1642 of the first ascents not a few travelers have set down their personal impressions of the mountain region.

By 1840 the genial and beneficent reign of the Crawfords—Abel, Ethan, Harrison, Lucy, and Thomas—a span of sixty years or more, was drawing to a close. It has been said with truth that the heroic age of the White Hills expired when Abel Crawford ceased to breathe. That age was now in its last decade. Harriet Martineau, who visited the mountains in the autumn of 1835, has left a pleasant picture of this interesting family and their hospitable inns. "The Crawfords," she says, "who live twelve miles apart, lead a remarkable life, but one which seems to agree well with mind and body. They are hale, lively men, of uncommon simplicity and manners, dearly loving company, but able to make themselves happy in solitude. . . . The elder Crawford has a pet album, in which he almost insists that his guests shall write. We found in it some of the choicest nonsense and 'brag' that can be found in the whole library of albums. We dined well on mutton, eggs, and whortleberries with milk. Tea was prepared at dinner as regularly as bread throughout this excursion."

In 1845–46 Lucy Crawford, wife of Ethan Allan Crawford, published The History of the White Mountains from the First Settlement of Upper Coos and Pequaket. Here is the simple story of Ethan Crawford's life— the stalwart Jötun of the mountains of Starr King, the Roland of the White Hills—so beset with adversity and ill-fortune of every sort, told in the quaint picturesque language of his patient, faithful, devoted wife. In her narrative the savageness and hardships of the wilderness, and the heroic qualities they nurse, are shown in one picture.

Each recurring season William Oakes, "well known as the most distinguished botanist of New England," says Asa Gray came hither to complete his collections of White Mountain plants begun many years before, and to prepare a flora of their alpine species for Dr. Jackson's *Final Report* on the geology of the state. In 1848 appeared in folio his *Scenery of the White Mountains*, with sixteen plates, from the drawings of Isaac Sprague—the first illustrations of real consequence pertaining to the region. This work was to have been followed, but for his sudden and untimely death, by a smaller volume, *The Book of the White Mountains*, which was "to contain," he says, "full descriptions of everything interesting at the White Mountains, and their vicinity, including a Flora of their alpine plants, with the mosses and lichens, and, also, a Complete Guide to Visitors." Oakes's descriptions are often eloquent, and marked by rare faithfulness and accuracy. "If the traveler would be carried back to the White Hills of New Hampshire," writes the Rev. Dr. Thomas Hill, sometime president of Harvard College, "if one would recall particular scenes, he must have recourse to the descriptive pen of Mr. Oakes, and the daguerreotyping pencil of Mr. Sprague, whose only fault seems to lie in the faithful prosaic accuracy of his drawing. A botanist could herborize in his foregrounds, a geologist theorize on his hillsides. He draws landscapes with minute accuracy, and they have therefore a value as portraits far above that of the beautiful idealized views which other artists give of the same spots."

In 1853 Professor George P. Bond, of Harvard Observatory, published a beautiful sketch map of the White Mountains—the first authentic map of the region—with a table of heights, bearings, and distances, and five lithographs from drawings of Benjamin Champney. This was followed a few years later, 1860–61, by Henry F. Walling's topographical maps, from actual surveys, of the northern counties of New Hampshire—Grafton, Coos, and Carroll—the mountain district.

Another work of permanent value belonging to this period is the Rev. Benjamin G. Willey's *Incidents in White Mountain History*. Mr. Willey was a brother of Samuel Willey, who with his family perished in the great slide of August 28, 1826. The first serious attempt to write the history of the region, it contains much valuable and interesting information concerning the White Mountain settlements and villages, Indian narratives and traditions, and also one of the fullest and best accounts of the deluge of 1826. The sketches by Mr. Champney add not a little to the attractiveness of the book. A smaller volume, bearing the title *Historical Relics of the White Mountains*, by John H. Spaulding, less trustworthy, of slight literary merit, and not to be classed with the foregoing, appeared about the same time. He was keeper of the summit houses, and the tarn at the foot of the headwall of the Great Gulf preserves his name. The book is chiefly a promiscuous collection of anecdotes and legends relating to the region. Henry Ward Beecher as an annual visitor to the White Mountains properly belongs to a later generation. But he was in 1856 at the Crawford House, then kept by J. L. Gibb, successor of Thomas J. Crawford, and has left an interesting account of his impressions in a contribution to the *Independent*, entitled "A Time at the White Mountains."

In the autumn of 1832 Nathaniel Hawthorne passed through the White Mountain Notch to Ethan Crawford's at the Giant's Grave, and thence climbed Mount Washington. The fruits of this brief visit appeared in sketches and narratives. Of his three allegorical tales, "The Great Stone Face," "The Ambitious Guest," and "The Great Carbuncle," the first was published in 1850, the same year as his masterpiece, *The Scarlet Letter*. The other two appeared somewhat earlier, and all were reprinted in *Twice-Told Tales*. Whittier, sometimes called the poet of the White Hills, was a frequent visitor to the mountain and lake district, and has celebrated their grandeur and beauty in song. "The Bridal of Pennacook," the ballad of "Mary Garvin," and "The Hilltop," all were written at this time. Among the poems inspired by the destruction of the Willey family, and properly

Tuckerman Ravine, the great glacial cirque on the
southeastern flank of Mount Washington.

belonging to this period, perhaps the most stirring is "The Willey House,"
a commemorative ballad of the White Hills, by Thomas W. Parsons, on
of the most powerful expressions of his genius.

Artists who were sketching in the mountains in the forties and fifties
were Chester Harding, who, in 1846, painted Abel Crawford in his old age,
Casilear, Kensett, Durand, and Champney—the latter settling at North
Conway in 1854—all were here. Frankenstein was painting "Mount Washington over Tuckerman's Ravine," "The Notch of the White Mountains
from Mount Crawford," "Mount Crawford from the Notch," and the cliff
which bears his name. In 1851 B. G. Stone painted the Crystal Cascade,
which he named the Crystal Falls, and Samuel Colman the romantic ruins
of "The Grand Gulf," a painting much admired by Starr King. And it was
about 1860 that Daniel Huntington painted "Chocorua Peak," and George
L. Brown his well-known White Mountain picture, "The Crown of New
England," now at Windsor Castle, which was painted from Martin's
Farm, near the site of the Mount Adams House, Jefferson Highlands.

This period was also rich in contributions to the natural history of the
region. Dr. Charles T. Jackson,[1] whose discoveries in etherization have

---

1. Dr. Jackson's observations in 1842 of ether anæsthesia, induced in himself, led, at his
suggestion, to the introduction of this practice into surgery four years later by Dr. Morton.

been of untold blessing to humanity and revolutionized the practice of surgery, was completing his survey as state geologist. His *Final Report* on the first geological survey of New Hampshire, an illustrated quarto volume of some 400 pages, appeared in 1844, and was highly valuable, alike for its geological, mineralogical, and agricultural information. In him the chemist, mineralogist, and geologist, practical and theoretical, were happily united. He was the first to call attention to many minerals and mineral localities which were previously unknown. "The single discovery of the ore of tin in New Hampshire," writes a contemporary, "is more than a return for the expense of the survey." Little if any of this metal had hitherto been found in America, although Hitchcock had a few years earlier discovered a single crystal of tin at Goshen, Massachusetts. "The actual number of miles we have journeyed in New Hampshire in three years," says Jackson, "nearly equals the diameter of the globe." The section from Haverhill to the White Mountains was surveyed by Dr. Jackson himself. The glacial theory of Agassiz he held as inadequate and not applicable, without modification, to the mountains of New England, a view in which he was supported by Hitchcock and other leading geologists of the time. He was a member of Abel Crawford's party in 1840, which was the first to reach Mount Washington on horseback by the way from the Notch. Two peaks in the region bear the name of Jackson, that in Bean's Grant having been dedicated to the geologist, it seems, by William Oakes. And to Messrs. Whitney and Williams, two of his pupils and assistants, belongs the credit of the first recorded ascent of Camel's Rump near the Canada line.

In 1841 President Hitchcock of Amherst College, who Sir Charles Lyell declared "knew more of geology and could tell it better than any other man he had met on this side of the Atlantic," with his glacio-aqueous theory of drift in mind, ascended Mount Washington and ten years later the Great Haystack. These visits were followed by a series of illuminating articles in the *Boston Recorder* on the geology and scenery of the White Mountains.

Agassiz, Hubbard, Lesley, Lyell, and brothers Rogers, and Arnold Guyot were studying the geological age of the White Mountains, their glacial phenomena, and otherwise enriching geological and geographical science. Here, in the summer of 1849, and for several years thereafter, Guyot was engaged in a study of the physical configuration of the Appalachian Mountain system, in the pursuit of which he investigated its principal chains and culminating groups from New England to Georgia. He was a careful observer, and his determinations of the numerous altitudes measured, usually by means of the barometer, especially of culminating points of the system, such as Mount Washington and Mitchell's High Peak, were remarkably accurate.

Among the botanists who were here in those years were Jacob Bigelow, William Boott—the brother of Francis Boott, the companion of Dr. Bigelow in their tour of 1816—Daniel C. Eaton, George Engelmann, George L. Goodale, Asa Gray, Thomas W. Higginson, William Oakes, Henry D. Thoreau, Edward Tuckerman, and the Honorable Amelia Matilda Murray. The Honorable Miss Murray, daughter of a bishop and granddaughter of a duke, was here in 1854, botanizing, sketching and writing. She was a maid of honor to Queen Victoria in 1837, the year of her accession, a friend of Lady Byron, and a correspondent of Dr. Gray. Thaddeus W. Harris, another scientific inquirer, was collecting in the mountains in the early fifties. Widely known as an entomologist, he was declared by Agassiz to have had "few equals, even if the past were included in the comparison."

A pleasing and adequate geographic nomenclature is difficult of attainment, and the application of names to familiar objects, such as mountains, hills, water-courses, and lakes, is often a thankless task. "What a pity," says Starr King, "that the hills could not have kept the names which the Indian tribes gave to them. . . . What a wretched jumble of names the highest peaks of the Great Range bear." And Professor Fay, in his presidential address to the Appalachian Mountain Club in 1882, expresses much the same sentiment: "I confess that it becomes an argument against the application of personal names," he observes, "when all the peaks of a group are named for men of a single class, as in our so-called 'Presidential Range.' This name is of itself its sufficient condemnation." Happily many of the Indians names, whose loss Starr King so justly deplores, have since either been restored or adopted.

Names of primitive origin are perhaps the most desirable, and ought, therefore, to be preserved and handed down to posterity. Those descriptive and characteristic, when discreetly used, may properly come next. Personal names, as applied to mountains, except in rare cases, are less appropriate. Nevertheless, not many probably would take exception to the names comprised in the following list, most if not all of which are closely identified with our period, an unusually fertile one in White Mountain nomenclature: Baldcap, Bigelow's Lawn, Black (Sandwich Mountain), Boott's Spur (Davis's Spur), Camel's Rump (now Pine), Cannon, Carrigain, Carter, Carter Notch, Clay, Crawford, Crawford Notch, Crescent, Crystal Falls (Cascade), Eagle Cliff, Echo Lake (Franconia Pond), Ethan's Pond, Field's Ridge, Flume, Giant's Stairs, Hayes, Hermit Lake, Imp,

The Notch House at the head of Crawford Notch,
as depicted in this early 19th-century engraving.

Iron, Jackson (Bean's Grant and Franconia), King's Ravine, Liberty, Little
Haystack, Nancy, Osceola, Oakes's Gulf, Pinkham Notch (?), Pitcher Falls
(Glen Ellis), Profile Lake, Resolution, Ripley Falls, Sleeper's Ledge, Stair,
Starr King, Tom (Willard), Tremont, Tripyramid (Saddle, Passaconaway),
Tuckerman's Ravine and Falls, The Twin Mountains, Webster, Wildcat
(Hight), Willey.

But the crowning glory of this fruitful period and of White Mountain
literature is The White Hills of Thomas Starr King. This work, which had
been foreshadowed in letters to the *Boston Transcript*, appeared in October, 1859, on the eve of his final departure for California. "This production," says his biographer, "is far more than a description of the White
Hills; its rich descriptions of every variety of landscape apply to all natural scenes, and bring out their inmost meaning. There is much of himself
in this volume, of his rare spiritual insight—much of what his cultured
and reverent eye saw in the beauty and the grandeur that God is creating
every day."

Starr King, the historian, painter, and poet of the White Hills, lived
weeks and months at the mountains, visiting and communing with them
at all seasons of the year. "The results of these rich and fruitful years are
before us," writes a distinguished contemporary: "This work lacks no

claim upon the general interest which such a work could proffer. In the lowest, yet to a novice the essential capacity of a guide-book, it is full and perfect, delineating in detail every route, with its periods, stations, and facilities. As a topographical manual, it leaves nothing to be desired, describing the whole face of the country, and entering into the minutest features of every striking view and every salient object. Its literary finish is exquisite. It is a poet's survey, and we never miss in a single page the poetic afflatus, which breathes on the writer's soul from the Creator-Spirit to whom 'the signs and wonders of the elements' utter praise. With his own magnificent prose-poem, Mr. King has tastefully interwreathed all the choice literature and poetry of the White Hills; and at the same time has put into fitting shape, not only the local history, but the rich legendary lore—much of it before unwritten—which has been handed down from the rude pioneers and among the hardy settlers in a region so prolific of wild and perilous adventure, and so well fitted to nourish weird and strange beliefs and imaginings."

Starr King was first led to visit the region, it seems, by a noteworthy article, entitled "The White Mountains," from the pen of the Rev. Dr. Hosea Ballou,[2] a founder and the first president of Tufts College, with whom he had long been on terms of intimate friendship. His first visit was in 1849, his last in 1860, and his genius has given our New England Alps an abiding place among the noblest mountains in literature.

---

2. Dr. Ballou, a careful observer, eloquent writer and mountain enthusiast, first visited the White Mountains about 1844.

1916

The Coming
of the Railroads

Frederick W. Kilbourne

From *Chronicles of the White Mountains*

*Perhaps the best-known history ever written about New Hampshire's great
mountain region is* Chronicles of the White Mountains *by Frederick W.
Kilbourne (1872–1965). Published in 1916 by Houghton Mifflin Company,*
Chronicles *is still considered the most thorough and comprehensive history ever
to appear in print. Its author was a Wallingford, Connecticut native who later
attended Yale University. It was while he was an undergraduate at Yale that
Kilbourne first began visiting the White Mountains, and it was during his
many years at the Brooklyn (N.Y.) Library, where he was in charge of publications, that he began amassing the historical information that led to his writing
of* Chronicles. *For many years, Kilbourne was also an active member of the
Appalachian Mountain Club, and he frequently contributed historical pieces to
AMC's well-read journal,* Appalachia.

As a glance at the map of the White Mountains region will suggest,
there is in this country probably no other summer-resort area, and certainly no other mountain district of anything like its extent, that is to-day
provided with such an abundance of railroad facilities, rendering it at once
easy of access and convenient for local travel. Indeed, this is so much the
case that it may be affirmed that, like some other parts of New England,
it is possibly oversupplied with such means of transportation. In these
automobile days the railroad has ceased to play so great a part as it once
did as a carrier of people to and through the Mountains, but in former days

it was an essential and very great element in the growth, and, indeed, in the very existence, of the region as a summer resort.

As a necessary preliminary, therefore, to an account of that development, as well as for its own intrinsic interest, a brief outline of the chief steps by which the railroads approached the Mountains from different points and of the building of the local extensions would seem to be pertinent at this point.

The first railroad to reach the region was the Atlantic and St. Lawrence Railroad, which was projected to run from Portland, Maine, to Island Pond, Vermont, and which was chartered successively in 1845, 1847, and 1848, by the three States it was to cross. Construction was begun July 4,

COURTESY LITTLETON AREA HISTORICAL SOCIETY

Workmen carry out the task of building the railroad through rugged Crawford Notch in the mid-1870s. This stereo view was taken near the top of the Notch, where the rail line clings to the side of Mount Willard.

1846, and was completed as far as Gorham, New Hampshire, early in 1852. The entire line from Portland to the western terminus in Vermont was opened in January of the following year. At the latter place this railroad was to connect with the St. Lawrence and Atlantic Railroad, a line from Montreal to that point in Vermont, the two roads, with the interchanged names, thereby forming a continuous route between the two cities. The

An engine and train on the Profile and Franconia Notch Railroad pause along the shore of Echo Lake.

COURTESY LITTLETON AREA HISTORICAL SOCIETY

A southbound Profile and Franconia Notch Railroad passenger train
passes over a wooden trestle on its way from Bethlehem Junction
to the Profile House in Franconia Notch, probably around 1880.

Canadian line was completed and opened for business in July, 1853. On the evening of the 18th of that month, the first train from Montreal arrived in Portland, where it was received with the ringing of bells, a salute of thirty-one guns, and various other formal and informal manifestations of joy at the consummation of this great work. About this time the amalgamation of a number of Canadian lines into one Grand Trunk Railway was effected, and to this system the Atlantic and St. Lawrence Railroad was leased for 999 years on August 8, 1853.

The route of the Atlantic and St. Lawrence Railroad, which is now known only by the general name of the Grand Trunk, and which is the one that has present interest for us, is, when approaching the Mountains, up the beautiful valley of the Androscoggin River, through Shelburne and Gorham. It thus passes to the north of the White Mountains, and so has been superseded for the most part, as a means of access to the region, by the railroads from the south and another railroad from Portland reaching directly the resorts among the Mountains. At the time of the completion of this first railroad to Gorham, there were only five public houses from which the summit of Mount Washington could be reached in a day, which statement will give the reader, familiar with the accommodations of to-day, some notion of the development of the region since the coming of the railroads.

The advance of the railroads from the south was a slow one, forty years elapsing from the time the early railroads out of Boston were opened before a traveler could reach the heart of the Mountains from that city entirely by rail.

The Boston and Lowell Railroad was opened for travel June 26, 1835. Three days before this opening of the road to Lowell, the Nashua and Lowell Railroad Company obtained a charter to build a road from the State line northwardly in the Merrimac Valley. The line was opened to Nashua, December 23, 1838. The surveys for the next link, the Concord Railroad, were made by Loammi Baldwin, Jr., William Gibbs McNeill, and George Washington Whistler,[1] the father of the artist, and the pioneer passenger train ran into Concord[2] Tuesday evening, September 6, 1842, a great gath-

---

1. Major Whistler went to Russia in 1842, to superintend the construction of the railroad from St. Petersburg to Moscow, and died in that country seven years later. William Gibbs McNeill was his brother-in-law.

2. A favorite route to New Hampshire from New York about 1850 was by steamer to Norwich, Connecticut, and thence to Concord via the Norwich and Worcester Railroad, opened in 1840, the Nashua and Worcester Railroad, and the Concord Railroad.

MOUNT WASHINGTON OBSERVATORY COLLECTION

An eastbound train on the Portland and Ogdensburg Railroad passes over Frankenstein Trestle in Crawford Notch. The trestle is 500 feet long and 80 feet high and was completed in June 1875, just two months before the railroad through the Notch was finished and opened to regular train traffic.

ering of rejoicing people on hand to welcome it. This was only twelve years after the first steam railway, the Liverpool and Manchester, was built.

North of Concord two lines were soon under construction, and in a little more than ten years Littleton was reached. Here, however, the advance was halted for two decades.[3]

The Northern Railroad of New Hampshire started from Concord, proceeded up the Merrimac to Franklin, and then struck over to a point on the Connecticut River near the mouth of its tributary, the White River. It was opened to Lebanon in November, 1847, and to White River Junction in the town of Hartford, Vermont, in June, 1848. There it connected with the Vermont Central Railroad (later the Central Vermont) and with the Connecticut and Passumpsic Rivers Railroad, lines then under construction. With the latter, which was in operation to Wells River as early as 1849, it formed a route much used, though somewhat less direct, by travelers to the Mountains in the early days as an alternative to the one about

3. A correspondent, "Pennacook," of the New York Herald, writing from the Flume House, June 15, 1853, speaks of the approaching opening of the railroad to Littleton, and adds, "No railroad should ever be constructed farther into these mountains than Littleton."

The Mountaineer steam engine and the "Great Cut"
at the top of Crawford Notch on the P&O Railroad.

to be mentioned. The Northern Railroad became part of the Boston and Maine system in 1890.

The Boston, Concord, and Montreal Railroad, the other line and the one which has more of interest for us as that which eventually became a link in the principal through route from Boston to the White Mountain region, was chartered on December 27, 1844. It was to start from Concord or Bow, and was to extend to some point on the west bank of the Connecticut River opposite Haverhill or to Littleton. Construction was immediately undertaken by the enterprising and courageous people who lived along its way, and on May 22, 1848, there was an opening of the road to Sanbornton (now Tilton). On this occasion the new engine, "Old Man of the Mountain," and cars painted sky-blue, were deemed peculiarly appropriate for a line whose future travel would largely consist of traffic to and from the White Mountains. Plymouth was reached in January, 1850, and Wells River, May 10, 1853. Late the same year, in December, the White Mountains Railroad was opened to Littleton. Twenty years later, this latter line became by purchase a part of the Boston, Concord, and Montreal Railroad.

In 1856, when the Boston, Concord, and Montreal Railroad, which was peculiarly a New Hampshire enterprise, was on the verge of bankruptcy, John E. Lyon took charge of it. To his courage, initiative, and persistency were due the extensions built into the north country beyond Littleton between 1869 and 1878.

This railroad-builder was, it may be mentioned in passing, concerned in many other enterprises connected with the development of the White Mountains as a resort. Besides being associated with Mr. Marsh in the Mount Washington Railway, he was instrumental in the rebuilding of the Pemigewasset House at Plymouth and in the building of the Fabyan House and of the Summit House on Mount Washington, and was one of the incorporators of the Moosilauke Mountain Road Company.

The further extensions of the White Mountains Railroad referred to were to Lancaster, to which point the road was opened October 31, 1870; to Groveton, reached on the national holiday two years later; and to Fabyan by way of Wing Road, to which terminus the road was opened July 4, 1874. Two years afterwards, the railroad was extended from Fabyan to the Base in time to be opened early in July, and thus the stage service over the turnpike from Fabyan to the Mount Washington Railway was superseded. The Profile House and Bethlehem were for some years longer accessible only by stage, but in 1879 a narrow-gauge road was opened to the former and in 1881 to the latter. These branch lines, which are operated only in the summer, remained narrow-gauge until 1897, when the change to standard-gauge was completed.[4]

What these extensions meant to the development of the region as a summer recreation ground and tourist center will be at once evident to any present-day frequenter of the White Mountains, when he recalls that for more than a score of years Littleton was the northern terminus of the White Mountains Railroad, and that Bethlehem, the Profile House and the Franconia Notch, the Crawford House and Notch, and other places were accessible only by long and tedious, and often otherwise unpleasant, stage rides.

The openings of two more branch lines remain to be chronicled. North Woodstock, now become a considerable summer resort, was connected by rail with Plymouth in 1883. Ten years later, a road twenty miles long was opened to Berlin. This started at the old terminus on Jefferson Meadow of the Whitefield and Jefferson Railroad, opened in 1879, at a point near to which starts the spur, opened in 1892, to the Waumbek Hotel, and passed through Randolph and Gorham.

All of these railroads in the Mountain region now form a part of the Boston and Maine Railroad system, which controls nearly all the railroads in the Granite State.

The lines up the Connecticut River from Springfield, Massachusetts, which city was connected by rail with Hartford, Connecticut, in 1844, were opened at various times. The principal links in the northern part of this the most direct route from New York City to the White Mountains were the Connecticut River Railroad, opened to South Vernon, January 1, 1849; the Vermont Valley Railroad, Brattleboro to Bellows Falls, opened in 1851; the Sullivan County Railroad, Bellows Falls to Windsor, opened in February, 1849, and sold October 1, 1880, to the Vermont Valley Railroad; and the Connecticut and Passumpsic Rivers Railroad, from White River Junction on. All these lines were eventually leased to the Boston and Maine.

Another important means of rendering the Mountains accessible by rail was undertaken in the early seventies in the construction of the Portland and Ogdensburg Railroad, so called, some one has facetiously remarked, because it started from Portland and never reached Ogdensburg. To two brothers, citizens of the State of Maine, belongs the credit for the building of this railroad, which vies with the Mount Washington Railway

---

4. I am indebted to the Boston and Maine Railroad, and particularly to Mr. G. E. Cummings, superintendent of the White Mountains Division, for information as to the time of this change of gauge on the Profile and Franconia Notch Railroad.

An engine and passenger car on Sylvester Marsh's Cog Railway, dubbed by some, the "Railway to the Moon."

as a conception and achievement and in scenic interest. General Samuel J. Anderson, of Portland, was the foremost promoter of the road and its first president. "Being," says Mrs. Mason in her article on Conway, "a gifted and persuasive speaker, it was easy for him to induce the town of Conway to raise five per cent of its valuation for the building of the road." John Farwell Anderson, of South Windham, Maine, was the engineer. Maintaining that the gorges of the Crawford Notch could be bridged, he accomplished the feat after it had been repeatedly declared impossible by other engineers. The company was chartered in February, 1867, and in four and a half years the line reached North Conway. It was opened to Fabyan in August, 1875. Some idea of the difficulties and expense of construction and operation may be gained from the facts that of the total ascent of 1890 feet

from Portland to Crawford's, 1369 feet are included in the thirty miles between North Conway and the latter place, and that between Bemis and
Crawford's the rise is 116 feet to the mile for nine consecutive miles. Such
structures on the right of way as the Frankenstein Trestle[5] and the Willey
Brook Bridge are striking evidences of the skill and genius of the engineer.

Less than a year after the Portland and Ogdensburg was opened to
North Conway, the Eastern Railroad, now a part of the Boston and Maine,
reached Conway. To-day the rail connection between the two, which form
together another through route from Boston to the Mountains, is at Intervale. In 1888, the former road fell into the hands of the Maine Central and
was renamed the Mountain Division of that railroad. The following year
the line was extended from Fabyan to Scott's Mills via the Twin Mountain House and Whitefield, thus completing a route passing entirely
through the heart of the Mountains. A later extension to the northward,
from Quebec Junction to North Stratford, opened in 1891, made the
Maine Central a means of access to the region from Canada.

5. The old trestle was replaced by a new steel one in 1895.

February 1926

Appalachian Mountain Club Trail System

Karl P. Harrington

From *Appalachia*

Karl Pomeroy Harrington (1861–1953) was no stranger to members of the early 20th-century New England mountain climbing community. The New Hampshire native, who graduated from Wesleyan University in 1882, and later taught there for some two and a half decades, for many summers frequented the North Woodstock area. While in summer residence there, he helped form the local trail club, the North Woodstock Improvement Association, in 1897. In 1919, at the age of 58, Harrington became a member of the Appalachian Mountain Club, and within a few short years was appointed AMC Councillor of Trails (1923–1925). During his tenure as Councillor, the club expanded its growing trail network into such areas as the southern Mahoosucs and across the entire Bond Range in the Pemigewasset Wilderness region. In their monumental hiking history, Forest and Crag, authors Laura and Guy Waterman noted that the soft-spoken Harrington had been described as the "archetypal absent-minded professor." They added: "He wore old suits when in the woods, complete with jacket, finding that 'the pockets of the coat were handy for sandwiches.'"

NOW THAT THE White Mountain trails of the Appalachian Mountain Club have been thoughtfully coordinated, and the most important missing links have been supplied, we may fairly speak of a trail "system." Tradition has it that some attempt was made, many years ago, to plan such a system on *a-priori* principles; but, if so, the plan speedily vanished into "innocuous desuetude," and trails for a time, like Topsy, "just growed." They

grew spasmodically for years, as one slope or another ridge flourishes in
nature according to the favorable conditions of sunshine, breeze, and fer-
tilizing rain. So the fond affection of various Councillors or other active
trail-makers, and their fostering enthusiasm for their favorite regions,
caused trails to spring up and blossom as the rose, on the Sandwich Mountains, for example, or in the Great Gulf, or on the heights adjoining the
Pemigewasset Valley. Of course, on this basis, certain regions were well developed, in some cases perhaps overdeveloped, while others remained terra
incognita. It is not so many years ago that the only trails on the Franconia
Range were those ascending Mt. Liberty from the Pool, and Mt. Lafayette
from the Profile House. In those earlier days the East Branch nexus of
trails did not exist, and no part of the Kinsman Ridge was accessible except the two peaks, and they only by the back door, virtually, that is, from
Easton. Trampers climbed Mt. Hayes from Gorham; but the vision of a
through trail over the whole Mahoosuc Range had not yet appeared to the
most imaginative soul among the Councillors of that era.

Our trails are entirely in the White Mountain region, because naturally,
for an organization whose home has always been in Boston, these mountains were the first objects of interest. Mt. Washington and its various approaches were rightly the earliest centers of attraction. The Presidential
Range, the Montalban Range, and the neighboring ridges and valleys were
long ago laid open to approach by horse or foot. Individual trails to other
prominent peaks followed. But the automobile and the consequent highway development, together with the various public camp-grounds maintained by the United States Forest Service, have invited travelers to pass
up and down every one of the famous "Notches" which are a characteristic of the White Mountains, and have brought them within easy tramping reach of every challenging height, every mountain tarn, and every
notable waterfall in New Hampshire. Trails have multiplied everywhere.
Local clubs and associations have prided themselves on making accessible
the beauty spots in their several districts. The United States Forest Service
has joined in the movement to open its large tracts of forest land to the
public. The New England Trail Conference has gathered the representatives of these various organizations and agencies, and urged coordination,
and worked toward the ideal of main highways of tramping travel between
them along our Appalachian Chain, with many local feeders all over New
England, as well as farther south. The rapid growth of summer camps, for
young people of both sexes, and the habit of taking large groups of boys
and girls from these camps on long hikes over the mountains, increased
the demand for through trails. In this out-of-door age many adults also

Nattily dressed late 19th-century hikers check out the
Lakes of the Clouds near Mount Washington.

like to break away from honking cars and jingling telephones for a week
or two, and breast the breezes, mount the cliffs, and rest beside some lovely
lake in the manner of the simple life.

Recognizing this trend of the age, our Councillors of Trails ("Improvements," as they used to be called) began years ago to work toward a rational trail system in New Hampshire especially. The process was both
positive and negative, the particular duty of the Appalachian Mountain
Club being to construct and maintain certain obviously needed lines of
trail not likely to be attended to by any other organization, and, on the
other hand, to relinquish to the care of local associations such trails as are
relatively non-essential for through travel, but are of prime local importance. So, for example, to the Wonalancet Outdoor Club, the Intervale
Improvement Society, the Randolph Mountain Club, and the United
States Forest Service, respectively, were turned over the trails on Sandwich
Mountain and Moat Mountain, through King's Ravine, and along Nine-
teen-Mile Brook. The Forest Service has also assumed most of the main
Presidential Range Trail from the Crawford House to the Madison Spring
Huts. Not less than sixteen trails thus transferred to the care of other or-
ganizations could be enumerated.

The time and money thus released found abundant occupation in assuming charge of important trails already constructed by local organiza-

tions, but in reality parts of a through system, or in constructing links to weld together widely separated trails. The Franconia Ridge Trail had been built in two sections, under different auspices, but was being maintained by the North Woodstock Improvement Association. After it passed under the control of the Appalachian Mountain Club, the Mt. Liberty Trail was relocated in the lower part, the Mt. Flume Trail was constructed at the suggestion of Mr. Jenks, the Kinsman Ridge Trail was constructed from Lost River to Kinsman Pond, and then linked up with another new route cut over "The Cannonballs" and Cannon Mountain to the Profile House by Messrs. Goodrich, Jenks, and others. Meanwhile Mr. Blood attacked the problem of connecting this western system of trails with those already in use in the eastern part of the mountains. The Twin Range Trail was already partly built. Blood laid out a trail through country often discouraging in its violent ups and downs, across Garfield Ridge, past lovely Garfield Pond, over the relatively isolated Mt. Garfield, and up South Twin, a task requiring three summers' campaigns to finish.

"North Fork Junction" had been established near the mouth of the North Fork of the East Branch of the Pemigewasset, and the East Branch trails were for a time focused upon it, and connection finally made with the Saco Valley by a trail down from Mt. Bond to the Junction, and one up the North Fork past Thoreau Falls and Ethan Pond to Willey House Station. The remaining link necessary for connection with the Presidentials without tedious road walking was over Mt. Webster. Jenks engineered the northern half of this, Blood, the southern end. Now one could tramp on forest trails from Lost River to Madison Huts or Randolph, or to Pinkham Notch, or through Carrigain Notch by using the East Branch railroad. Dr. Larrabee devoted much painstaking labor to the Wildcat Mountain region. A large part of the Mahoosuc Range was opened under the enthusiastic direction of Jenks and Goodrich, and by the indefatigable Harris, of the Worcester Chapter. Stetson and Harrington, with the help of G. R. Potter, opened the new link from Kinsman Pond to Mt. Liberty, and Whitehouse Bridge Trail, thus putting the upper Franconia Ridge on the main through route. The North Chatham trails have been joined to the Carter Notch by way of the Wild River country.

A kind fate has reserved it for the present writer to see completed under his administration the final links in rounding out two through routes from Lost River to Old Speck Mountain: Zealand Ridge Trail, from Mt. Guyot across to Thoreau Falls, eliminating the detour by way of North Fork Junction; Pine Link, from Madison Huts to Gorham; the rest of the Mahoosuc Range Trail, between Mt. Hayes and Gentian Pond; the southern end of the Twin Ridge Trail, over the Cliffs of Bond; Shoal Pond Trail, connecting the Ethan Pond Trail with the Carrigain Notch Trail; Lost Pond Trail, eliminating the highway walk for those wishing to reach Carter Notch from Pinkham Notch Camp; and the lower end of the Huntington Ravine Trail, making a direct route from Tuckerman Ravine Trail to the summit. Thus, starting over the Dartmouth Outing Club Trail from Glencliff, and using occasionally trails belonging to the Forest Service, a tramper can follow a general northeasterly direction along trunkline trails across the main peaks and ridges all the way to Grafton Notch, well over into Maine, with alternative routes between Kinsman Pond and Mt. Lafayette, Mt. Guyot and Mt. Washington (going by way of Carrigain Notch and over the Davis Path, if preferred), and the Presidentials and Gorham (choosing between the Carters and Pine Link). The one other important gap in the system, a trail from the end of the former East Branch railroad extension up past Norcross and Nancy Ponds and down by the graceful Nancy Cascades to Bemis, affording a direct approach (without several miles of dodging automobiles on the Crawford Notch road) to the Davis Path, has been persistently blocked by the owners of the timber land around Nancy Pond and Cascades, a unique experience in the history of the Club. Doubtless the relatively short pieces of A.M.C. trail on Mt. Cardigan and on Monadnock will before many years coalesce with other trails, some already constructed by other organizations, to complete the line to southern New Hampshire and to the trails in other States in southern New England and New York; while the pushing of the main trunk line on toward the goal of Katahdin may be confidently expected at an early day.

One thing calls for another. A few hundred dollars were appropriated for trails, only a few years ago; now the amount has risen to ten times that figure. From placing a half-dozen signs in a season, we have come to put up nearer a hundred. From hiring a local man or two to help clear trails, we have come to a trail crew hired for all summer, with a foreman, not to mention the skilled workmen who have been building our shelters for several years; for a necessary corollary of the trail system itself is a system of shelters where those using the trails may escape from wind, rain, darkness, and fatigue. And so, located in strategic spots, by unfailing water springs, we have now fifteen open shelters, which, taken with the huts and camps at Lakes-of-the-Clouds, Madison Spring, Pinkham Notch, Carter Notch, and Willey House Camp, make it impossible for a tramper anywhere on our trail system ever to be beyond reasonable walking distance from a comfortable place to spend the night or escape from stormy weather. It is amazing to consider the number of signs painted and placed by the veteran Jenks; but thus far, thanks to his enthusiastic generosity of time and labor, the sign problem has been simple of solution. The new problem of suitable trail bridges has forced itself upon our attention this year, and is discussed elsewhere in this number of *Appalachia*.

A rational trail system of nearly three hundred miles in extent, duly signed and suitably described in our own official publications, is now an accomplished fact, built and maintained for the general public as much as for our own members, and offering an opportunity to obtain an intimate knowledge of all the best, and best known, parts of the main White Mountain region, as well as many beautiful outlying districts, and ready to be connected with other parts of New England in the great movement for combining and coordinating the principal trails of the East.

All this has come about not without a good deal of hard work and much "roughing it"; while, on the other hand, many fond reminiscences will be lastingly connected with this work, in the minds of those who have had their fingers most deeply in the pie. It would be delightful to listen to all the trail stories of past pioneers in this work. Blood and Jenks have been kind enough to furnish some of the data already used in this article, and to express some of their sentiments in regard to it. Jenks writes: "Development of the Club trail system was, apparently, slow, unsystematic, and irregular. Especially, it was for many years almost entirely local, a succession of Councillors developing trails locally; that is, according to the locality where they summered or were otherwise particularly interested. Thus, North Woodstock was favored by Carpenter, Pray worked in the Sandwich region, Hart developed the Great Gulf system, Hart and Tyler reopened the Davis Path, and Perkins and the East Branch, and I suppose Larrabee was local to Jackson in the Stairs Col, and probably Cutter worked mostly on the Northern Peaks."

Blood supplemented the foregoing statement as follows, ultimately running into personal recollections: "The Garfield Ridge Trail linked the Franconia Ridge with the Twin Range and thus with the Ethan Pond and Carrigain Notch Trails to the Saco Valley, and the Webster Cliff Trail was opened as an emergency exit from the Lakes-of-the-Clouds Hut to the highway—a means of escape in times of severe storm. But even as Saul going out to seek his father's asses found a kingdom, so I, in attempting to carry out a business-like program, opened two of our most spectacular trails. They were cases where virtue was its own reward.

"All of these trails bring back memories to me personally.

"*Webster*—a perfect, nightmare of heat and thirst the last two days when working along the cliffs (how interminable the cliffs seemed!), matched by a dry comfortable camp site near the river and daily swims in the sandy pools.

"*Ammonoosuc*—how impressive was our first view down into the gorge from the ledges where the trail crosses the brook!

"*Garfield Ridge*—a three years' fight. How bitterly cold it was at Hawthorne Fall the first three days the first year, in low cloud and steady rain! What a fine fireplace we built! What a marvelous bench Ed Lorenz built, using only two nails! How much we ate—for want of any other occupation! What a desperate attempt we made the last day our second year to mark the trail to Lafayette, climbing over Garfield and stringing to timber-line on Lafayette and returning, all in one hectic day! The wonderful game of 'freeze out' with flapjacks on a rainy day, culminating in a draw between Jenks and Lorenz on a cake composed largely of uncooked malt breakfast food and seasoned with cinnamon! The third year with the camp at Garfield Pond, so delightfully described by Goodrich in his sketch on 'Rewards of Trail-Making,' in *Appalachia*.

"The mountains are dotted with the stone fireplaces we have built at all our camp sites. Is there anything more desolate than an abandoned camp site? Is there anything that makes you more homesick than to visit one of your own and think of the fun and good-fellowship enjoyed the previous year? To me these trails mean more than mere paths in the mountains. They mean my friends with whom I worked in cutting them—Jenks, the Goodriches, Blaney, Lorenz, Crawford—alas! No more with us—and others in later years."

As for the writer himself, many a page could be filled with the record of exciting, exasperating, or amusing experiences. One of my earliest important trail ventures was in connection with the location and cutting of the southern end of the route over the Franconia Ridge. Charles Henry Raymond, of Lawrenceville School, was my partner, and with us were three Frenchmen hired from among the idle hands of the moment at Lincoln. The task of reaching Mt. Flume was not inconsiderable, and involved the use of many logging roads in making the summit of Osseo Peak. From "Camp 3" we wound up and along Clear Brook, hewing our way on the right, and at length crossing on a big log, only to discover a good road on the left all made for us! Deciding then after the next crossing to leave this northward-tending valley, we struck through a very wet swamp into the hardwoods, and built a rude brush camp, the first night, near the last small brook. The next day was steep going till well into the afternoon, when a wonderfully graded road slabbing easterly was suddenly encountered.

Posing for a group shot above treeline on the Presidential Range.

That led us straight to the little notch between Osseo Peak and Potash Knob, amid showers. As nightfall approached, it was clear that we must camp, and equally clear that there was no water anywhere about. I tried to assume a Spartan indifference; but that didn't "go down" with the French axemen; and, realizing that we were likely to lose their services on the spot, I thought quickly and acted promptly. Seizing a tin pail, I bolted for the bottom of the mountain, and did a sprint of a half an hour or so that would have qualified a runner for any college track team. Reaching the camp site of the previous night and filling my pail, I made tracks back again, and reached the gang before darkness had settled entirely upon us, finding a camp built on an iniquitous side hill under a shelving rock, where rain was liable to drip in at any moment, and where sleep was highly problematical. A network of roads had to be followed next day, with slow cutting through balsam thicket, and careful search for possible access to the ultimate ledges of Osseo Peak, which was finally attacked only by climbing at the one feasible point up mighty roots and achieving a shelf where ladders have since been placed. More monotonous miles through tall timber along the ridge exhausted the patience of the Frenchmen, and the first trail was for the nonce left inchoate.

The first scouting for the Kinsman Ridge Trail from Mt. Kinsman southwards was done after arriving, nearly exhausted, at the summit shortly before sunset. Stetson was with me, and, fixing our eyes on the tiny lakelet in the sharp little notch far below, and establishing as firmly as possible the direction in mind for the goal of our immediate endeavor, we pushed our way through the tangle of scrub, and painfully crawled down the steep, letting ourselves drop over many a rock too huge to walk down. As darkness closed in, we lighted matches and other kinds of temporary flames, and advanced through rough and entirely untrodden country, where the rocks are all too big, toward the wished-for lake. The hours passed; it was getting toward the end of a somewhat imperfect day; the water did not appear. But our confidence in our sense of direction was destined to be justified; for suddenly, in the stillness of the forest, a single peep from a frog's throat directly ahead sounded out. It was still half or three quarters of an hour to the margin of the lake and an improvised bed on top of the springy swamp bushes; but the faithful frog guided us with absolute certainty, sight for once yielding to sound.

Another vivid picture in my memory is that of a dull afternoon on what was long known as "2650," a mean, long mountain with a top like a great platter, logged, burned, and newly grown over with thick bushes and young trees. At length I had solved the problem of several years, and after traveling over the rough, scratchy, blinding wilderness from Page Pond to the end of the new trail at the western end of "2650," turned back, rather late in the afternoon, to retrace my steps to the "Trail-Spree" camp on Dream Lake, with a satisfied feeling that the route for the balance of the trail was finally scouted out. Plunging and floundering around over the uncertain footing, as I hurried on in the waning afternoon, I reached at length the edge of a sharp little valley into which I did not wish to go, and coming face to face with a huge boulder towering above the vegetation, I managed to climb over burned stubs to its top, whence there was an excellent prospect. "Now," said I to myself, "I must go a bit to the left to avoid the precipice seen on the way over here." And, having determined on the course to be followed, I dived back into the thick and blinding growth, and walked for about a half-hour, hoping every moment to find myself descending around that summit and making my way down under the precipice to the valley beyond. Suddenly I noticed a strangely familiar boulder in front of me, and, half-dazed with the revelation, discovered that I was once more climbing the very same boulder I had left so long before. In a lonely rage I took my bearings once more, and started off again, to follow that proposed course, "keeping a little to the left." Alas! Another half-hour brought me a third time vis-à-vis with my boulder, and the afternoon was almost gone. "Three times and out!" was my ejaculation, and, abandoning the foolish notion of keeping "a little to the left" in a thicket, I made a bee-line for the point where I must wind around the height, and reached a rocky gully, down which I turned as twilight hastened on. How near was I to the precipitous place? Should I get down at all before nightfall? These queries kept me alert until at last, pushing away some branches with both hands, I found myself in a pocket of thick trees, and standing on a shelving ledge. It was too dark to see how far down it was to the bottom in front of me, or on either side, and I had no matches! Halted thus rudely on a rocky island in space, in the dark, what was I to do? For the answer to this interesting question, as the serials say, look for the next chapter!

But time and space fail for describing how I lay on my stomach under a rock while rain poured and thunder rolled around us on the ridge north of Lost River; or how I had to ford Gale River at torrential flood-tide without any diving bell; or how I experienced the thrill of discovery when, on following up a little brook, the water kept warm, and divining its source to be a pond, I suddenly came out on the shores of the hitherto uncharted Upper Gentian Pond. Oh, it's a great life on the trail!

Incidents in
White Mountain History

The Pioneering Spirit

Lucy Crawford

From *The History of the White Mountains, From the First Settlement of Coos and Pequaket*

The Crawford name is synonymous with White Mountain history and perhaps no book ever written about the region is more fascinating than The History of the White Mountains *by Lucy Crawford, wife of the pioneer settler, Ethan Allen Crawford. This book, written and copyrighted in 1845 and published the following year, "Is not only a White Mountains classic, it is a classic of Americana," wrote historian Stearns Morse in his introduction to a 1966 Dartmouth College reprint edition of the book. The Crawfords, starting with Abel (Ethan's dad), were among the first settlers in the area today known as Bretton Woods and Crawford Notch. Early in the 19th century they were responsible for establishing the first tavern, or inn, for travelers in the Whites, and they constructed several early footpaths up onto the nearby Presidential Range. Ethan Crawford (1792–1846) was also a noted hunter and fisherman whose outdoors exploits remains unmatched in White Mountain annals. Although Lucy Crawford (1793–1869) is credited as author of* The History of the White Mountains, *most of the events and stories told in the book are related by her husband, Ethan. The following excerpt tells of the tragic July 1918 fire that destroyed Lucy and Ethan Crawford's first home near present-day Bretton Woods.*

Early on the morning of the 18th of July, my family not being well, I went to our nearest neighbors for assistance. It was nearly eight o'clock when I returned with Mrs. Rosebrook, and not long after we had a son born, which weighed nearly five pounds. After doing what was necessary to be done at the house, at eleven o'clock I went to carry some dinner to our men who were at work on the Cherry Mountain road, one and a half miles from home. Grandmother desired me, on my return, to bring her some trout, as she said I must give them a good treat and do something extra for their services and my good fortune that morning. I accordingly, though reluctantly, obeyed her commands. The trout were in as great haste for the hook as I was for them. I caught in a few minutes, a fine string of good large sized ones. I was gone about one hour from home, and when on my return, the first sight which caught my eyes as I came out of the woods, was flames of fire ascending the tops of the chimneys, ten or fifteen in the air! I added a new speed to my horse, who was then under a good headway, and I was soon there. Here I found Lucy and her infant placed on some feather beds behind an old blacksmith's shop, where she could not see the flames of fire in the open air. I passed her immediately by and flew to the house, and tried to save something from it, but all in vain, the fire was raging, and to that height could not save a hive of bees, which stood a few rods from it. These were suffered to perish. There were no men there excepting a Mr. Boardman, from Lancaster, who, with his wife, on their return home from Saco, called for refreshments, and while this was preparing, Mrs. Boardman came into the room and inquired of Lucy how she did, and what she should say to her mother who lived three miles from them, when she should get home. After a little conversation and receiving thanks from Lucy for her kindness, she took her leave and went out. The room where Lucy lay was about ten feet wider than the other part of the house, which was built with these two rooms under ground. And there was a large poplar whose boughs and leaves touched the chamber window where grandmother slept. While in conversation with Mrs. Boardman Lucy saw smoke and leaves pass her window; but as she was much engaged and the wind shifted, she forgot to mention it. The girl, going into one of the rooms, heard the crackling of the fire overhead, and when she opened the chamber door, the flames met her. She immediately closed the door and gave information. In a few minutes Mrs. Boardman returned and said, Mrs. Crawford, do not be frightened, the house is on fire and cannot be saved; be quiet and keep still, you shall be taken care of; remember your life is of more value than all the property which is to be consumed. These words, coming in so friendly a manner, and from so good a woman, calmed all her fears, and, when left alone, she had the presence of mind to command herself without trembling. She arose and dressed herself, then went to the desk, which stood in the room, unlocked it, took out all the papers and other things of consequence from the drawers, and put them in a pine chest, which stood near by, then asked

Mr. Boardman to save it, which he did. She then went into another room and took out some drawers, and they were carried out and saved. She would have taken down the top of the brass clock, had it not been for Mrs. Boardman, who would, every time she saw her making exertions, admonish her by saying she was not aware of her critical situation, and as it hindered her by these arguments from doing much herself, Lucy gave up and was placed in an arm chair, and carried to the place where I found her. The infant was the last thing taken from the burning ruins, as Mrs. Rosebrook had taken it and laid it upon a bench in the barroom, for the house was built for a tavern. Mr. B. asked where it was? She said she knew, and ran in and brought it out. We had a pig shut up in a pen so near the building, that before he could make his escape, was burned. The noise of this pig attracted the attention of the other hogs and brought them to the place, and it was with difficulty that Lucy and one little brother of hers, four years old, who lived with us, could keep them from tearing everything to pieces. Beds all on fire—cheeses all around—hogs in the midst of them—all hurly burly; while the female party had much to do to keep safe what they had taken from the house, and Mr. Boardman had his horse and chaise to look after. As there was but little help, there could not be much saved. The day was fair, and the wind strong, and it blew in different directions, so that the bed on which Lucy lay caught fire three times, which she extinguished by smothering it with her hands.

The fire is supposed to have communicated from a candle, accidentally left burning in a kitchen chair, in the morning, in a tightly ceiled room, by our grandmother; and it was some time making its appearance, owing to the stillness of the air, as that was the place where it was discovered. Lucy having been unwell in the night, the old lady was called upon to come and see her, and after rendering her services, Lucy was better and desired to go to bed again. This, she was at first unwilling to do; but after a little persuading, she went. I gave her a new long candle, which she took and set in the chair, and then she lay down on the bed, not thinking to sleep, as she said; but she did fall asleep, and when she awoke, the sun shone brightly in her face, and thinking she had neglected Lucy, and unmindful of the candle, left it burning; coming out of the room, she shut the door after her and came down stairs.

Dear reader, my feelings at this time, may be better imagined than described; no inhabited house within six miles on one side, and twelve the other, my family in this destitute situation, all my carriages sharing the same fate with the buildings, and no means to convey them hence. As Mrs. Boardman was a feeble woman, and out of health, she could not think of giving up her chaise to carry away my family with; neither was it a desirable carriage for them. And while we were contriving some means to get them away, it seemed as though directed by the hand of Providence, a tin peddler happened along, and after we had put what things we saved into an old barn which stood at such a distance from the other buildings that it escaped the fire, he kindly emptied his cart of its contents in the field, and we placed some feather beds in his cart and put Lucy and her brother and the babe in it. I then gave the before mentioned trout to Mr. Boardman, helped them to their carriage, and they went their way, and we went ours. While on the way, the baby was uneasy, and Mrs. Rosebrook picked raspberries and gave them to the child, and to its mother. Grandmother and Mrs. Rosebrook on horseback, myself and the peddler on foot, made up our traveling party, and about the setting of the sun, and over a very rough road, we all arrived in safety at Mrs. Rosebrook's. The two girls we had living with us, staid and slept in the barn, and likewise the men, when they returned from work. I had laid in a good store of provisions for my family's use, as we were not always sure of a crop, and depended on buying. We had a small store pretty well filled with salt and salt fish. I had bought forty dollars worth of wheat and forty of pork. I had made two-thirds of a barrel of maple sugar, and when done sugaring, had taken the large potash kettle which I had used and brought across the Amanoosuc river, I walking over on a log, the kettle on my head, Uncle William helping me to put the kettle on my head; after putting it in a cart I brought it home. These and all other kinds of provisions were destroyed. Some new cheese, however, was saved; this was in the furthermost part of the house, where the fire came last. All my farming tools were destroyed, excepting those that the men had working with, such as plows, harrows, hoes, shovels, rakes, pitchforks, scythes, etc. In the morning we had enough and to spare; in the evening, nothing left but this new cheese, and the milk of the cows. . . .

The next day was the Sabbath; the horses were sent for, and the girls came down and joined us. One incident, by the way, I would just relate. The swallows, after losing their nest, followed the family, and the barns of Mr. Rosebrook seemed to be alive with them; they were actually partakers of our trouble.

Monday, my parents and Lucy's came to see what was to be done; and they agreed to move a small house, twenty-four feet square, which belonged to me, one and a half miles from where ours stood before it was burned; and sent an invitation to our neighbors, who immediately collected, with provisions for themselves and oxen, to draw the building.

My loss by the fire was estimated at $3,000, and there was no insurance. I was young and ambitious, but this shock of misfortune almost overcame me; and I was for some days quite indifferent which way the world went. I at length was constrained to arouse my feelings, and once more put my shoulder to the wheel.

My house was placed upon the spot, and left, with one outside door, and chimney up as high as the chamber floor; there were no windows and there was nothing but a rough, loose floor to walk upon. Yet we could not prevail upon Lucy to stay any longer than two weeks where she was. We therefore spread bedclothes for a carpet, and hung some up for a partition, to keep her from taking cold; and, thus situated, she was accidentally visited by several gentlemen and ladies from Portland. They seemed to sympathize with her, and afterward sent her several articles of furniture for the table. Lucy, however, took cold, which caused her some pain and trouble; and she was obliged to go back to Mr. Rosebrook's and remain there three weeks longer.

I hired two joiners, and went twelve miles for lumber, to work with, and while we were thus engaged, Colonel Binney, from Boston, with two young men, came along, by the way of Littleton, to my place. Finding us so destitute of everything, they staid but a short time, and they went down to father's. The young men wanted to go on to the mountain; they consulted him, and agreed to take him for a guide, with a man to carry provisions and other necessary things. They rode to the top of the Notch, then sent back their carriage, and proceeded to the woods. They had such difficulty in managing to get through; they, however, proceeded slowly; sometimes crawling under a thicket of trees, sometimes over logs and windfalls, until they arrived where they could walk on top of the trees. This may seem to some strange, but it is nevertheless true. They never reached the summit but managed to get along on some of the hills.

As the day was growing to a close, they returned to the woods, in order to pass the night, and erected a shelter for their protection. A dense fog arose and during the night it rained. In the morning, owing to the darkness, they could not tell the best way to proceed, but took the surest way, by following the Amanoosuc river, and came to my house. These men wore fine and costly garments into the woods, but when they returned, their clothes were torn and much injured by the brush, and their hats looked as if they had been through a beggar's press. They were much exposed all night, without fire or food.

In September, there came two gentlemen to my father's and engaged him to go with them to the top of Mount Washington, where they placed an inscription in Latin, which was engraved on a brass plate, and nailed it on a rock; they likewise filled a bottle and put it in a rock. The inscription was as follows, as I had it copied and kept carefully at home. (I vouch not for the Latin or translation being correct; it is at all events, a true copy, as found on the plate; and was translated, with the exception of the word "*perspire*," by a friend, who was afterwards in the vicinity.)

"*Altius ibunt, qui ad summa nitunteer*"—They will go higher who strive to enter heaven. "*Nil reputans, si quid superesset agendum*"—Think nothing done while anything remains to be done. "*Sic itur ad astra.*"—We go thus to the stars. "*Stinere facto per inhostales sylvas Rustribus pramptis feliciter superrtes. (Eheu quantus adest vius sudor!) Johannes Brazer, Cantabrigsensis, Georgius, Dawson, Philadelphiensis, hic posuerant ivid Septembris MDCCCXVIII.*" After passing inhospitable woods and surmounting abrupt ledges (how it made us perspire), John Brazer, of Cambridge, and George Dawson, of Philadelphia, placed this inscription here on the fourth day of Ides of September, 1818.

We succeeded in having a comfortable small house, for the winter of 1819. We had now many difficulties to encounter, owing to the limited size of our small house; it being at that time the principal, if not only market road then traveled by the people, who depended upon going to market in the winter with their produce, from the upper part of New Hampshire, and even west of Vermont; and the snow did not fall early to make a good sleigh path. When it did, our house was filled, and Lucy would many times have to make a large bed on the floor for them to lie down upon, with their clothes on, and I would build a large fire in a large brick or stone chimney, that would keep them warm through the night. It was no uncommon thing to burn in that fire-place a cord of wood in twenty-four hours, and sometimes more.

At that time my father thought it best to sell, as there was a chance, he thought; he being holden with me on the notes, I suppose, would like to have been liberated from them. He consulted with grandmother, and gave her and William a mortgage of his farm, at that time worth two of mine, so that there should be no incumbrance on my barn. But the man to whom we expected to sell, drew back, and we still remained, and struggled along as well as we could, through the winter.

1855

The Willey Slide

Benjamin G. Willey

From *Incidents in White Mountain History*

The Tenth Turnpike in New Hampshire, says an old Gazetteer, was incorporated in the year 1803, December 27th, to extend from the west line of Bartlett through the Notch of the White Hills, a distance of twenty miles. It occupied the site of a laid-out but never well-finished county road, which had been projected years before. The effects of the labors of the incorporated company were soon seen in the increasing travel. In a short time from its opening it became one of the best paying turnpikes in northern New Hampshire. The only outlet to the large portion of country north of the White Mountains, beginning then to be settled, its numerous advantages were not long in being appreciated. Prior to the extension of the northern railroads, and the opening of the numerous markets along their lines, its demand, as an outlet to the Coös, was much more strongly felt than at present. The original cost of the road was forty thousand dollars, its repairs were many and expensive, and yet its dividends were large, and its stock always good.

Portland, the nearest and most accessible of the seaboard towns, was, in those days, the great market for all this part of New Hampshire. Well can we remember the long train of Coös teams which used to formerly pass through Conway. In winter, more particularly, we have seen lines of teams half a mile in length; the tough, scrubby, Canadian horses harnessed to "pungs," well loaded down with pork, cheese, butter and lard, the drivers rivalling almost the modern locomotive and its more elegant train of carriages in noise and bluster. Hardy, resolute men were those early settlers of the Coös;

"——Rough,
But generous and brave and kind."

Besides this Coös travel, compelled, as it were, to pass through this gateway of the mountains, the mountains themselves had already begun to attract much attention. Visitors to them, though few in comparison with the large numbers which now resort thither, journeyed mostly in private carriages, and thus gave to their travel an importance far beyond what at the present time the same number would command.

The want of public houses on the road, especially through the mountains, to accommodate the increasing travel, was sorely felt. From the elder Crawford's to the old Rosebrook place, where recently stood the Mount Washington House, a distance of thirteen miles, there was no public house, indeed no occupied house. To appreciate fully the necessity there was for these places of shelter, one should pass north through the Notch in the depth of winter. The roads are then buried beneath the snow, piled up in drifts to a great depth. This is continually blown about by the wind so as to render impossible a well-beaten path. The traveller has, frequently, shovel in hand, to work his way through the mountains, the cold northern winds, concentrated by their passage through the Notch, blowing directly in his face, almost instantly penetrating and benumbing him.

To open, then, a public house somewhere on this distance, it was seen, would be not only a work of profit, but a kindness. For this purpose a house had been erected, some years previous to the time of which we write, by a Mr. Henry Hill, and is yet standing, being familiarly known as the "Willey House." It was kept by Mr. Hill and others as a public house for several years, but was at length abandoned, and, at the time of my brother's moving into it, had been untenanted for several months. It was in the fall of the year 1825 that he first moved his family into this house. It had been roughly used by the mountain storms and winds, and needed much repairing. The fall was accordingly spent in making it comfortable for the winter. He enlarged the stable, and made such other improvements as time would allow, to make it a comfortable shelter for man and beast. But, with all his most earnest labors, he was but imperfectly prepared for the intense cold and storms of those mountain winters. Still he was hailed as a benefactor, and often were he and his shelter greeted with as much warmth by the traveller in those mountain passes, as the monks of St. Bernard by the wanderers upon the Alps.

The winter passed, nothing unusual occurring, beyond the arrival and departure of his various company. In the spring further improvements were projected and commenced in his buildings, with the design of making them worthy of the increasing patronage. Travellers, who had been his guests, often gave us flattering accounts of his success, and not the least apprehension was felt for his safety. The first thing that particularly diversified his history and awakened his fears, was the slide which took place in June following the spring just referred to.

In the afternoon of one dull, misty day during this month, he and his wife were sitting by a window, that looked out to the north and west. Before them rose in all its grandeur the mountain which is called by their name, "Willey Mountain." The clouds and mist almost entirely covered the mountain; but, as they cleared up and the surface came out to view, they saw distinctly a large mass of earth beginning to move. It passed slowly on, increasing in volume and extent, stopping occasionally, as it were to take breath, and at last rushed into the valley beneath. This was quickly followed by another, less in magnitude and extent. These slides took place near the house, and did no injury beyond greatly exciting their fears.

They were startled by them, and took counsel from their fears at first to leave the place. It is said, and is probably correct, that my brother, under the first panic, was even about getting ready his carriage to carry his family to some place of greater safety. He felt for the moment that he must leave.

But still it is certain he did not leave the place. He grew more calm in a short time, and, not long after the period referred to, became almost entirely unapprehensive of danger. I never saw him after this event, but was told repeatedly that he apprehended no danger to himself or family from what had passed. In conversation with a person on the subject, in reply to a query as to his feelings in relation to the recent slides, he said, "Such an event, we know, has not happened here for a very long time past, and another of the kind is not likely to occur for an equally long time to come. Taking things past in this view, then," said he, "I am not afraid." This was certainly fair reasoning on the matter, and such as we might all well make under like circumstances, though now we can see, in the light of all that is past, how little it availed in respect to the calamity that awaited him so soon. His unsuspicious calmness did not protect him from danger. It rather presaged evil than good. It was the dreadful felt stillness that often, perhaps always, precedes the earthquake. Now we perceive that the events we have written above had a dreadful significance in them.

In August, succeeding the June we have just referred to, a storm took place in the region of the White Mountains, raging in and about the Notch with peculiar violence. It was memorable for its strength and for its

The Willey House in Crawford Notch, circa 1875, nearly 50 years
after the great avalanche killed the seven members
of the Willey clan and their two hired hands.

disastrous effects. It can never be forgotten while a single individual shall exist that lived anywhere near the place in which it transpired, or any care be taken to transmit the account of it to succeeding times. I lived at North Conway at the time of it, and can, therefore, best present what I have to say from that point.

Previous to the time in which this storm took place, there had been a long and heavy drought. The earth, under a fervid sun, had dried to an unusual depth. This prepared the way for the surface of it to be operated on more powerfully by any quick and copious rain. The soil, dried deep and powdered somewhat, would slide easier under the pressure of any accumulating waters, especially if the roots of plants that traversed it had been made tender by the long-continued heat that had been upon them. In this, perhaps, we have as good a theory of slides as any that can be made.

As the month verged towards its closing, signs of rain began to appear. Clouds gathered on the sky, and though they would disperse in a short time, quickly they would gather again. They continued to do this a number of days in succession, every day assuming more permanence than they did the preceding one. At length they became so condensed, that they gave rain, small in quantity to be sure, but some—a signal of what was to follow. In this way, things went on till the storm came on in its strength.

The great disaster, in the destruction of my brother and his whole family, consisting of his wife and five children, together with two hired men, took place on the night of the twenty-eight of this month, August. That day came on Monday, and the disaster took place some time during the night of that day. I was away from home on an exchange the Sabbath previous, and remember well all the circumstances and events of the gathering storm. On Monday, as I came home, I recollect I was hindered by the rain, occasionally falling in showers, so that, though I had but comparatively a few miles to come, I did not reach home till near sunset.

On my way, as I came up from the south toward my residence, I had the most favorable opportunity to note the gathering clouds. Their movements were all before me, and I had only to look and see them. I had often seen storms gather in the regions of those compacted and elevated mountains, but never before with such grandeur and awfulness. The clouds were not so rapid in motion as I had seen before, but their volume and blackness made up, and more than made up, for the want of speed. Their comparative slow movement, indeed, added greatly to the sublimity of their appearance. They reminded one of some heavy armed legions moving slowly and steadily to battle. As they sailed up the giant outline of mountain range extending from Chicorua peak northward for miles, till you come to the White Mountains, and then, pressing upon them, covering them fold after fold with their dark solemn drapery, I could but think of the march of Napoleon, and the measured tread of his infantry, loaded heavily with armor, moving on to some warlike encounter.

They were, in all truth, the very significant portents of a most affecting scene of destruction. As we anticipated things in the sequel transpired. At the close of that day, when the darkness was just coming on, it began to rain; and such a rain I never knew before. The way for it had been prepared, and now it came on in its fury. I was not conscious of all of it, especially the latter part. Being somewhat fatigued, I retired early and slept soundly. As it appeared afterwards, I slept calmly while others, not very far off, my kindred, even, were suffering and dying. Not long after midnight, I was waked suddenly by the slamming of a large door, on the barn, that was ajar and playing in the wind. I arose quickly and went out. As I passed round the corner of the house to go to the barn, which stood north, in the direction of the White Mountains, my eyes fell directly upon them. I saw something about them unusual. It was all clear overhead, not a cloud on the sky, and the moon shone brightly. The storm had passed off. On the White Mountains there lay, close down upon them, a large, dark covering of clouds. It appeared like a pall thrown over sugarloaves of unequal heights. Save this, all above and about them was clear and cloudless.

Out of them were seen, at short intervals, vivid lightnings. I heard no thunder; I saw only the lightnings. They continued till I had done my work, and returned to the house. These were unusual as we have said; but whatever there might be in them, peculiar in character, we may consider them now the after scene of the storm, just passed, and as impending the spot where death had just ceased its revel.

I had remained in the house but a short time when word came to my door that the intervales were being entirely covered with water, and that they must immediately be cleared of the cattle and horses that were upon them. As we came up from the intervales, having accomplished the object, we could but take notice of the marked effects of the storm on the White Mountains. There was plainly visible to the eye the terrible devastations it had produced. All the portions of them facing the south indicated clearly the desolating influences of the rains that had fallen so copiously on their summits and sides. I never saw such in all my life; and I had looked on those mountains, upon an average, scores of times every week for years. It was judged that more destruction of trees, and more displacing of rocks and earth, were made on the declivities of the mountain facing our post of observation, on that terrible night, than had been made since the country was settled. And this was but a part of the destruction produced. On the other sides of the mountains, quite round the whole circumference, were gorges and grooves, made deep even on the hard mountain surface, to show that the destroyer had been there.

We were so occupied on Tuesday, the day succeeding the storm, with what was directly before us, — that we could hardly think of anything else.

On Wednesday early, perhaps on Tuesday, suggestions were made a few times in my hearing respecting things about the Notch; starting the inquiry how the storm might possibly effect my brother and his family. They were but suggestions, however, indicating no particular anxiety in relations to their safety, as there was certainly none with myself or any of his kindred near me. As yet we had heard nothing from him up nearly to the close of Wednesday.

Near the close of that day our suspicious were, for the first time, really aroused as to the safety of my brother's family. Dr. Chadbourne, our physician, on his return from Bartlett, whither he had been on a visit to his patients, informed us that he had heard the whole family were destroyed. He had seen at Bartlett a man, who had just come down through the Notch, who had given him the information. So entirely unsuspicious had we been of any danger to them, and so unprepared for the reception of such tidings, that for the moment we were overcome.

Recovering somewhat from the stunning effects of such sad tidings, we went immediately to a sister's, who lived near. She had heard the same reports; but both of us, arguing rather from our hopes than the facts, were inclined to disbelieve the story. To satisfy ourselves, however, further on the subject, it was thought best to go at once to my father's, who lived two miles north of us, near Bartlett. Mr. Thompson, my sister's husband, and myself, accordingly set out.

We found him having received the news as we had, from the same source, and about the same in amount of information. He was entirely unimpressed with the correctness of the report, and immediately calmed our fears. He said he knew the Notch well, which was the fact, all its bearings and relations, and though he had heard what he had, still he did not think, from the best judgment he could make, that the family were destroyed. Though they were not in their late place of residence, he thought they were alive in some retreat, whither they had fled from the ruins of the storm. The idea that the family were all destroyed was too much for him to entertain. He thought that, notwithstanding all which had been reported, and all the danger that must have surrounded them that dreadful night, still they were among the living.

The calmness and reasoning of my father almost entirely reassured and convinced us that the rumors must be entirely incorrect. We sat some time conversing, and the evening was considerably advanced before we left for home.

It was quite dark, and very still. Our minds still occupied with the recent storm, and its terrible ravages, we were suddenly startled by a sharp, shrill voice, coming apparently from the river below us on the right, and saying, as we thought, "They are there." Breaking so suddenly upon the still night, it was like the shill cry of some bird of prey piercing the darkness. It was many minutes ere we could collect ourselves to come to any satisfactory conclusion concerning the voice. Being nearly opposite Mrs.

Lovejoy's, the mother of my brother's wife, we at length concluded that the family had had additional tidings from the Notch, and that one of the sisters was informing some one on our side of the river of the safety of the family at the Notch, and that they were all in their late home.

As we learned afterwards, we were correct in the conclusion at which we arrived; but not in the words of the speaker. It was "They are not there," instead of "They are there."

Much relieved by the contradictions of the first report by later news, as we supposed, we hastened home. Though we had seen on every hand the terrible ravages of the storm, — the mountains scathed and torn by the torrents, and the waters running in floods at our feet, before and behind us on all sides wasting destruction, — yet, so anxious were we that it should not be true, and so strangely forgetful of the awful danger which must have threatened our brother, that we retired to our beds almost entirely relieved of our anxiety.

But that delusive impression did not remain long. It did not continue through the night. The dawn of another day had scarcely come, when renewed tidings from the Notch made it quite certain that my brother and his family were destroyed. The manner in which these tidings were transmitted to us, at a certain point of their progress, it may not be uninteresting here to present. It shows how in all respects the whole scene of the Notch disaster was filled up with the most thrilling and soul-stirring incidents.

As I have said, my father was comparatively little moved under the first heavy tidings that came from the Notch. He reasoned them all down with his usual tact and calmness, and made them the occasion of little serious alarm to himself and others. But he must be corrected. He had come to a wrong conclusion, and a messenger was already on his way that would correct him. This messenger arrived in the adjoining neighborhood of my father about midnight, to which we have already referred, when that shrill female voice was heard in the darkness. He was there stopped by the Saco, swollen still with the effects of the recent storm. But he carried important tidings which must be communicated. He was sent for this very purpose. So, to get ears to hear them, he stood on the river's brink, the nearest possible point to my father's, and sounded a trumpet. It was a shrill blast, and startled all my father's neighborhood from their repose.

The startled sleepers, soon gathered on the river's bank, learned the sad tidings; but too truly confirming the reports of the previous evening; and then started most of them on their way to the Notch.

I did not hear that blast of the trumpet, — or those blasts, for the first was often repeated,—but those that did, say they never heard anything so impressive and solemn. At any time they would have been startling, pealing as they did through the darkness of midnight. But, under the circumstances before us, they were peculiarly impressive. The sad tidings of the evening before, though not generally credited, had yet left a deep impression and sadness on the minds of all in my father's neighborhood. With these feelings they had retired. Whether sleeping or waking, dim images must have been floating through their minds, from the evening's conversation, when suddenly they were roused by repeated trumpet-blasts, raising echoes from the mountains in almost every direction.

My brother, who heard these trumpet-calls, has often said he never heard anything to be compared with them for what was awe-inspiring and even dreadful in its character.

The confirmed reports soon reached all the relatives of the destroyed family. By daylight the news was spreading in all directions, and people were starting for the Notch. We went generally on foot, there being few horses in the train until they were intercepted by the swollen river. We passed this river in boats and on trees fallen across it, the bridges being mostly carried away. With little of interest to diversify our way, save some additional reports that my brother's family were destroyed, we approached the scene of destruction, entering the opening a hundred rods perhaps below the Notch House, which was still hidden from our sight by the intervening ascent. We met the first great slide, which had crossed our path on level ground, and even ascending some, so great was the force which propelled it from the base of the mountains. After passing this, which consisted of large rocks, and trees, and sand, and which was impassable, except by footmen, and reaching the elevation, we came in full view of the Notch House, and all the ruins that surrounded it. On our right stood in lengthened prospect the precipitous mountain, which had been driven by the fires and tempests of many succeeding years. On our left and in front, the mountains, though once covered with a wood of pleasant green, now presented their sides lacerated and torn by the convulsions of the recent storm. The plain before us appeared one continuous bed of sand and rocks, with here and there the branches of green trees and their peeled and shivered trunks, and old logs, which, from their appearance, must have long been buried beneath the mountain soil. With these the meadow which stretches along before the Notch House was covered, and so deep, that none of the long grass, nor alders that grew there, were to be seen. Moving on from this site, we came upon the next large slide, which continued till it met that of another, which came down below the Notch House, and within a rod of it. Thus far it was one continued heap of ruins, and, be-yond the house, the slides continued many rods. The one back of the house started in a direction, in which it must have torn it away, had it not been arrested by a ridge of land extending back of the house to a more precipi-tous part of the mountain. Descending to this point, the slide divided, and sought the valleys, which lie at the base; one part carrying away in its course the stable above the house, and the other passing immediately be-low it, leaving the house itself unimpaired.

Over this crude and extended mass of ruin we reached the house about noon. Many persons had already arrived there from both above and be-low the Notch. Some search had already been made for the bodies in that part of the slide, just described, which came down below the house. That not availing anything, there was a pause in this direction about the time our party arrived. The slide which we have referred to above as dividing back of the house, again united directly in front of it, and flowed on the bed of the Saco, down the valley. Following down this slide, the acciden-tal moving of a twig disclosed some flies which prey usually upon infected animal matter. Search was immediately commenced about this spot. This search soon disclosed one of the bodies. Immediately the news came to us, and we were soon crowding to the spot. It was no long time before the body first discovered was fully uncovered, and another not far off. These were the bodies of my brother's wife, and one of the hired men, David Allen. They were dreadfully mangled, especially my brother's wife. Scarcely a look of her, as seen in life, could be perceived about the remains. The body of my brother was soon found, near where those of his wife and hired man had been discovered. This was injured less than those of the two preceding. It could be recognized easily in any place by an intimate acquaintance.

All these bodies, after suitable time to make coffins from materials such as could be obtained there, were made ready for burial. It was decided to bury them near the house of their recent habitation, and let them remain there til they could be more conveniently moved to Conway the succeed-ing winter. One common wide grave was dug for them, and they were placed in its margin, to remain till the befitting and accustomed prayer at burial was performed. That prayer was made by a personal friend of my brother, and one who often ministered in holy things. The prayer was suited to the occasion, coming from a kind, sympathizing, pious heart. It was impressive as it came from the good man's lips; and then its impres-siveness was greatly increased from the circumstances under which it was made. In the echoes that were awakened by his voice, the very mountains around us seemed to join with him in describing the majesty of God, and imploring his mercy on our stricken hearts. When, with slow and distinct utterance, the minister, and the commencement of his prayer, referred to the magnificence of the Deity, as described by the Prophet Isaiah, saying, "Who hath measured the waters in the hollow of his hand, and meted out heaven with a span, and comprehended the dust of the earth in a measure, and weighted the mountains in scales, and the hills in a balance," the echo gave back every word of this sublime description in a tone equally clear and solemn with that in which they were first uttered. The effect of all this was soul-stirring beyond description. I shall never forget the tears and sorrows that marked the faces of many that stood around that open grave, on that solemn occasion. The minister who made that prayer was Elder Samuel Hasaltine, then of Bartlett, now living in Bethel. After the prayer we buried the bodies, —

> "And then, one summer evening's close,
> We left them to their last repose."

It was dark before the burial was completed, and we were compelled to spend the night in the house so lately left by the buried family.

The next day the most of us left for our homes. Some remained to make further search for the bodies yet undiscovered. In the course of the day, the body of the youngest child, about three years old, was found, and buried near those of its parents, without any special religious service. Search was continued still the succeeding day, and the body of the eldest child, a girl of twelve years of age, and the other hired man, David Nickerson, were found and buried in the same manner. The bodies of the remaining children, two sons and a daughter, have never been found. They were covered so deep beneath the piles of rubbish, that no search has ever come at them. From the magnitude of the slide, and the amount of matter thrown into the valley, it is more remarkable that so many of the bodies were found, than that these were not found.

The destruction was complete; no living creature about the premises escaped it, except by brother's dog, and his two oxen. He had two horses, which were crushed beneath the falling timbers of the stable. These had been dragged out and exposed to view when the party I was in first arrived on the fatal spot. The oxen were imperiled by the disaster, but escaped without any material injury. One of them was crushed to the floor by falling timbers, but not killed. The other, standing by his side, being more sturdy, resisted them, so that they broke over his back, and, when found, he stood upright amid the ruins about him. In this condition, one crushed to the floor, and the other standing, they remained from Monday night until the next Wednesday morning.

They were then released by a Mr. Barker, the man who first visited the scene of the ruins after it transpired. Coming down through the Notch, from the north, he reached the spot about sunset on Tuesday, and took up his lodgings in the vacated house for the night. When the hush of stillness and desertion, he first found about this house, became more settled, as he lay in his bed trying to compose himself to sleep, being weary, he heard a low moaning, as from some living creature. Under circumstances to interpret this most darkly, as being perhaps the suppressed wail of one of the family still living,—and, yet, not able to accomplish anything by rising, on account of the deep darkness in the house and about the premises, and unable to get any light to relieve it,—he lay terror-stricken and sleepless till the dawn of day. With the first ray of light he arose, and, after a little search, found the cause of his excitement. It was the crushed ox we have referred to, moaning under the pain and uneasiness of his situation. He immediately released him from his confinement, and soon proceeded on his way down toward Bartlett and Conway. This was the man that brought to us the first tidings respecting the great disaster.

So far we have sought to bring out somewhat minutely the points in the great destruction of my brother and his family, so richly deserving a record and the lasting remembrance of all who survive them. Here we might cease, perhaps; still there may be lingering inquiries, with some, demanding attention. How were the family destroyed? What were the main circumstances pertaining to the great event of their destruction? In what manner did the great slide from the mountain, directly back of the house, which was certainly the agent of their destruction, come to bear upon them so as to produce their deaths?

In attempting a reply to these queries there is obviously nothing to aid but conjecture. There is no definite knowledge within our reach to bring to such a work.

They all perished together, and this was rather remarkable. Some one or more of the children, since the moving of their parents to the Notch House, had generally been with their relatives in Conway. That they should all have been at home, then, at the time of the disaster, and all have perished together may be deemed as giving a peculiar aspect to the whole matter. Friends might have wished it otherwise, on some accounts, and yet, we must say, it was best as it was. No one survived to endure the deep anguish that must have come from the destruction of all his nearest kindred.

We have said if one of the family had survived we might have had some information about it. If even the family dog could have spoken, he would have told us more about the sad event than we now know. He would have described one of the most heart-rending scenes ever witnessed. He probably accompanied the family, as they commenced their march to death from their dwelling, but escaped by his superior sight and agility. We infer this from some contusions of his body discoverable when first seen after the disaster. This dog, to the best of his power, did try to inform some friends of the destroyed family of what had happened. Soon after this disaster, and before any news of it had come to Conway, this faithful dog came down to Mr. Lovejoy's and, by moaning and other expressions of deep inward anguish around the persons of the family, tried to make them understand what had taken place, but, not succeeding, he left, and after being seen frequently on the road between the Notch House and the res-

MOUNT WASHINGTON OBSERVATORY COLLECTION

Remnants of the 1826 slide that killed the Willey family but spared their home can be seen in (upper left) in this 1865 stereo view of the Willey House site.

idence of the family just referred to, sometimes heading north, and then south, running almost at the top of his speed, as though bent on some most absorbing errand, he soon disappeared from the region, and has never since been seen. He probably perished through grief and loneliness combined with exhaustion of body.

In the absence of any exact information, then, from any quarter, respecting the manner of the destruction of the family, we are shut up entirely to the force of conjecture, as we have said. That most commonly indulged is this:

The family, at first, designed to keep the house, and did actually remain in it till after the descent of most of the slides. From the commencement of the storm in its greatest fury they were, probably, on the alert, though previously to this some of them might have retired to rest. That the children had, was pretty evident from the appearances in the house when first entered after the disaster. My brother, it is pretty certain, had not undressed; he stood watching the movements and vicissitudes of the awfully anxious season. When the storm had increased to such violence as to threaten their safety, and descending avalanches seemed to be sounding "the world's last knell," he roused his family and prepared them, as he could, for a speedy flight, trembling every moment lest they should be buried under the ruins of their falling habitation.

At this hurried, agitating moment of awful suspense, the slide, which parted back of the house, is supposed to have come down, a part of which struck and carried away the stable. Hearing the crash, they instantly and precipitately rushed from their dwelling, and attempted to flee in the opposite direction. But the thick darkness covering all objects from their sight, they were almost instantly engulfed in the desolating torrent which passed below the house, and which precipitated them, together with rocks and trees, into the swollen and frantic tide below, and cut off at once all hope of escape. Amidst the rage and foam of so much water, filled, as it was, with so many instruments of death, they had no alternative but the doom which was before them.

Others have supposed that, as the storm increased during the night, thinking the stable a safer place than the house, being constructed of stronger materials, they went into the stable before the destructive slide come down which carried them away; and there they met death by the part of it which fell, and the mingled current of sand and timber which produced the fall, and were borne along on its course to where they were afterwards found. This conjecture arose, probably, from the fact that the remains of such of the family as were discovered were found very near the timbers of that portion of the stable which was carried away.

There is still another conjecture respecting the manner of the great disaster, suggested by a dream of my eldest brother, James Willey. In his dream he thought he saw the brother that was destroyed, and asked him why he and his family left the house, as they did, and thus exposed themselves to dangers abroad, when they might have been more safe at home. This has often been asked. In reply to this, my brother remarked that they did not leave the house until the waters rose so high in front, and came up so near, that they found they would carry away the house; so, to avoid being drowned, they took some coverings for shelter against the storm, and went out to the foot of the mountain back of the house, and from thence, soon after, were carried away by the great slide that came down in that direction.

This is an explanation of the manner of the disaster of which we might never have conceived but for the dream. But, when taken up from this source, it adjusts itself better to great facts in the case than either of the theories we have heretofore considered. It explains why a bed was found on the ruins near the body of the eldest daughter. That bed was needed as a shelter from the storm, in the retreat the family made to the base of the mountain.

The theory of the dream, too, explains why the family were all destroyed, and some did not escape. On the supposition of the first theory, that the family fled precipitately from the house when they heard the crash of the stable, and were soon engulfed in the part of the great slide that ran below the house, it has always seemed strange to me, at least, that such as were in the rear of the fleeing party did not pause, or recede, even, when they found those in the advance carried off by the moving mass, and, perhaps, giving a sudden outcry that there was danger in the way. But on the supposition before us, the family, just previous to the slide, were grouped together at the foot of the mountain. In this situation they would be an easy prey to the massive slide, coming upon them in its force, and be carried away before it in a body.

1927

Dolly Copp

George N. Cross

From *Dolly Copp and the Pioneers of the Glen*

The story of Dolly and Hayes Copp, early inhabitants of the Pinkham Notch area, is every bit as fascinating as that of Lucy and Ethan Allen Crawford. The Copps, wed on November 3, 1831 in Bartlett, lived together for 50 years in the remote wilderness of Martin's Grant. Here, where the winters were long, the summers short, and the wildlife bountiful, the Copps farmed the rugged land and welcomed hundreds, if not thousands of weary travelers into their cozy home, which Dolly had turned into an inn. George N. Cross, author of the 1927 booklet from which the following piece has been excerpted, was a longtime summer resident of nearby Randolph who, because of deafness, was forced at an early age to abandon a promising teaching career. In 1924, three years before publication of Dolly Copp and the Pioneers of the Glen, *Cross authored* Randolph: Old and New, *a centennial history of the unique mountain community at the foot of the Northern Peaks of the Presidential Range.*

FOR FORTY YEARS the Pinkham Notch road was the one highway between Jackson and Randolph and the north country, and the Copp home the one large dwelling between those places. Although it was never licensed as such, it naturally became a sort of tavern. Travelers in either direction usually stopped for a meal, or, if they arrived late, spent the night. Dolly's good food and comfortable beds became widely known. The price of entertainment was not exorbitant—"a shilling all round," that is, twenty-five cents for a meal, the same for a bed for each person and a quarter for the feed and care of a horse.

From the vivid memory of some of Dolly's long-ago guests still living it is possible to make a tolerably accurate pen picture of the Copp home and its mistress. By a door on the south side of the house, the traveler entered the living room, a large, low, square apartment. Opposite the door was a huge stone fireplace, in which usually blazed a hospitable fire. In the corner at the right stood a rude wooden loom and beside it a large spinning wheel; in the corner at the left a wide bed, covered with a handwoven, light blue coverlet. Near the fireplace ticked a "grandfather's" clock, the early history of which Dolly herself has handed down to us. The ancient timepiece is still preserved in one of the homes of Gorham. On the inside of the case is this curious little memorandum in Dolly's quaint and odd hand:

> "In the year of 1821 there were twelve of these clocks brought into the town of Jackson, State of New Hampshire, and sold for twenty dollars. I bought this one of Capt. Anthony Vinson [Vincent], who then lived on what was afterward called the Carlton place, Randolph. It was forty-eight years ago last September that I bought it and paid five and one-half dollars for it. It was for many years an excelent timckeeper.
>
> "DOLLY COPP"

Over the fireplace on wooden pins hung two long-barreled guns, one of them with a flint lock. Around the room stood several splint-bottomed chairs. From a crane a teakettle was suspended over the fire, and on a flat stone in front of it stood a frying pan and a tin baker.

In cold weather this living room served as kitchen and dining room also. The late Eugene B. Cook of Hoboken, who was once a storm-bound guest over night at the Copp farm, gave the writer many years ago a vivid description of Dolly's table as it was spread for supper before the fire. Of the food served that night Mr. Cook could remember nothing but that it was a very satisfying supper for a tired and hungry tramper. He recalled that the table was covered with a snowy, fringed linen cover that would make you modern housewives draw a long breath. Dolly raised the flax in the narrow flax field by the river, pulled and heckled the flax, spun it on the small flax wheel as she rocked Sylvia's cradle, wove it on the loom in the corner and bleached it in the sun and dew of the orchard behind the house. The table was resplendent with a silver teapot and sugar bowl, and delicate china ornamented with a narrow gilt band and tiny flowers. Of the silver pieces Dolly was frankly very proud. They were probably heirlooms, and as part of the bridal outfit had come up the trail lashed to the bridal car. In Dolly's heart, beneath the toil-worn exterior of the pioneer, lived the woman's love of the refined and beautiful.

COURTESY FLOYD W. RAMSEY

Dolly Copp

On the right of the fireplace was the huge brick oven of olden times in which each Saturday morning a fire was built. When it was hot the coals were raked out and the floor swept clean with an oven broom. Into the cavernous depths, with a long, pronged hook, were pushed a roast of pork, or venison, or bear, a pot of pork and beans, another of Indian pudding, and other delicacies of the pioneer's table. The oven was then sealed with a heavy wooden shutter and the savory viands left to simmer all night in the mellow heat and be drawn forth in the morning, a Sunday breakfast for a sturdy, hungry family.

At the foot of the bed stood a heavy wooden cradle painted red and furnished with a hand-woven coverlet of the same light blue as the one on the larger bed. Into that cradle in 1832 came Jeremiah, to grow up a stalwart son, a cheerful helper in every task of the farm, skilled in all the arts of forest and stream. In later years Jerry married and moved to Littleton, where he lived to a goodly age, famed as the most skilful trout fisherman in all the region. He died in Meredith in 1910.

In a year Jerry had to yield the warm, red cradle to baby Nat. Of Nathaniel's young manhood of great strength, courage and endurance there will be much to tell presently.

Five years later Dolly rocked in the little red cradle Sylvia, little Sylvia, the fittingly named joy of that woodland-girdled home, the one sweet and gentle element of that stern household. After ten years of rest in the attic the red cradle once more took its accustomed place at the foot of the bed to welcome Daniel, the last baby of the family.

Dolly makes a pleasant picture as she sits by the foot of the bed, one small foot resting on the cradle rocker, and occasionally gently nudging Dan's uneasy slumber, the other foot on the treadle of the flying flax wheel, her deft fingers drawing out the smooth, even linen thread. To be sure, twenty years of never-relaxing toil have wrought changes in the once girlish form—shoulders bent, figure stouter, face pinched and seamed with lines of care, the curly, flaxen hair replaced by a frowsy wig, contentment shining from her pale blue eyes, save an occasional flash of impatience in response to the angry snarl of the tangled wheel.

She is dressed in a gown of pale blue homespun, woven from the wool of her own flock, the plain, loose-fitting garment made by her own hands. It is fastened at the throat with a large, gold breastpin. Her sole other adornment is a necklace of gold beads, bright with years of wear and nervous fingering. Between the lips of her small, firm mouth is held a short-stemmed clay pipe, the comfort and solace of many toilsome hours. Such was Dolly Copp, a typical pioneer woman of the wilderness of Martin's Location seventy-five years ago.

1904

General Grant's Stagecoach Ride in the White Mountains

Alice Bartlett Stevens

From *The Granite Monthly*

"MOST EVERYBODY has forgotten all about it, I guess, but I remember it jest as plain as if 'twas yesterday. You see it happened way back in '69. It was sometime in the month of August—I don't recollect jest what time of the month it was—that word had got around that General Grant and a party was goin' to make a tour of the White Mountains. At that time [Edmund] Cox owned the best team of horses in these parts, eight matched chestnut-sorrel thoroughbreds. The leaders couldn't be brought for less than three thousand dollars cash. Every horse was as clean as a whistle; not a spot or blemish anywhere. They were as handsome a lot of horses as you ever see in harness, and, travel! They could go like the wind! So it was decided that when General Grant came—everybody knew how the general liked horses—Cox should be the one to meet the party at Bethlehem. Well, one day, seems to me it was the last part of the month, but I won't say sure, Cox got word about noon that General Grant would reach Bethlehem that night. I got wind of it, and long about three o'clock in the afternoon I sauntered over to the stable to take a look at the team as they was bein' hitched up. The 'Flume chariot' as they called it, was roomy; good springs; had a high box seat for the driver, and would carry a dozen or more.

"We all knew that Cox was goin' to break the record for fast stage driv-

130

ing, and there was some bets out amongst a lot of the stage drivers, who stood around waitin' for the start. Some said he couldn't make the run in less than two hours, while others there was who said he'd do well if he made it in two hours and a half; but Cox, he kept a quiet tongue in his head as he carefully looked over and tried every strap and buckle. All he said was that the horses knew that 'they had got to do their level best,' that he wouldn't say anything about the time now, but for all of us to 'just wait and see.'

"Don't talk to me about horses not knowin' or understandin'! You could tell by the actions of them horses, every one of 'em, that they knew somethin' unusual was goin' to happen. 'Twas all Cox could do to manage them as he was hitchin' up, dancin' and prancing' as they was led out of the stable. Their ears pricked up; their eyes full of fire, nippin' and strikin' out at each other, and, when the leaders came out and were put to, it took a man at the head of each horse to keep them from dashin' off. When Cox took his seat and gathered up the lines the horses broke away from us and bounded off like hounds. The minute they started, we was all pretty well worked up by this time, we all took off our hats, threw them up in the air and shouted: 'Cox is goin' to fetch the president! Hurrah for Grant! Hurrah for Grant!'

"As Cox would take plenty of time goin', we calculated that he would get to the Sinclair House in Bethlehem 'bout dusk. So, after an early supper that night I drove to the Profile House, along with a number of old stage whips, who wanted to be there when Cox and the presidential party arrived. Before I started I cautioned 'mother' to keep a sharp lookout, for she would see the president drive by at a pretty good rate of travelin'." As "mother" had already joined us and was sitting near by listening attentively she interrupted Uncle Ben Daniel at this point by saying, "Yes, I kept a pretty close watch all the evenin', settin' out here on the piazza, lookin' down the road every little while; pretty soon I heard a rumblin' noise and quite a clatter, but before I could scarce say to myself the president's comin', I see a great cloud of dust whirlin' up the road, and I started for the front gate. I had almost got to the gate when the cloud of dust whirled by. I couldn't see to make out a single figure in the stage, and the horses seemed to me to be spread out flat, and their bellies almost touchin' the ground. I hadn't time to hardly think before they was out of sight."

"'Yes,' responded her husband, laughingly, 'Mother was pretty well worked up and excited, but she was terrible disappointed 'cause she couldn't make out General Grant in that cloud of dust. Let's see, where did I leave off? Oh, yes, I was sayin' as how I went with a parcel of stage-drivers to the

Profile to wait for Cox. Well, after Cox got to Bethlehem he put up his team, gave them a good feed and rest, and in about two hours drove to the Sinclair House for his party. It was about seven o'clock as the president and his party walked out of the hotel. The general's keen eyes recognized at once the quality of the horses standing before him, and he stepped up to the driver and said, 'If you haven't any objections I will ride up here with you.' Cox answered him that 'It is pretty rough ridin' up here, General,' but, the president said, 'I can stand it if you can' and climbed up into the driver's seat. When the party had all taken their seats Cox gathered up the lines and away they started for the Profile.

"The telegraph operator at the Sinclair House sent a message to the Profile the minute they started. It was exactly seven o'clock. You remember that little barkin' cannon that is kept at Echo lake, about half a mile this side of the Profile—kept there to amuse the guests of the hotel who want to listen for the echo? Well, arrangements had been made that when Cox passed this point the gunner should fire off the cannon three times, so that those waiting at the Profile should be ready and on a sharp lookout for them. Well, 'long 'bout eight o'clock we had got word that they was on the road; the crowd of us stood near the hotel talkin' and waitin', when all of a sudden bang went the cannon! The guests all run out on the piazza. We all looked at each other, then we looked at our watches and we said 'It can't be! Look at the time!' but it was, for we could hear the clatter of the horses' hoofs comin', and before we heard the second signal from the cannon everybody was shoutin', 'Here they are! here they are! clear the road!' and in a flash they were right on us, comin' around a bend in the road into the large circle in front of the hotel, Cox holdin' the lines drawn hard up, and General Grant beside him holdin' on to his hat with one hand and onto the side of the seat with the other. The horses in a dead jump, white with foam. When Cox put on the brake and stopped the coach we all took out our watches. The drive had been made in jest fifty-eight minutes. The president, when he got down from the box seat, was a curious sight. He was covered with dust from head to foot. Mrs. Grant was in the party, and, if I remember, Miss Nellie Grant, and one of the sons was there, too. I don't remember the names of the others.

"We helped take care of the horses; I worked over one of the leaders a good while; they was all shaky and winded, of course, but not hurt a bit. After we got them rubbed down and fixed up for the night we all went into the hotel office. Somebody asked Cox how the horses was, and he said they could do it over again, but they was pretty stiff now, and would ache some all night. The president was anxious to know how they was too. He came into the office and give us a good account of the ride. He said the way Cox handled his horses beat anything he had ever seen, and that the further they went the better they traveled."

"You ask how did they ever make that three mile hill," added Uncle Ben Daniel, bending towards me, his face grown flushed and heated in the recount of these exciting details.

"How did they ever do it? Let me tell you. Them horses knew by the way the lines was held that there was somebody settin' beside the driver that when he set out to do a thing he done it. It was because General Grant was on the box seat. It ain't in the power of horse flesh to travel that distance in that length of time for any other man that ever lived!"

1870

How Sarah Whitcher
Was Lost in the Woods

William Little

From *The History of Warren*

*Although it may not rank among the most accurate New Hampshire town histo-
ries ever written, certainly* The History of Warren *by William Little (1833–
1893) is one of the most entertaining to read. Originally published in 1870,* The
History of Warren *was written to "preserve the Indian traditions, tales of
border wars, the memories of old proprietors and first white settlers, the legends,
anecdotes, and events of our mountain hamlet," wrote Little in his introduction
to the book. The author, an 1859 Dartmouth College graduate, made sure his book
was not your run-of-the-mill town history as he took many liberties in spicing
up events and happenings of the past. The result is one of the "most readable,"
if not entirely accurate town histories on record. William Little was a Warren
native and son of Jesse Little, a local physician. After attending Dartmouth, he
studied law at Albany (N.Y.) Law University and went on to become a successful Manchester, N.H. attorney. Following publication of* The History of
Warren, *Little was contracted to write a* History of Weare, New Hampshire.
This book was published in 1888, just five years before the author's death.

I T W A S T H E most beautiful Sabbath of June, 1783. Quiet pervaded the
haunts of men. The clatter of the mills had ceased, no rude cart rumbled
the stony path, the voice of the ploughman was not heard, and the woodman's axe was hushed and still. A mellow softness pervaded the air, the
woods, and the waters, and a thin haze of the most delicious and tender
blue, rested upon the mountains. All nature seemed in worship. The leaves

murmured melody in the light breeze, the brooks sent up the gentlest music from the mosses of their stony beds, the clouds like silent nuns in white veils worshipped in the sunbeams, and the birds sang psalms.

And yet there was no religious meeting in our mountain hamlet. The settlers with their families sat down in their homes or reclined in the shade of the trees about their dwellings, reading their bibles or engaged in silent meditation.

On Pine hill, Mr. John Whitcher dreamed the morning hours away, then suggested to his wife that they pay a visit to Chase Whitcher, their relative, who lived by the wild roistering Oliverian at the Summit. The idea was agreeable to Mrs. W., and in a few minutes they were ready for the pleasant walk along the bridle path through the woods.

Their little girl, Sarah, not yet four years old, lispingly asked her mother if she could go, but was told she must stop at home with the other children, and they would bring her something nice on their return.

And then they walked rapidly away across the ridge, and down toward babbling Berry brook, admiring not a bit the dewy wild flowers in the path, and hardly noticing their delicious perfumes as they crushed them beneath their feet. In an hour they were at Chase Whitcher's by the Oliverian.

The day was spent most agreeably. The new fields of full blown clover and honeysuckle, and on the borders of which the bright purple cranesbill was just blooming, were alive with the music of the vireo, blackbirds, and the wood-thrush, and the mild fairy-like hum of the myriads of wild bees sipping their nectar from the delicious flowers. Among the grasses they found the sweetest wild strawberries, and they passed the hours talking of the wonders of the deep forests where they would go hunting in autumn, speculating how high was the mighty precipice of Owl's head, and what an abundance of blueberries were growing on its summit.

It was only when the sun was sinking behind Webster-slide mountain in the west, that they said good by, and the few stars that shone out struggled through the rifts of the rainy clouds and the moon was scarce seen at all. But the bright light that streamed from their cabin window was cheerful and made their home doubly inviting.

"What made you leave Sarah up at the Summit?" said one of the older children almost as soon as they entered.

"We did not leave her," instantly replied the father, astonished.

"She is certainly not at home. Where can she be?" each one exclaimed, and then the dread reality burst upon them in a moment. Lost! Lost! Sarah is lost in the woods!

Mr. Nathaniel Richardson tells that the ruddy face of Mr. Whitcher

turned pale, but he said, "Trust in the Lord;" that Mrs. Whitcher's countenance lighted up with afright, and the other children gathered closer to
them, not knowing what to do. Reuben Whitcher who was present, seized
the dinner-horn and started instantly for the woods. Mrs. Whitcher followed him, then came back and with the older children went to Mr.
Stephen Richardson's to spread the alarm. The father seemed as if smitten down, then agitated paced to and fro in front of the house, then hurried away in the woods alone. The nearest neighbors came, shouting and
hallooing in the forest; then built great fires that gleamed through the
trees. Thus passed the night.

When her parents were gone little Sarah followed after them, then
missed the path and wandered in the woods.

As she — "Mrs. Dick French" — told the story in after years, it was a
new world for her; the giant forest extended itself interminably, and the
huge old trees looked as if they grew up to the skies. Among their roots
was the young wood sorrel, its beautiful white flowers with brown spots
about the stamens; then she gathered handsful of wild peony with deep
red flowers, with leaves that curled over the purple and yellow flowers of
the adder tongues, like Corinthian capitals. In the branches above were
strange birds that she had never seen before. The Canada jay, called sometimes carion bird, because it robs the hunter's traps almost before his back
is turned, with slate colored back and white breast, sent its strange wild
note deep in the forest. Large owls in velvety sweep, flew by her. Squirrels
chattered and scolded one another, and their companions the partridges
clucked before her, or flew away with heavy, rumbling flight. Once an eagle
screamed above her; and she started back affrighted as a wild cat sprang
past her.

All day long she wandered on; her little hands full of flowers, her mind
filled with strange indefiniteness, hoping continually to find her father and
mother. But she did not meet them, and no cart tracks, no cow paths, no
spots or blazes on the trees were to be seen.

Despairing, at last exhausted, her feet scratched and bleeding by the underbrush, she sank down on the thick moss by the great rock that stands
by the old beaver meadow, at the foot of the Cascades on Berry brook. "It
is night now. Darkness has come down on the woods. She is alone. The
wind is heard on the mountain. The torrent pours down the rocks. No hut
receives her from the rain, alone in the thick woods of the valley. Rise
moon from behind thy clouds. Stars of the night arise. Give light to her,
sitting alone by the rock of the mossy stream."

Something is coming. She hears a strange sound; the underbrush is crackling, a black form appears in the darkness. Frightened the tears rolled down her cheeks. It is a great shaggy black bear. He came close to her, smelt of her face and hands, and licked the blood from her feet. She was no more afraid of him than of her own great dog at home, and dared to stroke his long, brown nose, and put her arm around his neck. Then he lay down beside her, she placed her head upon his shoulder and alone in the thick woods, with the dark clouds of the sky for a covering, she was quickly asleep.[1]

Two days afterwards the foot prints of the child and the bear were found in the sand and mud of the brook.

None slept in John Whitcher's house during the long hours of that terrible night. The father was out in the woods, the children sat down with woe pictured on their faces, while the mother would not suffer a door or a window to be closed, but listened to every sound, and started at every leaf.

In the morning, the exciting rumor of "John Whitcher's child lost and supposed to have perished in the woods," seemed to speed itself, on the wings of the wind, sounding along the borders of Beech Hill, startling the wild solitudes of the East-parte region, arousing the rugged yeomanry of the Height-o'-land, the brave boys of Runaway pond and the Patchbreuckland, charging them all to pack up their dinners and hurry away to the search in the woods.

In an incredible short time all the dwellers in the hamlet were moving towards Pine hill. Col. Obadiah Clement left his oxen yoked, mounted his horse and galloped swift away up the bridle path, passing Jonathan Clement and 'Squire Copp, with their sons, who, leaving their hoeing, were hastening in the same direction with tin dinner horns in their hands. Joshua Merrill, Joseph Merrill, Stevens Merrill, and 'Squire Jonathan, seized their axes and ran. Joseph Patch, with his long barrelled gun, and his neighbors, came up at a rapid pace, and a little later in the day, Lunds, Clarks, and Tarletons came over the mountain.

All day long they hunted. Col. Clement and his friends went down through the maples to Black brook, and Kelly pond, then climbed up by Oak falls, and beat the woods as far as Wachipauka pond under Webster slide. 'Squire Copp blew a loud blast with his horn on the shore. "No response came from the far glimmering passionate sound but its own empty echo, " hurled back from the mountain face.

Stevens Merrill and others, with Joseph Patch crossed Berry brook and went through the dark forest to the very foot of Moosehillock mountain.

---

1. Sarah Whitcher's, otherwise Mrs. Dick French's, own statement.

Chase Whitcher, Stephen Richardson, and a host of others hunted along the bridle path, and then explored the Oliverian up what is at present High street, as far as the dark passes on either side of Black mountain. The women and children hunted for long hours, but in vain.

The night came, and one after another the parties returned empty from the search. Despair seemed to have taken possession of the grief-stricken parents, and a feeling of sadness pervaded the whole settlement.

On Tuesday morning the entire town renewed the search. As the day wore away, people began to arrive from the neighboring lands. They came from Wentworth and Romney, from Orford, Piermont, Haverhill, and Newbury. At night, one of the last men to come in, reported that he had found the track of a child and of a bear on Berry brook. "She is torn in pieces!" "She is eaten up!" every one said, and Mrs. Whitcher was nearly frantic.

The next day they searched on the Summit, going over the ground thoroughly; but night brought no success. "She is hopelessly lost." "She will never be found." Yet at the earnest request of the agonized mother they promised to continue the search one day more.

Thursday the woods were alive with people hunting. The long hours slowly wore away, when about noon a Mr. Heath who had walked the whole distance from Plymouth, came to the house. Mrs. Stephen Richardson who was cooking a bushel of beans for the people's supper, and Mrs. Obadiah Clement, were alone at John Whitcher's. Mrs. Whitcher was still searching in the woods.

"Give me some dinner," said Mr. Heath, "then show me the bridle-path to the north, and I will find the child." While he was eating, he stated how he heard last evening that little Sarah Whitcher was lost, and that three times in the night, he dreamed that he found her lying under a great pine top, a few rods to the south-east of the spot where the path crossed Berry brook, guarded by a bear.[2]

The women smiled, but partly believed it might be so, for people had different notions then from what they entertain now. Some believed in witches, ghosts, and goblins, and all had a certain kind of faith in dreams; at any rate the women wished his dream might prove true; they felt so sad at the loss of the child; they wished so much it might be found.

---

2. Samuel Merrill, who resided at the East-parte, and lived to be 84 years old, often told about the lost child. He believed in Mr. Heath's dream as much as in his own existence. There were hundreds of people in Warren of the last generation who believed implicitly in Mr. Heath's dream.

Just then Joseph Patch came into the clearing, heard Mr. Heath's story, and said he would accompany him.

An hour went by; the sun was going down on the last afternoon of the search, which would be given up that night, and every one felt that little Sarah was lost forever.

Suddenly a gun was heard; every soul in the clearings and the woods listened. Another report, then another. It is the agreed signal of success. "Thank God! the child is found." "Is it dead or alive?"

They found her just where Mr. Heath said they would; but no bear was to be seen. When she woke up, she said, "I want to go to mother. Carry me to mother." When asked if she had seen any one, she said, "a great black dog stopped with her every night."[3]

Joseph Patch took up the half famished child in his arms and carried her home. On the bridle-path they met many people, and they ran before, hurrahing, waving their hats and green boughs to tell the good news, how all on account of a wonderful dream the child was found alive. Some said the bear guided her to the path. Mrs. Whitcher was so overjoyed that she fainted. Mr. Whitcher could not say a word, but smoked his pipe as hard as he could, to keep his feelings down, and the rest of the children were so glad that they cried and laughed by turns.

Tradition has it that the Rev. Mr. Powers was present and offered a prayer of thanksgiving, and then all the people sang Old Hundred. However that may be, we know that they ate all the baked beans[4] that Mrs. Richardson had prepared, and everything else they could find cooked on Pine hill. Then they blew their tin horns as though the 4th of July had come; shouted and hurrahed again and again, while those who had guns fired volley after volley till all the powder in the settlement was burned, so much did they rejoice that the lost child was found.

<hr />

3. Nathaniel Richardson's statement.

4. Nathaniel Richardson, son of Steven Richardson, also gave many incidents about the search, and told of the beans.

1994

The Famous
Cherry Mountain Slide

Floyd W. Ramsey

From *Shrouded Memories*

Retired English teacher Floyd W. Ramsey (1931–) lives in Littleton, N.H., and has been writing about true historic events of the North Country for the past 15 years. In late 1994, he self-published a collection of 20 such historical pieces in the popular book, Shrouded Memories, *currently out-of-print. The Willey Slide, excerpted from* Shrouded Memories, *was published earlier this year in booklet form by Bondcliff Books, also of Littleton.*

THROUGH MOST OF June of 1885, New Hampshire residents grumbled about the wet and unseasonably cold weather. In early July they had more reason to complain. Violent thunderstorms had moved into the area. And, wherever these thunderstorms struck, tragedy followed. For example, on South Street in Littleton, lightning did considerable damage to the house of Theophilus Carbonneau. It also mangled the foot of his ten-year-old daughter, crippling her for life.

In Lancaster, Moses Kimball and his son-in-law were examining a sick cow in the pasture when lightning ended the animal's life. The impact threw Kimball violently backwards, and his son-in-law temporarily lost his eyesight.

At Jefferson Mills an errant ball of lightning entered the home of Charles Morse. As a consequence, two beds were set on fire and his wife was rendered insensible for a time.

Then on Wednesday, July 8, the weather took another unpredictable turn. Local thermometers shot past 90. This heatwave, however, was shortlived. The next afternoon the thunderstorms returned accompanied by high winds. Trees were uprooted, bushes and shrubs blew away, and telephone and telegraph poles were extensively damaged.

That Friday morning damage by the storm reached its climax by unleashing one of the most destructive landslides that has ever occurred in the White Mountains. At the time of the catastrophe, the homes of John Boudreau and Oscar Stanley stood in the path of a million tons of debris that were traveling at express-train speed down 3600-foot Cherry Mountain in Jefferson.

The day before this dramatic occurrence, Oscar Stanley, 49, a hardworking, highly respected farmer who lived near Jefferson Meadows on the south side of the Cherry Mountain Road, was caught out in the storm. Shortly after lunch that day he had set off for Whitefield in his buggy to buy materials necessary to set up a cookstove in his nearly completed new home.

Following the destruction of his former home by fire on the night of June 4, for five long weeks his widowed mother, Moranda, 74, his wife Ellen, 37, and his three daughters—Della, 18, Grace, 9, and Mora, 5—had been staying a half-mile north at his father-in-law's, John M. King. As for himself, he had been sleeping in his barn, which sat on the opposite side of the road near the newly laid tracks of the Whitefield and Jefferson Railroad.

Initially he had worked on the rebuilding alone. However, after collecting what little house insurance he had, the money enabled him to hire two Whitefield brothers, Moses and Cleophas McDonald, to help with the carpenter work. His regular hired hand, Donald Walker, 23, who was engaged to his daughter Della, took care of the farm work. At the end of each exhausting day, the four men slept on beds set up in the barn. Every morning Della and Grace walked over to make the beds, and to sometimes serve dinners in the barn when the weather was disagreeable.

Now, with the haying season near and all but the ell completed, Stanley decided to move his family into the uncompleted house the next day. Preparing the meals there, he knew, would save valuable time. For the moment, though, his return from Whitefield was delayed. Finally, at 9:00 that night, he arrived back at the barn.

On Friday, July 10, when he awakened his men at daylight, he was disappointed to find that it was still raining. Despite this fact, he led the brothers across the road to the house following a quick breakfast, while Don Walker remained behind to milk the cows.

Unknown to any of them, shortly before 6 A.M. lightning struck the bald spur known as Owl's Head which crowned the north side of Cherry Mountain. At nearly the same time two thunderclouds collided directly over the summit, releasing a deadly downpour. Minutes later giant boulders were dislodged forty feet from the top. When they landed on the saturated, clay-based covering of the steep north slope, the covering collapsed and began following rain-swollen Stanley Brook down the ravine.

Screaming and twisting its way for a mile and a half down the mountain the slide grew in volume and velocity. Along the way it picked up nearly a million tons of earth and stone along with thousands of feet of fir, spruce birch, and ash. When it broke out into the open meadow just above Boudreau's shanty-like house, it swallowed a bridge that crossed the ravine. Its first victims were Silas Marshall's cattle that were pastured just below there.

Boudreau, asleep when the slide began, was awakened by the deep rumbling that it made. At first he thought it was distant thunder. However, as the deadly roar increased and his house began to shake, he ran to a window and saw a sight that paralyzed him with fear. All he could mutter was, "Mon Dieu! See him come!"

Miraculously, Boudreau and his family were spared only because a bend in the channel of Stanley Brook turned the slide toward the opposite side of the ravine. Though his house was left standing, the main body of the gigantic mass plowed down the middle of his land. As it flew by, some of the debris landed within twenty feet of his door and huge logs were hurled into his garden.

A quarter of a mile beyond, Oscar Stanley's attention was distracted by the same peculiar rumbling sound that awoke Boudreau.

"What is that?" he asked over the sounds of saw and hammer.

One of the McDonald brothers shrugged and replied, "Only a train on the road."

As the noise grew louder, a strange vibration could be felt in the house. Stanley now felt an inexpressible feeling of fear. "Boys," he said, "it is something terrible. Something awful is happening."

Going to the door, he looked toward the mountain. Through the gently falling rain he saw a forty-five foot high mass, which was at least a hundred feet wide, rushing toward the house. As rolling boulders banged against each other, flashes of fire shot out from the sides.

Stanley screamed, "I'm going to get out of this! The mountain is coming down!"

Propelled by the horror of the moment, the three men ran toward a wooden fence which stood on higher ground just west of the house. Momentarily looking back, they saw the monstrous mass engulf the house. Arriving at the fence, one of the McDonald brothers was literally thrown over it by the force of the wind given off by the slide.

Stanley himself had the narrowest escape. He came within eight feet of being drawn into the debris.

Hurtling across the road, the slide instantly destroyed the barn. Then, with its fury spent by the level ground, it slowed down and spread out over twenty acres of field. It finally stopped just short of the railroad tracks.

The road, now rendered impassable, was covered by fifteen feet of debris spread out over 495 feet. Trees, boulders, and the remains of the house were all a part of it. Where the barn stood, only the roof would be seen above the mud.

Trembling uncontrollably, the three men remained behind the fence watching waves of watery mud eight to ten feet high undulate past. Several minutes later they realized that the danger was over.

Stanley looked down at the barn roof and cried, "Don Walker is a dead man!" But Walker wasn't. Hearing Stanley's voice, he painfully cleared dirt and gravel from his mouth and hoarsely shouted, "Help!"

Reacting immediately, Stanley ran to the roof and crawled in under an open corner. Working his way over the debris, he saw a hand pushed up through the mud. He also spotted Walker's head sticking out of the rubble.

Of that moment Stanley later said, "I found where he was buried in the ruins of the barn though he looked like a dirty log. I somehow lifted a stone from his back that weighed, I should think, four hundred pounds. Also another from his neck. His right leg was all twisted up in the roots of a tree, and his face was plastered with mud."

After Stanley was joined by the McDonald brothers, the three of them dug away the debris holding Walker down. Before he could be dragged out, his boots had to be cut off to free his feet. Once he was removed from under the roof, it was evident that his legs were severely damaged. He also had deep cuts about the face and head, and his body was extensively bruised.

Laying Walker gently on a bed of straw, the men put together a crude litter. When it was finished, he was carried to an open field. Here the decision was made to move him to John King's house while one of them rushed to Jefferson Depot to telephone Whitefield for emergency help.

Following the call, a special train immediately brought Doctors Patten, McGregor, and Morrison to the disaster area. When word of what happened finally caught up with Doctor Charles H. Burnham, the overworked

COURTESY FLOYD W. RAMSEY

This photograph of Oscar Stanley and his one-horned cow
proved quite popular with sightseers in the weeks and months
following the June 1885 Cherry Mountain landslide.

local physician, he rushed by team down from the village. Doctor Gove
later arrived from the Twin Mountain House.

While being examined, Walker told the doctors he heard and saw the
slide coming. He said, "I rushed for the door, but the wind was blowing
toward the mountain and had carried the sound from me. Otherwise I
might have heard the noise in time to escape."

Wincing from the pain that racked his body, he continued, "When I
got to the door, I had trouble pushing it open. I got out of the barn just as
the avalanche struck. It threw me into the shed which opened from the
barn. When it was over, I lay there buried up to my neck, having no idea
how I would get out until I heard Mr. Stanley's voice."

As the doctors made a second examination of his injuries, Walker
mumbled, "I never expected to get out alive. But, I'm all right, doctor, except for my legs."

To give him hope the doctors shook their heads in agreement. They
knew his chances for recovery were doubtful at best. His left leg was found
to be broken in several places below the knee, and his right leg was bru-
tally crushed.

Knowing Walker was in good hands, Stanley took the opportunity to
search for his missing livestock. At the same time the McDonald brothers looked for their tools. Though three cows, a calf, two hogs, a pig and
the tools were never found, one cow was discovered alive where the stable

once stood. Unfortunately she was buried up to her neck in mud, and she was missing a horn.

After being dug out and examined, she was also found to be suffering from a dislocated shoulder, several fractured ribs, and a broken neck. Despite these injuries, she survived for a time to be seen, pitied, and photographed by hundreds of visitors to the slide.

Before the morning was over, Stanley also unexpectedly found his horse, Jack. Unlike the cow, he had only a minor head injury.

While this was going on, telegraph wires were humming with news of the calamity. Jefferson, Whitefield, Lancaster, Twin Mountain, Bethlehem and Littleton were gripped by excitement. People were soon on their way to the scene in droves. Those who knew that the Boudreau and Stanley houses were in the path of the slides were emotionally prepared to encounter a scene of devastation and death as tragic as the Willey Slide which occurred in Crawford Notch on August 28, 1826. At that time, Samuel Willey, his wife, five children, and two hired men were buried by the avalanche.

Meanwhile, as the throng flocked to the scene, Ellen Stanley walked over the slide area. She was staggered by the desolation and confusion she found. Not only was their home gone, but also the furniture and personal possessions they had stored in the barn since the night of the fire. And before her, forty acres of cultivated land lay buried under twenty feet of mud.

Oscar later told her that he estimated there were at least 400,000 feet of timber scattered over their property. He fixed their loses at between $3,000 and $4,000.

While the Stanleys were pondering how they were going to survive, the next morning several dozen tourists left Boston on the 9:30 Boston & Maine Railroad with the intent of visiting the slide. Neither the Stanleys nor the other 965 residents of Jefferson realized the impact that these summer visitors were going to have on their quiet life in the months just ahead.

By that Sunday alone, thousands of people had trampled over Stanley's and Boudreau's property on sun-hardened mud. Quickly taking advantage of the opportunities presented, enterprising locals set up makeshift tents and sold everything from full meals to cigars. To justify capitalizing on the disaster, part of the money they took in went to the Stanleys, part to suffering Donald Walker, and they pocketed what was left.

The following Tuesday, which was July 14, Walker not only turned twenty-four, but it was also the day that he was scheduled to marry Della

Stanley. Instead, he died at 1:00 P.M. following the amputation of his right leg. His mother Mary was holding his hand when the end came.

The $25 he had received as his share of the proceeds made at the slide the previous weekend went toward his funeral expenses.

Then more tragedy followed. The Saturday following the funeral, Oscar Stanley's brother-in-law, Asa J. King, began to exhibit symptoms of insanity at his father's house. Emotionally distraught since the slide, Walker's death aggravated his condition. Before long he was driven to Lancaster where Doctors Mitchell and Stockwell officially declared him insane. By order of the Overseer of the Poor he was committed to the asylum at Concord, New Hampshire.

When Sunday, July 19, arrived, a young lady from Lancaster, who admitted she was a "Sabbath breaker" was among the twenty-six carloads of passengers who rode to the slide by train. Describing what she saw, she wrote: "Just opposite where stood the Stanley house, is erected a stand for Mr. Stanley's benefit where everything eatable, from a twisted donut up to elaborate cakes and flaky pies are dispensed to the hungry crowd. Mr. and Mrs. Stanley made their headquarters here during the day, and both of

The Stanley family poses for a photograph amidst the ruins of their Jefferson farm. Pictured are, l–r, Ellen Stanley, Grace, Mora, Della, and Oscar Stanley.

them seemed polite unassuming people, answering any and all questions with the same patient air.

"A little below the stand is a placard marking the spot where Donald J. Walker met his death. The large stone is still lying there as found across his body. Many pieces were broken from it to be preserved as relics of the slide, and many a mother will point to these mementoes and tell her children of the sad fate of Donald J. Walker.

"A little distance along is another placard telling us where the cow was buried beneath huge timbers. Also the horse. They now stand in a tent curtained off, and a boy outside admits all whose curiosity is sufficient to invest ten cents.

"We missed seeing a hen that came out unscathed through this upheaval. The boy in charge told us, 'Three fellows came along, pushed me aside without paying, went in and threw the hen out.'

"A look under the barn reveals to sight broken bedsteads, remnants of chairs, broken dishes, a crushed table, and many other spoiled furnishings of household goods . . ."

Though the young lady hinted at the rowdyism there, she failed to mention that alcoholic beverages were also being sold. Littleton and Lisbon excursionists returned home that same day to report that many people there were intoxicated, and that "a disgraceful row had ensued among the lower classes."

Adding to this complaint, ministers and priests from Jefferson to Dalton were attributing poor church attendance "to the absence of those who went to the slide with the multitude to do evil."

Stung by the mounting criticism, the following Sunday the Jefferson selectmen and twenty police officers were at the slide. Before the day was out, arrests had been made. One party from Berlin was caught selling rum and fined $100. By the next Sunday, the police reported everything was quiet and under control.

In an attempt to recoup more of his losses, on July 22 Stanley sold a half interest in his farm to Frank P. Brown of Whitefield for $1,500. In announcing the sale, Brown said, "The land is now to be enclosed, and to have erected upon it a restaurant and a stable for the accommodation of the horses of sightseers who will be charged ten cents admission to view so much of the slide as lays upon the farm."

At this time John Boudreau made it known that he was also enclosing his land, but was only charging "five cents a peep."

Following his announcement, he not only fenced in his land, but he also began charging ten cents to anyone who crossed his property to hike up the slide.

By the middle of August Stanley was still competing against Boudreau for the tourist trade. Running a daily coach to Jefferson Depot, he personally picked up sightseers. Boudreau attempted to outmaneuver him by opening a toll road. Once it was operational, tourists coming from the Twin Mountain House could now reach his property without first driving to Stanley's.

By the end of August the railroads were running excursion trains to the slide seven days a week at reduced rates. This not only created more headaches for the Jefferson selectmen, but Oscar G. Barron, one of the most influential hotel men of this time, also warned them that he was going to make trouble for the town if the Cherry Mountain Road was not satisfactorily repaired, particularly the section running from the Carroll line to the slide.

To meet his request, the town spent $500 just on the section he specified. However, their troubles were far from over. By year's end, due to the heavy expenditures required to maintain all of the Jefferson roads and bridges strained by the unusually heavy traffic to the slide, the town was shocked when it was discovered that it was heavily in debt.

That autumn, as the tourists finally headed home, Stanley got out of the slide business altogether. On October 29 he sold the remaining half of his farm to Frank Brown for $2000. For good measure, he threw in an additional twenty acres.

Following the completion of the sale he moved his family up to Jefferson Hill, which was then a long line of summer hotels and boarding houses. In the years ahead, he got involved with a number of land transactions there. For a short time he owned Cherry Cottage, and was later listed as the proprietor of the Waumbek Cottage.

Following his death at 79, his wife lived with their youngest daughter near the Jefferson Hill Library. When she died at 83, she was buried next to him in the lower section of the Forest Vale Cemetery on the Meadows Road.

All three daughters were tall, attractive women, even in their old age. Following their marriages to local boys, they lived out their lives close to one another on Jefferson Hill where they could see Cherry Mountain whenever they liked. Ironically, Della and Mora both died at 86 from bronchial pneumonia. Grace lived to the age of 92.

On close examination, Della has to be numbered among the victims of the slide. Subjected to the trauma of losing her fiancé, Donald Walker, on their wedding day, she was further shocked by the profiteering her father participated in following Walker's funeral. He later disappointed her again when he became a "tavern operator," as she put it. To her dying day she would never talk about either the slide or her father with her grandchildren.

As for John Boudreau, like the slide, he just eventually faded from sight altogether.

The Golden Years of Tourism

Among the Clouds

Excerpted from *Among the Clouds*

Among the Clouds, *the mountaintop tourist newspaper published daily in the summer months on Mount Washington, was founded by Henry M. Burt in 1877. Mr. Burt, whose previous newspaper publishing experiences included stints in Boston, and Bellevue, Nebraska, among other places, was editor of the paper until his death in 1899. His son, Frank H. Burt, succeeded his father and was editor/publisher until June 1908, when a disastrous summit fire completely destroyed the paper's office just days before the busy tourist season was to begin. The paper was revived in 1910, and continued to be published at the base of the mountain until its final season in 1917. The following articles appeared in* Among the Clouds *during the seasons spanning 1877 to 1879*

Mount Agassiz and Its Surroundings

(September 6, 1878)

Among the many places of interest in the White Mountains, few, if any, afford greater pleasure to the visitor, or give better satisfaction, considering the effort or expense required, than does a visit to Mount Agassiz. It is situated about one mile from the Sinclair House in Bethlehem and nearly south from the village. It has an elevation of nearly 2,500 feet above the sea, and is one thousand feet higher than the street, with an easy ascent of three fourths of a mile, making the distance from the street to the summit only one and three-fourths miles. The mountain commands one of the most beautiful landscape views to be found in the whole region, and while it lacks that grand and extensive view to be seen from Mount Washington, the whole surrounding country, especially the Franconia range, seems to be within reach of the enraptured beholder. Standing upon the balcony of the observatory on the mountain, looking toward the south over the beautiful valley in Franconia and Eastern [Easton] for a distance of six-teen miles, the eye rests upon the bold symmetrical form of Moosilauke, as it stands boldly out in the distance. Still farther on and a little to the right, at a distance of ninety miles from here, Ascutney is seen as though it was a cloud coming up out of the horizon. "Right about face," and our eye rests on the Bow-Back mountain in Canada, sixty miles to the north of us, and 150 miles from Ascutney, between which points we have a fine landscape view of some of the most beautiful valleys in the region.

The view from east to west, though not as extensive, is of more interest to most travelers, as it takes in the Presidential range on the east and some of the most important mountains in Vermont on the west. Some say the distant peak of Mount Marcy is seen on a clear day, without the aid of a glass, just showing itself in the dim distance. Some 30 miles to the north-east, in the direction of and beyond Whitefield, standing out like a bold sentinel, with an almost unchangeable appearance from spring to winter, the rugged and barren forms of the white marble mountains in Stratford, known as Percy's Peaks, meet the gaze. They are the first to attract atten-tion on account of their striking white appearance in midsummer, when all about is green and beautiful.

Among the more important of the mountain peaks to be seen from here, commencing with Moosilauke and going toward the left, are Kins-man, Cannon or Profile, which has three peaks, the center being the high-est, and the northern one on which the "Old Man" has taken up his abode. We would say just here that on a good day, by the aid of the glass which is always to be found at the observatory, the "Old Man's" features can be dis-tinctly seen. On the north of Cannon are Eagle Cliff and Mount Lafay-ette, Haystack, Twin, Hale, Jackson, Clinton, Pleasant, Franklin, Monroe, Washington, Clay, Jefferson, Adams, Deception and Cherry. Then come Pliny, Starr King, the south peak of Pilot, Percy in Stratford, Prospect, Pleasant and Orne. Still following around to the left we see Bow-Back in Canada, Cow and Burnside in Guildhall, Owl's Head near Lake Mem-phremagog, in Canada, Burke and Umpire near Burke, Jay Peak sixteen miles southwest of Newport, Vt., Elmore, Mansfield, Camel's Hump, Mt. Tom, Equinox, Killington Peaks and Ascutney, in Vermont, Sugar Loaf and Haystack in Haverhill, and Black Mountain in Warren. There are many other peaks to be seen from here of less importance, but which make the view still more to be admired.

We also have some fine valley views from here. The Franconia valley, to which reference has already been made, is one of the most level in the region, and contains many thrifty farms. The Ammonoosuc, another of the beautiful mountain valleys, can be seen from Fabyan's to Littleton, a distance of nearly twenty miles. Round and Montgomery ponds are in full view. In the northeast can be seen the form of the Slumbering Giant.

One of the prettiest bird's-eye views of a country village is to be seen from here, as looking down the valley of the Ammonoosuc, the eye rests upon the village of Littleton, one of the most thrifty and stirring towns in New Hampshire. Though having a population of only about 1,500 inhab-

Mount Agassiz and its first toll house and road to the summit.

itants, it is the business center of the entire region. It has some thirty stores, all doing a thriving business, five churches, Free Masons, Odd Fellows and other lodges, and institutions which make it the banner town of this section. It also has one of the finest school buildings and the best facilities for education. To the northeast, nestled on a beautiful slope of land facing the west, is the village of Jefferson, a favorite summer resort, while at our feet as it were is Bethlehem, with its large hotels and numerous boarding-houses, noted for its high elevation and health-giving air. It is the most noted resort in the mountains for the victims of hay fever.

One of the greatest attractions which Mount Agassiz presents is its easy ascent, which can be made by carriage or on foot. It is only three fourths of a mile from the base to the summit, and an ordinary person can make it in forty minutes, without hurrying and with very little fatigue. The road is kept consistently in good condition, and there is therefore none of that hard climbing up irregular bridle-paths, which accompanies the ascent on foot of mountains like Lafayette. There is no suffering from thirst, as there is always an ample supply of good cold water at the house at the base and at the observatory on the summit. A good glass is kept at the observatory for the use of visitors.

Among the other things of interest, the visitor should not forget the echo, as it is one of the finest in the mountains, repeating five times. The echo from a single instrument resembles a full orchestra in the neighboring forest. This has not that volume which characterizes the echo at Echo Lake, but for sweetness of sound it is unsurpassed.

There have been up to the present from 1,500 to 2,000 visitors on the mountain this summer. The proprietor informs us that he intends to make a number of improvements for next year, arranging the observatory so it can be closed on windy days, so that parties will not be obliged to sit in a draught after walking up the mountain. For the benefit of those who wish to stay in Bethlehem and at the same time have the advantage of a mineral spring, we would say that the proprietor has on his premises a good iron and sulphur spring, where plenty of water can be obtained.

The Mountain Echoes

(August 30, 1877)

Mr. Burr of the Hartford Times, alludes in a recent letter to the various and wonderful echoes in the White Mountains, and of that of Echo lake in the Profile Notch, he says:

We stopped, on our return, at Echo Lake, and had the attendant wake the echoes for our benefit. First he loaded and fired a cannon—not a full-grown Dahlgren, but a "son of a gun," bearing the name relation to a big one that a "Colt" bears to a big horse pistol. He put in three-quarters of a pound of powder, and rammed down a whole sheet of the New York Herald for wadding—setting off the gun with a slow match. The echo of the report went crashing through the wooded mountains at the east side of the lake, and kept reverberating for the space of fifteen seconds by the watch. A steep and wooded north shore would greatly heighten the effect; but, as it is, it is a striking echo. Then a horn was brought out—a sort of bugle without keys—and we all "took a hack at it." The echo was very fine; more distinct than that at Mount Agassiz in Bethlehem, but not so delicate and eerie. Mr. Corliss, the proprietor of the latter mountain, once brought out for me his gun, and then his horn, and tested both on the crags, while we staid up on the tower. The hour was sunset, the air was still, and the western sky was aflame with the glories of the departing day above the distant peaks of Vermont, while above us to the east and the south towered the giants of the White Mountain and Franconia ranges, bathed in their changing opaline and purple lights. When the horn was sounded, there came back from the nearer hills, but seemingly from the Franconia mountains, such delicate and airy music as might have greeted the coming of the Titania, or Queen Mab. It was as if the whole band was playing, off in the mountains, but so faintly (yet clearly) as to suggest a band of elfin musicians, mountain gnomes and sprites, playing among the upper crags on fairy horns. The sinking sun, the purple mountains, the hushed and charmed air, all conspired to heighten the delicate and spiritual character of the echoing stream, till we could hardly help repeating the matchless word-music of the one world's poet who has grasped and expressed the sensation in words which are themselves, the music they describe:—

> "Oh hark! Oh hear! how thin and clear
> And thinner, clearer, farther going!
> From near and far, from cliff and scar,
> The horns of Elfland faintly blowing!
> Blow, bugle, let us hear the purple glen replying,
> And answer, echoes, answer—dying, dying, dying."

These mountains are full of echoes. There are "echo lakes," and "echo hills," and echo places unnumbered; and the echoes come back across the roar of pouring mountain torrents and foaming cascades. We did not stop to get them all, either on the Glen side of Mount Washington, or in returning from the Profile mountain, but after leaving Echo lake we stopped the horses at an obscure woodland path and followed the path till it turned back and down across a wild glen, crossed by a rustic bridge, and there we found a little house, a frame covered very tastefully with bark, and the whole showing good architectural taste. Rustic seats, arranged about the gorge, were fitted to trees in the woods. Inside the home was a table; and the place seemed to be used for practice by the brass band of the Profile House and Echo lake.

A sudden shower gave us a wetting as we drove home towards Bethlehem; but it heightened the wondrous effects of light and color on the mountains. From a high hill overlooking Bethlehem we saw in the distance the valley of the Connecticut, the town of Littleton, the New Hampshire hills and settlements north of it, and away in the west such a sunset in Vermont as one rarely witnesses even here. Looking back at the mountains we had left, we saw the giant peak of Lafayette, and the tops and slopes of all his family of the Franconia range, bathed in a swimming sea of purple mist, over which was arched a magnificent rainbow. In the west the clouds were breaking; and the sinking sun, partly disclosed in a gulf of blue, touched with molten gold, just above the Green Mountains of Vermont, kindled among the broken clouds such an intensity of hues of burnished copper and liquid gold, infusing even the sea green-tinted sunny blues, as to lift the very soul in ecstasy, and suggest in its gleaming cloud-pillars and its unutterable glory, the opening of the gates of the Celestial City of which the Bedford allegorist has told.

This daily play and frolic of the lights and shadows on the mountains is indeed a wonderful feature of the scenery among the White Hills. Every afternoon—unless it is absolutely cloudy—three magnificent aeriel light and shadow dances are displayed along the principal slopes. Colors, strange and beautiful, rest on the great mountains. The effect is particularly fine toward sunset. Mr. Prime's language, which once I considered essentially exaggerated, is literally correct. But it seems that not everybody has eyes to see, or even ears to hear.

Base-Ball on the Mountain

(August 8, 1878)

To the Editor of Among the Clouds:

It may not be known to the world below that the base-ball fever has not been checked by the lofty elevations of Mount Washington, and that an exciting match game was played yesterday on the "Cow Pasture," near the seventh mile-post on the carriage road, between nines from the employ-ees of the Glen coach company and the Mount Washington railway. Ex-tensive preparations were made for this game, the ground being cleared of rocks and the base lines laid out by Superintendent Charles Locke, of the Glen road. The game was called at 3:15 P.M., the grand stand and the sur-rounding grounds being filled with interested spectators. The railway nine went to the bat first, Mr. Taylor batting a terrific ball over the head of Mr. Philbrook, centre field, towards the Gulf of Mexico. Amid tremendous cheering Mr. Taylor reached his third base in safety, and would have scored a home run, had not Mr. Philbrook, by wonderful exertion, secured the ball just as it reached the edge of the Gulf, and assisted him out at home base. The next two batters were put out on flies to Mr. McCormick at short-stop and Mr. Dresser at second base, and the nine was out without a score. The same fortune awaited the Glen nine, the principal feature of the playing being a beautiful fly catch by Mr. Morrill, right field. In the second inning Mr. Judkins, captain of the railway nine, made a remarkable heavy bat, sending the ball through the top of a coach standing at the other end of the field, and scored a home run. The two who followed him struck out. Mr. Horne made a run on errors, and Mr. Butterworth was put out by the catcher on a foul tip. Mr. Sands, captain of the Glen nine, excited universal admiration by a home run in the second inning. (We are re-quested to state that he never stopped till he reached home, making the longest time on record.) Messrs. Cameron and Twitchell each scored a run, and at the close of this inning the score was 3 to 2 in favor of the car-riage road. In the third inning both sides became dissatisfied and disgusted with the umpire's rulings, and during the dispute which followed, the rain began falling and the game was broken up. It was unanimously resolved to adjourn to Tuckerman's Ravine, where a reception was given the players by their friends, in the spacious and elegant parlor of the Snow Hotel.

Franconia Notch
Fall of a Great Cliff

(July 24, 1878)

Mr. W. C. Prime, who spends the summer months at the Profile House, writes from his cabin on Lonesome Lake concerning the changes in the mountains and the fall of a cliff:

"The last winter has worked more changes on the hills hereabout than any winter of the quarter of a century I have known them. One becomes very familiar with great hills, and every feature gets to be known, so that a slight change is recognized. You would think it hardly possible that they could have so impressed their outlines on the eye and mind that you would miss a tall tree from a lofty ridge, or see a change in the shape of a great cliff from which a few rocks have fallen. But it is so.

I think I did not tell you of a grand sight I saw last fall, which showed me how these mountains crumble away.

You remember the vast range of granite cliffs which bound the western side of the Pemigewasset valley, rising a thousand feet out of the forest, and extending a huge wall of bare rock, without a tree or shrub, for two miles. The Old Man, the great rock face, is the northern end of these cliffs.

I went down from the cabin to go to the Profile House toward evening. My horses, with the buckboard, were waiting for me in the clearing. As I came out of the forest path into the sublime amphitheater, which I always think as grand as anything I ever saw in Alp or Lebanon country, the purple evening light was filling all the valley, like a great cup with wine, and overflowing the edges where the high mountain ridges glowed with deeper tints. It was profoundly still. No sound was heard but the lapse of the river over its bed. It was very grand, very beautiful, and very lonely, for my driver and myself were the only human beings within two miles.

As I took my seat in the buckboard and lifted the reins, a sound like the discharge of a hundred cannon roared through the valley. The horses sprang forward, and as I threw myself back on the reins I looked up.

Near the top of the western cliff, 1,000 feet above me, on the sheer side of the rock wall, a great fragment, as large as a house, had just parted in the solid mass, and was grinding its slow way down, held by the ragged edge of its own fracture. The next instant I saw above it on the flat front of the cliff a hundred zigzag lines running here and there, out of which puffed white smoke made by the friction of the cracking and crashing masses. It was but an instant, and then a portion of the top of the cliff, 200 or 300 feet in breadth, fell perpendicularly. The first sound had been the cracking of the single rock, which had been sort of a key-stone holding the masses above it. The direct perpendicular wall was about three hundred feet. It came down thundering on the rocks below and shaking the valley like an earthquake. The mighty masses—thousands of tons—broke into fragments, bounding into the air, and rolled and plunged five hundred feet more down the slope of old debris, the remains of similar catastrophes in old days. Here they vanished in the dense forest which skirts the base— vanished, but the sounds continued as old trees were sheared down by flying rocks that plunged along among the undergrowth with a hideous sound of destruction.

It was all over in less than thirty seconds, perhaps in less than fifteen. Then a cloud of white smoke, dense and thick, rose slowly in the calm evening air, passing gently over the very spot the rocks had left, until it overtopped the cliff, when it took the rosy light of the sun and southerly air, and floated slowly up over the Profile House. Fisherman on Profile Lake heard and felt the sound, and thought it was an earthquake. The stillness that followed was that appalling sort of silence which all know who have experienced the sensation of sudden calm after a terrible explosion. But my horses trembled from head to foot, and looked into every recess of the woods as we drove homeward, seeking the invisible source of danger.

It is not easy to measure the size of a mass of rock falling from a mountain top. The mass was much larger than the entire solid contents of a block of tall houses three hundred feet long. It does not often happen to a man to have the chance of seeing such a weight fall three hundred feet perpendicular, and plunge down a slope of several hundred more.

It is in this way that the mountains are decaying. Along the same cliff I can see that numerous changes have occurred since last year. There is no doubt that in time the Old Man will disappear. Already a rift is visible in the cliff behind his forehead, and some day that point of the mountain will fall into the valley. If you have never seen him, it would be just as well to hurry up your visit, for I am afraid it will not be many years before it will exist only in pictures.

First Winter Visit to the Summit of Mount Washington

(September 4, 1878)

Rosendale, N.Y., Aug. 20th, 1878

To the Editor of Among the Clouds:

It is not the spirit of boasting, or a vain wish to crowd my name into a prominent place in Mount Washington history, that bids me claim the honor of being the first man who ever stood on the top of Mount Washington in the winter. I had been taught to believe that any one who could succeed in climbing over the ice and snow to the top of Mount Washington in our cold New England winter weather, would very surely find the wind so thoroughly filled with cutting frost that being breathed would create a hurried inflammation of the lungs and cause sudden death. Having had several seasons' experience in business on Mount Washington, I formed an opinion that to attempt to visit that famous place in winter would not be altogether a foolhardy undertaking. Having made my plan known to an artist by the name of White, and to a young gentleman by the name of Brooks, we three left Lancaster early on the morning of February 10, 1862, and after traveling all day over a road made nearly impassable for sleighs by deep drifts, we arrived at the Glen House about dark. After partaking of a good substantial supper and thereby gladly realizing the kindness of Mr. Thompson, who was then proprietor, we said good night, and started at 8 o'clock in the evening up the mountain on our daring expedition. The full round moon was shining brightly, as with ample packs filled with blankets and provisions, we walked cheerfully up the new carriage road on snow-shoes. The night was cold and still and clear, while highly excited as we were by the thought of the adventure before us, the spring of our snow-shoes on the glittering crust was music for us, while the great tree shadows thrown across our path, and the white winding road contrasting with the dark evergreen thickets on either hand, combined to make our night walk quite varied in incidents, and not very wearisome. It was past midnight when we arrived at the Ledge (half way up) and here the fire-scathed trees boldly relieved by moonlight the glittering, ice-covered ledge, and a dark old shanty in the background combined, with other objects, to form a very wild picture. This shanty had been built by the road workmen, and on breaking it open we found a rusty old stove in which we kindled a fire, and after taking a lunch we spread our blankets on an old frost-covered straw bed, and drowsed till day-break. At sunrise we started for "tiptop" without our snowshoes, and very soon began the labor of advancing by cutting steps in the ice. When we halted to rest we could but remark the death-like silence that reigned around us; not one breath of wind, not one sound of running water, for beneath a wintry robe every waterfall was chained. How like blank solitude was the stillness! Yet its loneliness was pleasantly enlivened by the wonder and wide-spread landscape beneath and around us, that afforded ample scope for admiration. Far away and near at hand, arose hundreds of glittering peaks. A thousand pyramids of smoke hung above a thousand dark piles that were roughly set in wide white margins. What a vast host of hopes and fears and joys and sorrows, were grouped in all those mortal homes so far below us! Yet we must not stop to speculate, for the task before us is to be accomplished slowly and carefully. Up about five miles we came to a wide acre of ice where we could not possibly advance one foot without cutting deep steps. It is not fiction to declare that as the pieces of ice went whirling down like a heavy shower of hail, at least eight hundred feet below, a shudder such as teaches poor mortality its weakness came over me. One false step or careless motion would have sent me down, down, and added another name to the victims of rashness.

About six miles up we came to a drift that covered many acres, and here, not being able to follow the carriage road, we wandered a long distance over ice-like snow that had been thrown by some hurricane power into mighty fanciful waves and shapes. At one place we climbed over the tops of a dwarf tree growth that had the appearance of a buried wilderness. Here we took a lunch, and looking southward saw a long line of storm clouds, with rainbow-tinted border, whirling wildly over the lower peaks and ever and anon a heavy gust of wind gave fearful warning for the coming night. Up we started, yet gained our object slowly, for at one time when I had slipped down, I looked, and both my companions were down, but

Mid-winter inside the Summit House on Mount Washington, Feb. 11, 1862.

John H. Spaulding

remembering the old adage that "misery loves company," I kept silent. As we approached the "tiptop," a heavy black cloud hanging low down was wildly whirling over, and as the wind, with a roar like thunder, drove the wintry mass toward us, we stopped to rest. Holding a short counsel, I agreed to go forward, while my companions leaned against their packs. I had penetrated the dense cloud but a short way before being coated with snow and frost, and as I fancied how I looked, me thought perchance I was a small personation of Old Winter. I found the Tip Top House completely covered with crusted snow, and all of the two houses to be seen was a little of the two gable ends of the Summit House. Words are a very important medium by which to picture the scene around me. The two houses stood out in bold relief, like two giant white mounds, and every rock heap and high point about the summit were to be seen through a thick covering of glittering ice. Vast crusted leaves of snow stood out from the jagged points in all the imaginable and fanciful shapes that the frost ever painted on window glass. On going back to meet my companions, they expressed wonder and beholding my thick layer of snow-like frost, and together we came back through the cloud. On leaving the summit the season before, my plan for an anticipated winter trip was to make headquarters of the old Tip Top House. Finding that house entirely covered, we succeeded in making an entrance by way of a gable and window into the attic of the Summit House. Feeling our way around through the blank darkness, after removing the snow, we brought up from the lower room a small stove, and after making a fire we piled around the stove a barricade of mattresses and prepared to pass the night as best we could. To obtain our wood we were obliged to cut the snow and ice from a window of the Tip Top House and take from it a pile prepared for our purpose the season before. Two days' labor and excitement, with our midnight walk up to the Ledge, had imposed quite a tax on our power of endurance, and though the heavy wind swept by with an unbroken roar loud as thunder, we slept till late in the morning. On getting up and looking out, we found our habitation surrounded by a winter hurricane. We prepared to make ourselves as comfortable as possible. The extent of our hopes and fears in such a situation cannot be presented by words, yet, without a wish to unnecessarily tax the reader's patience, allow me to add that we stayed two days and two nights on the top of Mount Washington—experiencing the effect of a wild snow hurricane that lasted thirty-six hours; enjoying one of the most magnificent sunrise scenes that imagination can picture; saw moonlight on a hundred glittering peaks, and wallowed down the mountain through an unmeasured snow depth, well satisfied with our trip.

J. H. S.

P.S. The interior of both houses we found much deranged by the storms of winter. Midnight darkness reigned within, but by the aid of a lamp we looked around and found snow and ice from three inches to three feet thick in every direction, through the different rooms. The furniture was all most curiously set in white, feathery casings, and in one room we found a cord that was suspended from overhead had assumed the appearance of a glass tube some two inches in diameter. The cloth roofing and wallpaper was in many rooms torn down by the action of the frost, while on the walls and overhead icicles and snow wreaths hung all around in fanciful forms. The darkened windows with the thick covering without, combined with the ceaseless, thunder-like roar of the almost everlasting wind, gave the whole scene around us a most chilling air of dread and consolation. What now would be regarded as commonplace and hardly worthy of mention, was to us full of apprehension and fear of disaster. We had braved the superstition as well as false reason of past ages, and dared to undertake what was never before accomplished, and with a raging storm around us a great part of the time we spent there, it need not be regarded as wonderful. If we had some serious fears of what the result of our undertaking might be. "So mote it be."

We left our names in pencil on the tiptop register (as the ink was frozen), Franklin White, C. C. Brooks, and J. H. Spaulding.

1892

Echoes of the Week

From *The White Mountain Echo and Tourist's Register*

The White Mountain Echo and Tourists' Register, a rival summer tourist newspaper of the better-known Among the Clouds, was based in the popular resort community of Bethlehem. Established in July 1878 by founder Markinfield Addey, The Echo covered events and happenings not just in bustling Bethlehem, but all over the White Mountain region, including such distant tourist communities as Jackson, Conway and Gorham. One of the best read sections of the paper was the "Echoes of the Week" column, which featured the social news of the various tourist communities served by the paper. The following excerpts from this column are taken from the 1892 tourist season.

July 9, 1892

After a year's absence, Mr. Arthur Cowing resumes his old position of tonsorial artist at the Sinclair House.

Root beer will soon be on draught at Smith's Drug Store, Bethlehem.

The Boston Saturday Evening Gazette is authority for the statement that "revised versions of pretty waiter girls will enumerate food at White Mountain hotels."

Mr. Herbert Hapgood, of Boston, will this season be in charge of the office at the Uplands, Bethlehem, while Mr. E.J. Cheever, of Manchester, N.H., will perform a like duty at the Turner House.

Professor J. Rayner Edmunds [*sic*], of Harvard University, is increasing the indebtedness to him of mountain travelers by building camps in the ravine of the Cascades, Mt. Adams, being aided in the work by Messrs. C. E. Lowe and H. H. Hunt.

Mr. and Mrs. F. H. Shapleigh have arrived at the Crawford House, and Mr. Shapleigh is now settled in his well known studio for the summer. He passed the month of June in Jackson, and shows as the result of his work there, charming pictures of old apple orchards in bloom, picturesque farm houses, and quiet country roads, all of which will be sure of a quick sale.

The baseball season in Bethlehem was opened on the grounds of the Maplewood on Saturday with a game between the Bethlehem nine and a team from Maplewood Cottage. The latter nine was victorious, the score standing 22 to 15 in their favor. The feature of the game was the wonderful playing of Mr. J. A. Frazer, the genial clerk of the Cottage, who succeeded in capturing the eye of more than one fair spectator.

The Councilor of Improvements of the Appalachian Mountain Club, requests the members to exam and report to him before October 15, whether the Club Record Cylinders (Metal) are to be found on the following mountains, and if so, when and by whom placed: Liberty, Lafayette, Lincoln, Garfield, Cannon, Guyot, Flume, Field, Monroe, Pleasant, Clinton, Clay, Passaconaway, Chocorua, Tremont, Hancock, Anderson, Bond, Kinsman, Iron, Twin (north or south), Royce, Starr King, Carter (south peak), Castellated Ridge, King's Ravine, Kineo, Webster and Franklin: Also the condition of the following Club Paths and Camps: Paths:—Boy Mt. from Mt. Adams House; Moat Mt.; Tuckerman's Ravine; Tecumseh Mt.; Black Mt. (Sandwich Dome); Bridal Veil Falls (Mt. Kinsman); and Ktaadn (from Sherman): Camps:—Imp Mt.; Ktaadn; and Mt. Liberty.

July 16, 1892

Col. O. G. Barron and Mr. J. Chisholm left Fabyans on Saturday for a day's fishing, and returned with four hundred and fifty speckled beauties, proving their skill as fishermen, and that the streams in the vicinity are well stocked with trout.

Bowling scores have been running high at the Look-off, Sugar Hill, of late, Saturday last having been an especially lucky day. Mr. Goodnow of Boston, led with a score of 244, followed by Mr. Lacroix, of Lynn, who scored 207. Miss Sibyl Collar, of Boston, broke the season's record in ladies' bowling with a score of 202.

The large painting of Mount Washington and the Presidential range as seen from the Maplewood, which has just been completed by Mr. Edward Hill, has been hung in the main parlor of the hotel, where it is attracting considerable attention. It represents the grand scene as it appears at sunset of an autumn day when the snow-capped peaks are flushed with the last rays of the setting sun. Mr. Hill is to have a studio in Cruft's Block, Bethlehem, above the Echo office, where he will have on exhibition paintings of mountain scenery.

July 23, 1892

Mr. James H. Fasset, of Nashua, N.H., who was the centre rush of the Dartmouth Championship Football Team in '90, is making a tour of the White Mountain region on his bicycle.

Sweetser's White Mountain Guide, $1.50; The White Mountains by Rev. Julius H. Ward, $1.75; and The White Hills, by Rev. Thomas Starr King, $2.50; are on sale at the office of *The White Mountain Echo*, Bethlehem. Mailed free on receipt of price.

The first passenger train over the new spur track from Jefferson Meadows to Jefferson Hill arrived on time Saturday. The train consisted of a passenger and baggage car combined, and the through Boston parlor car, both of which were crowded with passengers for the maiden trip. The engine was decorated with flags and streamers and saluted the new station as it approached with prolonged blasts from its whistle. During this week only the express trains will be run to the Hill, but afterwards all trains will depart for and run to the new station.

August 13, 1892

The Hillside House, Bethlehem is entertaining Admiral Chauncey Thomas, of the U. S. Navy. The gallant admiral is accompanied by Mrs. Thomas.

Master Irving Heidelshimer, but eight years of age, has entertained several of the guests of the Fabyan House with musical selections played on the violin. For one of his age his execution is wonderful.

Mr. Jean Paul Selinger, the artist, and Mr. W. W. Swornsbourne, the leader of the Glen orchestra, climbed up into Tuckerman's Ravine one day last week, and while Mr. Selinger was making a sketch of the marvelous snow arch, a magnificent eagle came and perched on a rock near them.

The championship doubles in tennis were played at Goodnow's, Sugar Hill, last Thursday resulting as follows: Miles and Tracy Hopkin, Sunset Hill vs. F. S. Hoppin and Baldwin, Sunset Hill, 6–3, 6–3; Robbins and Soleliac, Look-Off vs. Brown and Balthar, Goodnow's, 6–4, 6–4; T. Hoppin and Miles, vs. Blodgett and Wright, Look-Off, 6–0, 6–0; VanPray and Bailey, Goodnow's vs. Robbins and Soleliac, 6–2, 6–2. Finals, Miles and T. Hopkins vs. VanPray and Bailey, 6–3, 6–2, 6–3. A large delegation from each hotel was presented to cheer the contestants and the Sunset Hill House guests were enthusiastic over their representatives on their return.

The new road from the Profile House to the top of Cannon Mountain is completed. Eddie Clark who is eight years old made the first ascent on horseback. He also rode to the Cannon, a position which can be seen from the Profile House.

A party of seven ladies and gentlemen from the Randolph Hill House, under the leadership of Dr. W. G. Nowell, of New York, are enjoying a camping trip on the great range. They are making their headquarters at the stone hut between the summits of Mounts Adams and Madison.

The Crescents of Littleton, visited Maplewood on Friday, and crossed bats with the latter nine to the great discomfort of the former. The Maplewoods were reinforced by the aid of Carter, the famous Yale catcher, who, however, deserted his customary position in the field and entered the box, doing deadly destruction with the ball, twenty-two out of twenty-eight being struck out by him. For the first three innings the teams were evenly matched but Merrill's pitching was soon knocked all over the field, ten runs being scored off him in one inning. After that the Maplewoods had things all their own way, the score, when the game was called, being 15 to 3.

August 20, 1892

Lieutenant Chauncey Thomas, of the U. S. Navy, a guest of the Hillside House, Bethlehem, was reported in last week's Echo, through a stretch of the imagination of its informant, as a "gallant admiral." The Lieutenant naturally rebels against this unauthorized elevation, but it is to be trusted that his modesty will be rewarded by the *Echo* being enabled sometime hereafter to speak of him correctly under the title it has given him erroneously.

LOST — On Monday, August 15, between Bethlehem and Sugar Hill, a ladies black Persian shoulder cape. Finder will be rewarded by leaving it at the office of *The Echo* or by forwarding it to L. E. Treadwell, Sunset Hill House, Sugar Hill.

The Mountain View House, Whitefield, has recently floated a fine United States flag from its cupola. The flag and staff were presented to the proprietors by the guests of this summer who have taken pleasure in thus commemorating the Columbian year. The presentation was made on Tuesday evening when the guests had assembled for a game of progressive euchre. Mr. Benjamin Johnson, of Lynn, Mass., was chosen to make the presentation, particularly in view of the fact of his many visits to Whitefield, which began in his boyhood. He voiced the feeling of all the donors in saying that the gift was an expression of the friendship which had grown out of the accidental relation of landlord and guests. Mr. W. F. Dodge and Mrs. Van Dodge accepted the colors with pleasant words of response. All present them joined in singing two verses of the well-known "America."

The Rev. John Peacock, secretary and treasurer of the Hay Fever Association, is again a guest at the Highland House, Bethlehem.

On Monday the tally-ho of the Sinclair House, Bethlehem, took the following company to the Twin Mountain House: the Misses Whitfield, Parmelee, Allison, Florence Allison, Laura Pease, Louise Pease, Smith, Carrie Smith, Milne, Dewey and Redfield, and Mrs. Terry, and Messrs. Howard DeForest, Austin, Spaulding, Parmelee and Whitfield.

Sept. 10, 1892

Some White Mountain houses are throwing out bait to catch young bachelor boarders by providing bachelor's apartments at reduced rates, so that young men may be "on tap" for the tennis court and ball-room. A cute Kentucky summer hotel man attracts them in this wise: He promises the first single masculine who applies for board that he will take him in for one week free of charge on the condition that he is the possessor of a dress suit.

Simultaneously with the flitting of the August guests come the September birds of passage, and the Crawford keeps well filled with people who know so well the delights of the place in autumn. This of all others is the time to ramble through the picturesque wooded paths, scent the falling leaves and get magnificent views at every turn. The walks around Ammonoosuc Lake and Merrill Spring with its diverging paths to "The Rambles" and "Red Bench" are especially attractive.

The Crawford party on the Summit Friday night enjoyed sliding upon the lee of the floor of the old Tip Top house, which is now left open to the weather.

It is rumored that an ascent of the Crawford bridle path, on horse back, is to be made, or attempted, this week. That last time this was done was in 1878, and portions of the path are now in bad condition.

H. Beal of the Phillips Andover foot ball team, ran down Mount Washington by the carriage road to the Glen House last Sunday morning in forty-eight minutes. This is within nine minutes of the record.

The Sugar Hill Improvement Association and its wide-awake citizens are taking active precaution to prevent cholera from obtaining a foothold among them, and are removing every cause that might tend thereto.

Sept. 17, 1982

The prospects for a large autumn business on Sugar Hill were never better than at the present time. The Sunset Hill House had every room in the hotel and Annex filled last Sunday, and throughout this week there were more arrivals than departures. The views from Sugar Hill can now be seen to the best possible advantage.

One day last week Mr. Edmund S. Munroe, of Washington, 70 years old, walked from Intervale to the Glen House.

The Profile House will close October 1, after having had the most successful season for seven years, and the best September known since the house has been open.

Mr. J. Rayner Edmands, of the Appalachian Mountain Club, and of the Harvard Observatory, and Mr. Eugene Seligman, of New York, guided by Ed. Wells, of the Glen, have been directing the clearing of the Madison path.

Among guests at Crawford's during the last few days have been found General Anderson, formerly President of the Portland and Ogdensburg R.R., and Mr. Merrill Sands, who is accompanied by his mother, Mrs. Edward Sands.

Mr. John Reece, of Boston, a guest at the Profile House, has undoubtedly taken the best picture of the Old Man of the Mountain that has ever been secured by a camera. The picture was taken from the summer house on Profile Lake and clearly shows all of the rock formation. It is reported that Mr. Greenleaf has had it copyrighted.

August 1, 1878

From Fabyan's
to the Summit

From *Among the Clouds*

THE FOLLOWING description of a trip to the summit of Mount Washington, by the railroad, is an extract from a letter written recently by Mr. Henry L. Lamb of Albany, and printed in the Watertown Daily Times:—

The greatest attraction in this region is that of Mount Washington. Twice a day from the Fabyan House a trains run to the base of the mountain and returns, a distance of six miles. At the base of the mountain, passengers change cars and take a seat in a car that runs up the mountain on the mountain railroad. This wonderful road was chartered by the state on the same principle that one might have been chartered to the moon. At the time the road was projected the projectors were subject to much ridicule. We had the pleasure of riding from St. Albans [Vt.] to Littleton [N.H.] with Sylvester Marsh, the president of the mountain road, who gave a very interesting detailed history of the same. Mr. Marsh was the projector and inventor. He was called crazy for several years simply because he intimated that a locomotive, pushing cars loaded with people, could be made to run up the side of the mountain. What is known as the base of the mountain, the place where the passengers change cars for the mountain road, is really far above the base. In running from Fabyan's out to the base there is an elevation of something like 1,200 feet. The length of the mountain railway is about three miles. The total rise from the lower station to the summit is 1,980 feet to the mile, about one foot in three, but averaging through the entire course about one foot in four.

The road-bed is constructed with special reference to safety and durability, of heavy timber clamped to the rocks and braced and secured in the strongest manner. The track is of the usual gauge, with rails of usual railway pattern, and a central safety rail, constructed of two parallel bars of angle iron, with cross bolts of one and one-half inch round iron, at intervals of about four inches. Between these bolts play the cogs of the centre wheel of the locomotive. In addition to the atmospheric brakes, instantaneous in their action, which are in use besides the ordinary brakes, is a firm iron support dropping into the notch-rim of the driving-wheel, which effectively prevents the descent of the train in case of injury to the machinery. After the passengers have examined the arrangements for safety they generally feel no alarm or apprehension of danger. The road in part has now been in operation eleven years, and so far no accident, not one even so slight as to scratch a finger, has ever occurred.

The Mt. Washington Railway engine, "Tip-Top,"
poised for another ascent of the mountain.

Crossing Jacob's Ladder, the steepest grade on the railway.

The locomotive is of novel construction, being made with special reference to the steep inclination of the road, and, when standing on a level track, appears sadly out of balance. Safety and power are attained in the construction at the expense of speed, which is not sought. The locomotive is always below the train, pushing the coaches upward as you ascend and preceding them in the return down the slope. The cars have seats leaning at an angle, facing toward the base of the mountain.

The ride up the mountain is a grand sensation, one of the grandest of a lifetime. The sensation of the balloon may be as fine, we hope to be able to explain sometime. We made the ascent, with about forty others, in one hour and twenty minutes. Along the road are water stations; at one of these stations our train stopped a few minutes. Telegraph wires extend along the

Tourists driven to the railway's base station by horse-drawn carriages
prepare to board a summit-bound train.

road to the Summit. It is our impression that no three miles of road in the
world afford such a succession of wild and startling views as the passenger
enjoys on the steep inclination of Mount Washington. Glimpses of the
wide valley below, through which wind the mountain roads, as well as the
bold landscape, filled with grand and startling outlines, growing and mul-
tiplying as one goes up, are seen and admired. Near the Summit is found
a monument, which stands to the memory of Miss Lizzie Bourne of
Maine, who in 1855, in her great anxiety to reach the top of the mountain,
died from exposure before she was able to reach the Summit. The monument marks the spot where Miss Bourne perished.

Arriving at the top of the mountain, we saw what seemed to us the
grandest sight of all. The view one obtains from this point, which is 6,291

feet above the level of the sea, can scarcely be imagined by one who has not been there. The day we were up was clear and bright, and there seemed to be no end to the distance one could see. Portland harbor, nearly a hundred miles to the east, could be plainly distinguished. To the south, objects as far away could be seen. The sight of little villages scattered here and there below us, added to the charm. To the west one can hardly see beyond the peaks of the Green Mountains, 40 or 50 miles, but the view is grander than words can picture. The Fabyan House below, a distance of probably eight miles direct, looks like a travelling picture gallery. Upon the mountain is a hotel, the Summit House, the U. S. signal service station, a printing office owned and occupied by Henry M. Burt, who publishes each day a handsome paper giving the arrivals at the Summit and other hotels, the state of the weather, and much interesting news, besides a large and varied assortment of advertisements of hotels, which are gotten up and displayed with much taste.

The signal station on the mountain is operated the same as any signal station. Two men are here employed by the government. They get along very pleasantly during the three summer months that the Mt. Washington railway is running, but in the winter it isn't so nice. In the winter they are the only occupants of the Summit. Once every week one of them goes down after their mail, by a route familiar to them. They change about, or in other words, take turns in making the trips for the mail. Enough provisions are taken up in the fall to last all winter. Snow comes very early here and remains very late. There are no trees or vegetation at or within a mile and a half of the top of the mountain. Scarcely anything but stones of all sizes can be seen. In the sunlight they present a white appearance, and sometimes are mistaken at a great distance for snow. On rainy or cloudy days nothing can be seen from the Summit, from the fact that the observer is among the clouds, or possibly above them. Those who ascend the mountain on a day that is not clear and delightful, lose much of the charm. To the people who remain on the Summit over night, the sun rises very early. Sunrise here is very beautiful, and the landlord rings his guests up at 4 A.M., to witness the spectacle. Some get very mad at being called so early, but when they look out and see the sight, they return their gratitude to the landlord at once.

1882

Crawford's

Samuel A. Drake

From *The Heart of the White Mountains: Their Legend and Scenery*

Tourist's Edition

Boston-born Samuel Adams Drake (1833–1905) was a frequent visitor to the White Mountains in the years following the Civil War, of which he was a veteran. Another of Bent's "Classics," The Heart of the White Mountains, Their Legend and Scenery, *is Drake's contribution to the vast amount of White Mountain literature left us from the 19th century. The book, which describes Drake's travels across the Whites, features several articles that he originally wrote and had published in* Harper's Magazine *during the summer of 1881. Other books of regional interest authored by Drake include* On Plymouth Rock, Nooks and Corners of the New England Coast, *and* Old Landmarks and Historical Personages of Boston.

ALL WHO HAVE passed much time at the mountains have seen the elephant—near the gate of the Notch.

Though it is only from Nature's chisel, the elephant is an honest one, and readily admitted into the category of things curious or marvellous constantly displayed for our inspection. Standing on the piazza of the hotel, the enormous forehead and trunk seem just emerging from the shaggy woods near the entrance to the pass. And the gray of the granite strengthens the illusion still more. From the Elephant's Head, a title suggestive of the near vicinity of a public-house, there is a fine view down the Notch for those who cannot ascend Mount Willard.

The Crawford House, being built at the highest point of the pass, nearly two thousand feet above the sea, is not merely a hotel—it is a water-shed. The roof divides the rain falling upon it into two streams, flowing on one side into the Saco, and on the other into the Ammonoosuc. Here the sun rises over the Willey Range, and sets behind Mount Clinton. The north side of the piazza enables you to look over the forests into the valley of the Ammonoosuc, where the view is closed by the chain dividing this basin from that of Israel's River. But we are not yet ready to conduct the reader into this Promised Land.

My window overlooked a grassy plain of perhaps half a mile, the view being closed by the Gate of the Notch, now disfigured by snow-sheds built for the protection of the railway. The massive, full rounded bulk of Webster rose above, the forests of Willard tumbled down into the ragged fissure. Half-way between the hotel and the Gate, over-borne by the big shadow of Mount Clinton, extends the pretty lakelet which is the fountain-head of the Saco. Beyond the lake, and at the left, is where the old Notch House stood. This lake was once a beaver-pond, and this plain a boggy meadow, through which a road of corduroy and sods conducted the early traveller. The highway and railway run amicably side by side, dividing the little vale in two.

This pass, which was certainly known to the Indians, was, in 1771, re-discovered by Timothy Nash, a hunter, who was persuaded by Benjamin Sawyer, another hunter, to admit him to an equal share in the discovery. In 1773 Nash and Sawyer received a grant of 2184 acres, skirting the mountains on the west, as a reward. With the prodigality characteristic of their class, the hunters squandered their large acquisition in a little time after it was granted. Both the Crawford and Fabyan hotels stand upon their tract.

Of many excursions which this secluded retreat offers, that to the summit of Mount Washington, by the bridle-path opened in 1840 by Thomas J. Crawford, and that to the top of Mount Willard, are the principal. The route to the first begins opposite to the hotel, at the left; the latter turns from the glen a quarter of a mile below, on the right. Supposing Mount Washington a cathedral set on an eminence, you are here on the summit of the eminence, with one foot on the immense stairway to the cathedral.

Our resolve to ascend by the bridle-path was already formed, and we regarded the climb up Mount Willard as indispensable. As for the cascades, which lulled us to sleep, who shall describe them? We could not lift our eyes to the heights above without seeing one or more fluttering in the play of the breeze, and making rainbows in pure diversion. President Dwight, in his "Travels," has no more eloquent passage than that describing the Flume Cascade. How many since have thrown down pen or pencil in sheer despair of reproducing, by words or pigments, the aerial lightness, the joyous freedom; above all, the exuberant, unquenchable vitality that characterize mountain water-falls! Down the Notch is a masterpiece, hidden from the eye of the passer-by, called Ripley Falls, which fairly revels in its charming seclusion. Only a short walk from the hotel, by a woodland path, there is another, Beecher's Cascade, whose capricious leaps and playful somersaults, all the while volubly chattering to itself, like a child alone with its playthings, fascinates us, as sky, water, and fire charm the eyes of an infant. It is always tumbling down, and as often leaping to its feet to resume its frolicsome gambols, with no loss of sprightliness or sign of weariness that we can detect. Only a lover may sing the praises of these mountain cascades falling from the skies:

"The torrent is the soul of the valley. Not only is it the Providence or the scourge, often both at once, but it gives to it a physiognomy; it gladdens or saddens it; it lends it a voice; it communicates life to it. A valley without its torrent is only a hole."

They give the name of Idlewild to the romantic sylvan retreat, reached by a winding path, diverging near the hotel, on the left. I visited it in company with Mr. Atwater, whose taste and enthusiasm for the work have converted the natural disorder of the mountain side into a trysting-place fit for elves and fairies; but where one encounters ladies in elegant toilets, enjoying a quiet stroll among the fern-draped rocks. Some fine vistas of the valley mountains have been opened through the woods—beautiful little bits of blue, framed in illuminated foliage. One notes approvingly the revival of an olden taste in the cutting and shaping of trees into rustic chairs, stairways, and arbors.

After a day like ours, the great fires and admirable order of the hotel were grateful indeed. If it is true that the way to man's heart lies through his stomach, the cherry-lipped waiter-girl, who whispered her seductive tale in my too-willing ear at supper, made a veritable conquest. My compliments to her, notwithstanding the penalty paid for lingering too long over the griddle-cakes.

The autumn nights being cool, it was something curious to see the parlor doors every now and then thrown wide open, to admit a man who came trundling in on a wheelbarrow a monster log fit for the celebration of Yuletide. The city guest, accustomed to the economy of wood at home, because it is dear, looks on this prodigality first with consternation, and finally with admiration. When the big log is deposited on the blazing hearth amid fuses of sparks, the easy-chairs again close around the fireplace a charmed circle; and while the buzz of conversation goes on, and the faces are illuminated by the ruddy glow, the wood snaps, and hisses, and spits as if it had life and sense of feeling. The men talk in drowsy undertones; the ladies, watching the chimney-soot catch fire and redden, point out to each other the old grandame's pictures of "folks coming home from meeting." This scene is the counterpart of a warm summer evening on the piazza—both typical of unrestrained, luxurious indolence. How many pictures have appeared in that old fireplace! and what experiences its embers revived! Water shows us only our own faces in their proper mark—nothing more, nothing less; but fire, the element of the supernatural, is able, so at least we believe, to unfold the future as easily as it turns our eyes into the past. If only we could read!

When we arose in the morning, what was our astonishment to see the surrounding mountains white with snow. Like one smitten with sudden terror, they had grown gray in a night. Striking, indeed, was the transformation from yesterday's pomp; beautiful the contrast between the dark green below and the dead white of the upper zones. Thickly encrusted with hoar-frost, the stiffened foliage of the pines and firs gave those trees the unwonted appearance of bursting into blossom. Over all a dull and

Strolling along the road through Crawford Notch near the narrow Gateway, just a short distance from the Crawford House (seen in the background).

brooding sky shed its cold, wan light upon the glen, forbidding all thought of attacking the high summits, at least for this day.

Dismissing this, therefore, as impracticable, we nevertheless determined on ascending Mount Willard—an easy thing to do, considering you have only to follow a good carriage-road for two miles and a half to reach the precipices overlooking Saco Valley.

Startling, indeed, by its sublimity was the spectacle that rewarded our trouble a thousand-fold. Still, the sensations partook more of wonder than admiration—much more. The unpractised eye is so utterly confounded by the immensity of this awful chasm of the Notch, yawning in all its extent and all its grandeur far down beneath, that, powerless to grasp the fulness and the vastness thus suddenly encountered, it stupidly stares into those far-retreating depths. The scene really seems too tremendous for flesh and blood to comprehend. For an instant, while standing on the brink of the sheer precipice, which here suddenly drops seven or eight hundred feet, my head swam and my knees trembled.

First came the idea that I was looking down into the dry bed of some primeval cataract, whose mighty rush and roar the imagination summoned again from the tomb of ages and whose echo was in the cascades, hung like two white arms on the black and hairy breast of the adjacent mountain. This idea carries us back to the Deluge, of which science pretends to have found proofs in the basin of the Notch. What am I saying? to the Deluge! it transports us to the Beginning itself, when *"Darkness was upon the face of the deep. And the Spirit of God moved upon the face of the waters."*

You see the immense walls of Mount Willey on one side, and of Webster on the other, rushing downward thousands of feet, and meeting in one magnificently imposing sweep at their bases. This vast natural inverted archway has the heavens for a roof. The eye roves from the shaggy head of one mountain to the shattered cornices of the other. One is terrible, the other forbidding. The naked precipices of Willey, furrowed by avalanches, still show where the fatal slide of 1826 crushed its way down the valley, traversing a mile in only a few moments. Far down in the distance you see the Willey hamlet and its bright clearing. You see the Saco's silver.

Such, imperfectly, are the more salient features of this immense cavity of the Notch, three miles long, two thousand feet deep, rounded as if by art, and as full of suggestions as a ripe melon of seeds. I recall few natural wonders so difficult to get away from, or that haunt you so perpetually.

Like ivy on storied and crumbling towers, so high up the cadaverous cliffs of Willey the hardy fir-tree feels its way, insinuating its long roots in

Guests and horse-drawn carriages from two nearby hotels
pass by the railroad depot at Crawford's.

every fissure where a little mould has crept, but mounting always like the
most intrepid climbers. Upon the other side, the massed and plumed forest advances boldly up the sharp declivity of Webster; but in mid-ascent
is met and ploughed in long, thin lines by cataracts of stones, poured down
upon it from the summit. Only a few straggling bushes succeed in mounting higher; and far up, upon the very edge of the crumbling parapet, one
solitary cedar tottered. The thought of imminent destruction prevailed
over every other. Indeed, it seemed as if one touch would precipitate the
whole mass of earth, stones, and trees into the vale beneath.

Between these high, receding walls, which draw widely apart at the outlet of the pass, mountains rise, range upon range. Over the flattened Nancy
summits, Chocorua lifts his crested head once more into view. We pass in
review the summits massed between, which on this morning were of a
deep blue-black, and stood vigorously forth from a sad and boding sky.

From the ledges of Mount Willard, Washington and the peaks between
are visible in a clear day. This morning they were muffled in clouds, which
a strong upper current of air began slowly to disperse. We, therefore, secured a good position, and waited patiently for the unveiling.

Little by little the clouds shook themselves free from the mountain, and
began a slow, measured movement toward the Ammonoosuc Valley. As
they were drawn out thinner and thinner, like fleeces, by invisible hands,

we began to be conscious of some luminous object behind them, and all at once, through a rift, there burst upon the sight the grand mass of Washington, all resplendent in silvery whiteness. From moment to moment the trooping clouds, as if pausing to pay homage to the illustrious recluse, encompassed it about. Then moving on, the endless procession again and again disclosed the snowy crest, shining out in unshrouded effulgence. To look was to be wonder-struck—to be dumb.

As the clouds unrolled more and more their snowy billows, other and lower summits rose above, as on that memorable morn after the Deluge, where they appeared like islands of crystal floating in a sea of silvery vapor. We gazed for an hour upon this unearthly display, which derived unique splendor from fitful sun-rays shot through the folds of surrounding clouds, then drawing off, and again darting unawares upon the stainless white of the summits. It was a dream of the celestial spheres to see the great dome, one moment glittering like beaten silver, another shining with the dull lustre of a gigantic opal.

I have since made several journeys through the Notch by the railway. The effect of the scenery, joined with some sense of peril in the minds of the timid, is very marked. Old travellers find a new and veritable sensation of excitement; while new ones forget fatigue, drop the novels they have been reading, maintaining a state of breathless suspense and admiration until the train vanishes out at the rocky portal, after an ascent of nearly six hundred feet in two miles.

In effect, the road is a most striking expression of the maxim, "*L'audace, et toujours de l'audace,*" as applied to modern engineering skill. From Bemis's to Crawford's its way is literally carved out of the side of the mountain. But if the engineers have stolen a march upon it, the thought, how easily the mountain could shake off this puny, clinging thing, prevailing over every other, announces that the mountain is still the master.

There are no two experiences which the traveller retains so long or so vividly as this journey through the great Notch, and this survey from the ledges of Mount Willard, which is so admirably placed to command it. To my mind, the position of this mountain suggests the doubt whether nature did not make a mistake here. Was not the splitting of the mountains an after-thought?

July 6, 1889

White Mountain Hotels

From *The White Mountain Echo and Tourists' Register*

At the start of each summer tourist season, The White Mountain Echo and Tourists' Register *would devote nearly an entire issue to the many hotels and inns scattered across the White Mountains region. This rundown of operating tourist homes would typically include a description of the building and property, the array of services and amenities offered, and daily and weekly rates. The following White Mountain hotel guide was taken from the July 6, 1889 issue.*

Franconia Notch

The Franconia Notch is undoubtedly one of the leading attractions of the New Hampshire Hills. Starr King says: "The narrow district thus enclosed contains more objects of interest to the mass of travelers than any other region of equal extent within the usual compass of the White Mountain tour. In the way of rock culture and waterfalls it is a huge museum of curiosities." Its principal features are Echo Lake, with its marvellous reverberations, its steamboat, and the neighboring peaks of Lafayette and Eagle Cliff; Profile Lake and the Basin; the Gloomy Pool, the Flume, with its fine cascade; Georgianna and other waterfalls, and Cannon Mountain and neighboring rocky eminences. There are good bridle and foot-paths to the summits of Lafayette and Cannon Mountains and a carriage road to Bald Mountain.

Profile House, Taft and Greenleaf, delightfully situated in the midst of all this grandeur, is the largest hotel in the district, and first-class in every respect. It possesses accommodations for 550 guests, its rates being $4.50 per day for transient board, and by the week $21 in June and September, $24.50 in July, and $28 in August. The Profile and Franconia Notch Narrow Gauge Railroad, from Bethlehem Junction (ten miles in length), leads direct to the house; while there is a stage line through the Notch to the North Woodstock Station of the Pemigewasset Valley Railroad (ten miles).

Flume House, Elliott Brothers, at the Southern end of Franconia Notch, accommodates 150 guests at $3 per day for transient board, and per week $12 to $17.50. This house has lately been extensively enlarged and improved, and, as it opens early and does not close until late in the season, offers a desirable stopping place for early and late tourists, who here find themselves in the midst of the most enchanting scenery. This house is five miles distant from the North Woodstock Station of the Pemigewasset valley Railroad and five miles from the Profile Station referred to above.

The Glen

The beautiful Glen, delightfully situated at the eastern base of Mount Washington, and between it and the Carter Range, is completely hemmed in by lofty hills. Far removed from the noise of the steam whistle, it possesses an attraction to the lovers of retirement peculiarly its own, so far as the White Mountains are concerned. It is approached from the south by fourteen miles of staging from Glen Station, on the White Mountains line of the Maine Central R.R., the route lying through Jackson and the Pinkham Notch, and past Goodrich and Jackson Falls; and from the north by eight miles of staging from Gorham up the charming valley of the Peabody. Another carriage road eight miles long leads to the summit of Mount Washington and the railroad station. Its most immediate attractions are Glen Ellis Falls and the Crystal Cascade, the grandest of the White Mountain cataracts; the Emerald and Garnet Pools, Osgood's Falls, Raymond's Cataract, Carter Dome and Tuckerman's Ravine.

Glen House, C. R. Milliken & Co., accommodates 400 guests, the rates being $4.50 per day, with a reduction for June and September. This entirely new house, one-half of which was erected three years ago, is now fully completed, and its management will be even superior to that which in past years won for the former house such renown. No expense has been spared in furnishing this elegant establishment with every appliance for comfort in accordance with fine taste, and in which the equipment of the dining-room is a special feature. Throughout everything is of the best, nothing has been slighted and no expense has been spared. The hotel is located in the midst of the beautiful scenery described above, being built upon the lower slope of the Carter Range, with views of Carter Dome and Wildcat to the south, the valley of the Peabody to the north and the noble peaks of the Presidential Range to the west.

The Glen House at Pinkham Notch.

Mount Washington

The crown of the monarch of the hills is the Mecca to which all true believers in the beauty of White Mountain scenery invariably direct their steps. The marvellous railroad and the carriage-way which climb the mountain's sides are well known, and have been so often described that it is needless to particularize them here; while it is impossible for either pen or pencil to properly portray the extent and grandeur of the sight revealed to the eye from the lofty summit of the towering peak, where mountain and defile, lake and river, town and village, field and forest in many a county and in several States are brought at a single glance within the compass of the human vision. On account of its elevation, 6,293 feet above sea level, the crest "forms," says Mr. Sweetser, "an Arctic island in a temperate zone, having the same climate as Greenland, at 70° N. latitude. This peculiarity is shown not only in the temperature, but also in the vegetation which there exists." On top is a small hamlet consisting of old and new Summit House, Tip-Top House, Railroad Engine House, Signal Service Observatory, and Tower, and in summer it is quite a busy place, through the crowd of tourists brought to it by the railroad from Fabyan's on the west side, and by the carriage road on the east. The places of interest within a short distance from the summit are the Alpine Garden, Bigelow's Lawn, Tuckerman's Ravine with its snow arch, etc.

Summit House, Barron & Merrill, proprietors (E. W. Powers, Manager); accommodates 200 guests, who are amply protected against the frequent chilliness of the climate, incident upon the great altitude of its location, by the rooms and corridors being kept comfortably warm. It contains all the conveniences of a first-class hotel, and has post-office, telegraph station, etc.

The White Mountain (or Crawford) Notch

It is almost needless to refer to the scenery in this renowned Notch, as it forms an important point of interest to all White Mountain visitors. With Mount Webster on the east and Mounts Willard and Willey on the west, with the Silver and Flume Cascades and Ripley Falls and many other grand scenes between them, this favorite locality contains sufficient to feast the eye to satiety, and its charms are plainly visible either from the road or the railroad passing through it. Near its northern gate are the Elephant's Head, Saco Lake and the foot of the carriage road leading to the summit of Mount Willard, which is easy of access and presents from its crest one of the grandest mountain scenes in the country.

Crawford House, Barron & Merrill (C. H. Merrill, Manager), situated on a high plateau and about quarter of a mile from the entrance of this famous Notch, has accommodations for 400 guests, the rates being, transient, $4.50 per day, and per week $17.50 to $25 in June and September, and $21 to $28 in July and August. The table of this establishment is noted for its excellence, the heating of many of its rooms by steam renders it a desirable abode in cold weather, while the comfort of its guests is promoted by repeated additions and improvements, including elevator, etc. Telegraph and post office in the house. Since the season of 1886 all the sleeping apartments have been either renovated or entirely refurnished. A station on the White Mountains line of the Maine Central R.R. is near the house, which is but two miles from the summit of Mount Willard, whither coaches convey guests.

Fabyan's

Located in the very heart of the mountains, at the junction of three rail-roads, Fabyan's has rapidly risen from a single house to the distinction of a village, and has now become a great centre of railroad travel. Here the lines of the White Mountains Division of the Concord R.R., the White Mountains line of the Maine Central R.R., and the Mount Washington Railroad converge, causing an almost continued succession of arriving and departing trains, which convey passengers to and from the summit of Mount Washington and every part of the Great Republic.

Fabyan House, Barron & Merrill (Oscar G, Barron, Manager), situated near the railroad station and opposite Mount Deception, accommodates 400 guests, the rates being, transient, $4.50 per day, and per week $17.50 to $25 in June and September and $21 to $28 in July and August. This house,

The dining hall of the Fabyan House at Bretton Woods.

recently greatly improved by the addition of an elevator and other modern appliances, is one of the largest mountain establishments, and from its central location forms an eligible point from which to visit the leading features of the district, as numerous trains leave the adjoining station daily for the summit of Mount Washington (which is clearly visible from the house), for the Crawford and Franconia Notches, and for the principal mountain resorts. Since the season of 1886, a large open fire-place has been constructed in the entrance hall, and all the sleeping apartments have been either renovated or entirely refurnished. Telegraph and Post offices in the house.

Mount Pleasant House, Barron & Merrill (Oscar G. Barron, Manager), lies about half a mile southeast of the Fabyan House, and has accommodations for 250 guests, the rates for transients being $2.50 to $3.50 per day, and those per week $12.50 to $21. This house has been leased by the proprietors for the purpose of supplying tourists with accommodations at cheaper rates than are charged at their other establishments, though in internal comforts it is hardly their inferior, containing, as it does, a passenger elevator and electric bells, being lighted by gas, and for cool weather having its rooms pleasantly warmed by steam. It has telegraph and post-offices in the house; telephonic communication with the Crawford, Fabyan and Twin Mountain Houses; and stations of its own on the White Mountains line of the Maine Central R.R., and on the Mount Washington Railroad, which render all points of interest in the region readily accessible. It commands fine views of Mounts Washington, Pleasant, Deception and other peaks, and is the only house from which the mountain railroad is in full view from base to summit.

The Twin Mountains

Nearly half a dozen miles to the west of Fabyan's and seven or eight miles east of Bethlehem, the Twin Mountain Range rises from the southern bank of the Ammonoosuc, and running at right angles to the stream, stretches to the southward in the direction of the eastern bank of the Pemigewasset. Its principal members are the North and South Twin and Mounts Guyot and Bond. The Twins are each about 5,000 feet high, a depression of only 200 feet separating their summits. A path has been constructed under the auspices of the Appalachian Mountain Club, to the summit of the South Twin, whence is visible one of the grandest sights of the mountain upheaval in the whole White Mountain region, interspersed with thriving villages and pictures of the illimitable wilderness, where nature's handiwork is exhibited in its normal state. It is expected that this path will eventually descend to this wilderness, and after passing through it in an easterly direction, ascend to the Thoreau Falls, nearly the easterly source of the Pemigewasset, and then connect with a contemplated path from the Crawford House in an opposite direction.

Twin Mountain House, Frank A. Cofran, proprietor, situated on a terrace north of the Ammonoosuc, accommodates 300 guests, the rates being $4 per day for transient board, and $15 to $25 per week in June and September, and $17.50 to $28 in July and August. The table, ever noted for its superior excellence, is kept up to its former standard. The water supply and sanitary arrangements are perfect in every respect. The peaks visible from this hotel, viewed from east to west, are the Baby Twins, Mount Hale, the North Twin, hiding the summit of its southern brother; Mounts Garfield, Lafayette, Cleveland and Agassiz; while a view of the upper peaks of the Presidential Range may be obtained near by. It is the annual resort of many persons of culture, and especially of sufferers from hay-fever. It has a station of the White Mountains Division of the Concord R.R., where express trains pass daily for distant places, while local trains bring every part of the mountain region within a few hours' compass.

Bethlehem

The village of Bethlehem, situated upon a lofty plateau nearly 1,500 feet above the sea level, with a fretwork of mountain eminences fringing the horizon in every direction, draws tens of thousands to it annually to enjoy its magnificent scenery and imbibe its invigorating mountain air, kept pure by a perfect system of drainage. These advantages have made it the headquarters of the United States Hay Fever Association, whose meetings are held in the village. It now possesses more than thirty hotels and boardinghouses; Protestant, Episcopal, Methodist and Congregational Churches; a public hall; and is supplied with water from reservoirs situated on neighboring hills; while more than three miles of brick and plank walks permit pedestrian exercise to be taken, even immediately after a refreshing shower, without fear of wet feet. The streets, which are well lighted by night, are kept continually sprinkled during hot weather, and all necessary appliances are provided for the suppression of fire. Every point of interest in the mountains can be brought within a day's excursion either by road or rail, and there are pleasant half-day rides to places in the more immediate vicinity, such as Howland's Observatory, Mount Cleveland, Echo Farm, Around the Heater, Cherry Valley, etc., while Mount Agassiz, Cruft's

Ledge and Strawberry Hill are within comfortable walking distance. All trains of the White Mountain Division of the Concord R.R. connect at Bethlehem Junction, three miles east of the village, with a narrow gauge railroad, for Maplewood and Bethlehem. Tourists are also enabled to reach Bethlehem by a stage line running in connection with trains stopping at the Littleton station of the same railroad, five miles west of the village.

Maplewood Hotel, Ainslie & McGilvray, is the handsomest and one of the most extensive structures of its kind in the mountains, having accommodations, with the private cottages in connection, for over 500 guests. The transient rates are $4.50 per day; special rates for the season. This elegant establishment possesses a large hall for entertainments, etc., has an elevator, is lighted with gas and electricity, is perfectly drained, has the Presidential and Northern Ranges of mountains in full view, and is located within beautiful grounds, 800 acres in extent, comprising tennis and croquet lawns, observatories, wooded walks, etc. There has been erected near the Hotel, and now ready for the enjoyment of guests, a fine Casino comprising spacious ball-room and entertainment hall provided with stage, etc., several billiard-rooms and bowling-alleys, gentlemen's smoking-rooms and Ladies' parlors with open fire-places, art gallery and studios; while a stone tower contains a reading-room and library. This building is lighted by electricity, and broad verandas and observation windows command views of adjoining base-ball grounds. The Maplewood has post and express offices of its own, and a station on the narrow-gauge branch.

Sinclair House, Durgin & Co., is a large modern hotel in the centre of the village, covering the site of the original establishment, the first of its kind in Bethlehem. It can accommodate 300 guests; the charges being for transient board, $3.50 per day, and by the week $15 and upwards, according to location of rooms and period of stay. The house has all modern conveniences, billiard, bath and hair-dressing rooms, is lighted with gas, well supplied with water, perfectly drained, delightfully situated, and commands a fine view of the surrounding hills. Adjacent to the hotel are base-ball grounds, tennis and croquet lawns, bowling alleys, and play-grounds for children. Telegraph office in the house and post-office opposite.

Avenue House, G. C. Edmunds, accommodates 75 guests at $2 per day for transient board, and $8 to $15 per week, according to situation of room and period of stay. This house, standing back a little distance from the main street in well-kept grounds, has recently been renovated throughout and tastefully painted in colors, the grounds enlarged and beautified and supplied with croquet lawns, etc., and every provision made for the comfort and enjoyment of guests. Good livery in connection.

The Maplewood Hotel in Bethlehem.

Bethlehem House, Simeon B. Phillips, accommodates 50 guests at $2 per day for transient board, and from $8 to $15 per week, with reduced rates for September and October. This hotel, greatly favored in its location, in Congress Avenue, and a short distance off Main Street, is free from dust, and consequently an annual resort for catarrh and hay-fever sufferers. The new proprietor has had the house in great part refurnished and thoroughly renovated. It has large, airy chambers, and a home-like table provided with milk, cream and vegetables from its own farm. Broad piazzas extend entirely round the house, ensuring a cool and shady retreat, even during the heat of the day. Livery in connection.

Highland House, J. H. Clark, on Main Street, at the west end, accommodates 85 to 100 guests. It possesses spacious apartments, with closets, open fire-places and baths, hot and cold water on every floor, electric bells, and all other modern improvements, and has fine lawn tennis and croquet grounds. The house from its advantageous situation commands views not only of the Presidential and Starr King Ranges, but most extended western views, including the valley of the Ammonoosuc and the Green Mountains beyond, with the resplendent sunset effects peculiar to the region.

Hillside House, Mrs. E. S. Davis & Son, on Mount Agassiz Road, accommodates fifty guests at $2 per day for transient board, $8 per week in June and September, and $9 to $14 in July and August. It is situated on high ground facing Mount Washington, and with Mount Agassiz in full view to the south. The rooms are large and airy, the drainage is perfect, and every attention is paid to the comfort of guests. Warm rooms for September and October boarders. Livery stable in connection.

Howard House, F. E. Derbyshire, accommodates sixty guests, at $2.50 per day for transient board, and from $10 to $15 per week, with special rates for September and October. This old-established and favorite house is centrally located on Main Street, within two minutes' walk of railroad station and post and telegraph offices. Its lawns are large and well kept. Lawn tennis and croquet grounds. Fine piazza. Good livery in connection.

Maplewood Cottage, Charles B. Goodwin, nearly opposite to and northeast of the Maplewood Hotel, accommodates 100 guests at $3 per day for transient board; special rates for the season. This well-kept and comfortable boarding-house opens in early June and closes in late October, and its guests are privileged to enjoy the social advantages of the Maplewood Hotel and the Casino with their delightful surroundings. Being heated by steam and lighted with gas, with cheerful fires in open fire-places, it is peculiarly adapted for visitors desirous of prolonging their stay in the mountains until the change of foliage.

Mount Washington House, C. L. Bartlett, on Park Avenue, accommodates, with adjoining cottages, 60 guests at $2 per day for transient board, $ 7 to $10 per week during June and September, and $10 to $14 in July and August. Pleasantly situated forty rods from Main Street, and ten rods from railroad station, it commands mountain views from every window, forty peaks being visible from the front piazza alone. Good table and excellent livery, with large farm in connection. Water on every floor.

Prospect House, Mrs. Geo. W. Phillips & Son, situated in its own beautiful grounds, one-third of a mile from railroad station, accommodates eighty guests at $2 per day for transient board, and $7 to $10 per week in June and September, and $8 to $12 in July and August. The mountain views obtainable from this house are more extensive than those commanded by any other in Bethlehem, it being the only one from which both Mounts Washington and Lafayette with their neighboring heights, are visible. Rooms with fires for fall boarders. Good livery. Farm and woodlands of 140 acres in extent.

Ranlet's Hotel, D. W. Ranlet, corner of Main Street and Park Avenue, is an exceedingly comfortable hotel of wide reputation, well merited. Its *cuisine* is of the very best; house heated throughout; broad piazzas on three sides; fine playgrounds and an unobstructed view of mountain scenery in all directions. Terms reasonable; open June to October.

Turner House and Cottages, J. N. Turner & Son., Main Street, on Turner's Farm, midway between Maplewood and the Sinclair House, accommodates seventy-five guests at $2 to $2.50, and $8 to $15 per week, according to location of room. These houses are delightfully situated amid handsome shade trees, and possess a spring of water noted for its coldness and delicious purity. Turner's is the oldest and one of the most popular boarding-houses in the village. Entirely new carriages and livery.

The Uplands, F. H. Abbott, at the west end, accommodates 100 guests at $2 per day for transient board, and from $8 to $15 per week. This first-class house, situated on high ground, and separated from the main thoroughfare by terraced lawns, is superior in every respect and is thoroughly warmed for the comfort of fall guests. Plumbing entirely reconstructed on scientific principles. Since last season the house has been enlarged to nearly twice its former capacity. On the front is a handsomely furnished parlor 30 ft. × 40 ft., a large commodious office and cosy reception-room. The whole structure has been renovated and fitted up with a view only to the comfort of its guests. Tennis court and croquet ground on large lawn.

North Conway

The charming village of North Conway is not only the oldest of the White Mountain resorts, but is unsurpassed by any for beauty of locality and picturesqueness of surroundings. It is seated on a terrace that overlooks the Saco and its marginal intervales, the position affording it every facility for perfect drainage. The valley in which it nestles is about three miles wide, and is bordered on the east by the Rattlesnake Range, and on the west by the White Horse Ledge, with Kearsarge raising its peak to the northeast, and Moat towering skyward to the southwest, standing like two sentinels to guard the entrances. Within these limits the lover of nature is enabled to find many a scenic gem—the Artist Falls and Artist Ramble, Sunset Hill, and its extensive view up the Saco Valley, Echo Lake, Diana's Bath, and the Cathedral, that wondrous resemblance to the interior of a basilica, but the handiwork of the Great Architect. North Conway is topographically divided into three districts—the village proper, the Intervale and Kearsarge Village—nearly two miles apart, all three within the limits of a walk or drive "around the square." Added to these, Lower Bartlett, just above the Intervale, claims to be considered as one of the North Conway family. Rambles through the wooded walks, which connect these localities, are not the least of the many attractions to draw people to this popular resort. Conjointly they possess nearly thirty hotels and boarding-houses, with places of worship for Protestant Episcopal, Baptist, Congregational, Methodist, and Swedenborgian denominations. The village proper is now provided with water-works, the supply being derived from the head waters of Artist's Brook, and during hot weather the streets are kept cool by repeated sprinklings. It is but a day's excursion from North Conway to Crawford Notch, Fabyan's and Mount Washington, to the Glen and the Glen Ellis Falls, and to Chocorua; while Jackson and its two fine water-falls, Humphrey's Ledge and Dundee and Ridge roads, with their magnificent prospects, are each within an afternoon's drive. North Conway and Intervale have stations on the White Mountains line of the Maine Central R.R., and the former is the terminus of a branch of the Boston and Maine Railroad. The sunsets of North Conway have such a peculiar attraction that they drew from Starr King this lavish praise: "Coleridge asked Mont Blanc if he had 'a charm to stay the morning star his steep course.' It is time for some poet to put the question to those bewitching elm-sprinkled acres that border the Saco, by what sorcery they evoke, evening after evening, upon the heavens that watch them, such lavish and Italian bloom. . . . For pomp of bright, clear, contrasted flames on a deep and transparent sky, the visitors of North Conway, on the Sunset Bank that overlooks the meadows, enjoy the frequent privilege of a spectacle which the sun sinking behind the Notch conjures for them, such as he rarely displays to the dwellers by the Arno or the inhabitants of Naples."

Sunset Pavilion, M. L. Mason, separated from the main street by a lawn, accommodates 150 guests, the rates per day for transient board being $3 and $3.50, and those per week $8 to $10.50 in June, September and October, and $8 to $17.50 in July and August. No hotel in the White Mountains has a more beautiful situation, being located on the famous "Sunset Bank," which forms the western wall of the plateau overlooking the intervales of the Saco, on which, sheltered by the mountains, rests North Conway village. An ample lawn of about five acres, shaded with elm, maple and Balm of Gilead trees, is one of the charms of the hotel, which has a piazza twelve feet wide and three hundred feet long surrounding it. Pure, running water on each story, also electric bells, fine large bath rooms, and large, light and pleasant chambers. A good livery stable is connected with the house. Recent additions comprise a new kitchen with modern appliances and a large hall for dancing, sixty feet long by thirty wide, open to the roof, and connected with the house by a covered walk. A fine orchestra in attendance.

Intervale House and Cottages, Stephen Mudgett & Sons, accommodates 300 guests, the transient rates being $3 to $3.50 per day, and those per week from $10.50 to $14 in June, September and October, and from $17.50 to $21 in July and August. This hotel, the largest east of Crawford Notch, commands views of unlimited extent and rare beauty. Recent extensive improvements include a fine dining-hall, seating 300, and a new entrance hall. The house has broad verandas, electric bells, hot and cold water on every floor, a perfect system of drainage, pure water from a mountain spring, and its own telegraph office. P.O. address, Intervale, N.H.

The Ridge, Barnes & Dow, located on a knoll in Kearsarge village, with a carriage drive from the main road, accommodates 100 guests at $2.50 per day transient board, $8 per week in June, September and October, and from $10 to $15 in July and August. This new hotel possesses one of the finest locations in the whole White Mountain region, has over 250 feet of broad piazzas, and excellent rooms with large closets, many of the apartments being provided with facilities for warmth during the fall. Electric communication has been introduced, and hot and cold water supplied to every floor. The *cuisine* is unexcelled. First-class livery. Post and Telegraph Offices in the house. Address Kearsarge, N.H.

Bellevue House, John A. Barnes & Sons, at the Intervale, accommodates 100 guests at $2 per week for transient, and $8 to $14 per week, with special rates for June, September and October. The prospect embraces the meadows of the Saco, the grand peaks of the White Mountain Range, and the many neighboring hills. The interior is tasteful, with hard wood floors, charming coloring, easy, handsome staircases, graceful chandeliers, and great picturesque fire-places. The capacity of the hotel has recently been more than doubled. It has 300 feet of piazzas, pure, running water on each floor, and bath room; the chambers are models of comfort, the beds being furnished with woven wire and hair mattresses. A good livery stable. P.O. Address, Intervale, N.H.

Eastman House, Alfred Eastman, accommodates 100 guests, at $2 per day for transient board, and $7 to $10.50 per week, according to requirements. This old-established and favorite house is replete with every comfort for the enjoyment of guests, is agreeably located in the centre of the village, and near to the post office, churches, railroad stations, etc., and has an extensive and well appointed livery stable in connection.

The McMillan, Frank S. Plummer, accommodates seventy-five guests, at $2.50 to $3 per day for transient board, $8 to $17.50 per week. Great improvements have lately been made to this house; the interior has been entirely renovated and refurnished, a new office constructed, and bathroom, lavoratory and pool-table added; while the piazzas have been extended 150 feet, so as to command a view of the Saco Valley and the Mount Washington Range, making in all a promenade of 500 feet. Special attention paid to this table. Drainage and sanitary arrangements perfect. The reputation of this house dates back to the last century, and its charming location, with its surroundings of stately trees and grassy lawns renders it free from dust and noise and makes it especially attractive to summer guests. A good livery is in connection, and a stage meets all trains.

North Conway House, L. J. Ricker, Jr., near the post office and Boston and Maine Railroad station, accommodates 100 guests, the rates being $2 per day for transient board, $7 to $10 per week in June, September and October, and $7 to $14 in July and August. This house, open the year round, was last season extensively enlarged and refurnished; ladies' parlor, dining and billiard-rooms and new apartments were added, and the grounds extended by the addition of a new lawn to the adjoining flower garden. From its central location the house is well adapted for both travellers and summer boarders.

Randall House, J. T. Randall, on Main Street, accommodates fifty guests, at $2 per day and reasonable terms per week, according to room and period of stay. Situated in the centre of the village, this house commands extensive mountain views, and has large and well furnished rooms with beds supplied with good mattresses. Pure spring water. Shady lawn for hammocks, and open lawn for tennis and croquet. There is a good livery in connection.

Jackson

The little village of Jackson is remarkably favored in the grandeur of its locality, and has consequently become the summer sketching-ground of some of the leading painters of the country. It is virtually surrounded by mountains, and is situated on the Wild Cat River, a tributary of the Glen Ellis, which it enters near by, both streams abounding in trout. Jackson Falls on the former, and Goodrich Falls on the latter are foaming rapids whose characteristics have been transferred to many a canvas. The village is only three miles distant from the Glen Station of the White Mountain line of the Maine Central R.R., and lies on the stage route between North Conway and the summit of Mount Washington, which latter is brought within sixteen miles of Jackson by a branch mountain road lately constructed. The village is also twelve miles from the Glen and eight from North Conway. Among other places of interest within easy driving distance may be named Carter and Pinkham Notches, Glen Ellis Falls, Winnewetah, Crystal and Appalachian Cascades, and Tuckerman's Ravine to the north, and Thorn Mountain, Mounts Bartlett and Kearsarge and the Ledges of Conway to the south. It possesses a Union church, in which ministers of all denominations officiate during the season.

Wentworth Hall and Cottages (late Thorn Mountain House), M. C. Wentworth, is an establishment unsurpassed for elegance and convenience in the mountain region. It remains open until October 10, and affords accommodations for 250 guests, the rates being $4 to $5 per day for the transient board, and from $21 to $28 a week single, and $35 to $60 a week double rooms. Every effort is made to provide for guests the comfort and pleasure of a refined and cultivated home. Warmth is afforded in cold weather by open fire-places and steam heat. The *cuisine* is acknowledged the best in New England; all vegetables, milk and cream, being produced on own farm, the former, in abundance in the early part of the season in extensive greenhouses. A handsome dining-hall is supplied from a kitchen under a separate roof, and guests are thus relieved from the odor of cooking. The house is provided with electric bells, spacious dancing-hall, billiard-room and 800 feet of piazzas. The grounds, handsomely laid out with fountains and flowers, contain tennis courts, croquet lawns and shrubbery. The sanitary arrangements are perfect, a large volume of water from Jackson Falls flowing continually through closets and drains. Extensive stables with fifty stalls, and apartments for coachmen and grooms are situated some distance from the house. A park of twenty-five acres is being artistically laid out with walks, bridges, pavilions, etc.

Iron Mountain House, Willard A. Meserve, accommodates ninety guests at $2.50 per day for transient board, with special terms by the week, open from June 1 to November 1, also through the winter for parties then desiring to visit the mountains. The house, which has been greatly enlarged and improved since 1886 and is nearly new, is furnished in a superior and tasteful style, and the pleasure and comfort of guests is studied in its various departments. All the public rooms have open fires, and arrangements are made for heating halls and rooms through September and October. The table is first-class and supplied from a farm connected. Pure water from living springs, perfect drainage, and excellent livery. Telephonic communication with line to Portland and with Western Union Telegraph Office at Glen Station.

Randolph

The town of Randolph is highly favored in its location among the northern peaks of the White Mountain region. The village is 1,200 feet above the sea-level, and lies on the main road from Jefferson to Gorham, which passes over the crest of a hill 600 feet higher than the village, from which eminence may be obtained excellent views of Mounts Madison and Adams and the remarkable gorge of King's Ravine. Randolph abounds in numerous beautiful walks and drives, among which are those to Mossy Glen, Ice Gorge, Salamacis, Cold Brook and Triple Falls, Pond of Safety, Look-Out Ledge on Randolph Mountain, King's Ravine, Jefferson Highlands, Crystal Cascade, Glen Ellis Falls, and the Glen House. The summit of Mount Washington is reached by a delightful carriage ride of sixteen miles by way of the Glen; and the immediate neighborhood abounds with sparkling streams which afford recreation to the angler. There is a Union Church on the Gorham road about two miles from the Ravine House. The nearest railroad stations are at Gorham, on the Grand Trunk Railroad, six miles distant, and at Jefferson, nine miles distant.

Ravine House and Durand Hall, A. N. Watson, accommodates fifty guests, $7 to $10 per week, with reasonable reduction to families and parties. Many improvements have been made in this well-known hotel since 1886; open fire-places and hot and cold baths have been added, and a lawn tennis court laid out; a fine parlor, with open fire-place and large sleeping apartments have been built; and the dining-room has been enlarged to double its former capacity. Water is supplied from Crystal Spring. The house stands near the centre of the town, at the base of Mount Adams and Madison, and is conveniently situated for tourists.

Jefferson,

or Jefferson Hill, as it is locally called, occupies a lofty position, about 1,500 feet above sea-level, and its advantageous location renders it exempt from hay-fever and thus makes it a resort for persons afflicted with that malady during the period of attack. Its elevation also places it in full view of the great Presidential and Franconia groups of mountains, with the Willey Mountain in Crawford Notch between; and with the Green Mountains observable in the west, beyond the valley of the Connecticut. It is not a very difficult walk to the summit of Starr King Mountain, whence a more extensive prospect can be obtained. Many pleasant excursions may be made from Jefferson, as the summit of Mount Washington, Gorham, the Glen, Crawford Notch, and Bethlehem are each within a day's visit; while Lancaster, Whitefield and Stanley's Slide may be visited in a half day's trip. It has places of worship belonging to the Baptists and Methodists. The railroad station is three miles distant, at the terminus of the Whitefield and Jefferson Railroad.

The Waumbek, owned by the Jefferson Hotel and Land Co., and managed by Messrs. Plumer & Porter, of the Laurel House, Lakewood, N.J., is open from June 1 to October 1, and accommodates 250 guests. Transient rate $4 per day. The hotel is finely located on the south slope of Starr King Mountain and commands a grand view of the great White Mountain and Franconia Ranges. It has all modern improvements, is heated by steam and has a perfect drainage system. Since last season it has been materially improved both externally and internally. The old front has been replaced by a handsome one in colonial style and additions made giving new office, parlors, and sleeping rooms. Since the Waumbek came into the possession of its present proprietors, it has been in great part newly furnished, and table and service are in every way first-class. It therefore now takes rank with the best of the Mountain Houses, and guests will find at it every comfort, and may be assured of the same liberal and courteous treatment characteristic of the highly popular Laurel House.

Maple House, F. W. Collins, Manager, accommodates 50 guests at $2.50 per day or $10 and upwards per week. This pleasant house, which has been greatly improved and beautified, fully enjoys the magnificent view obtainable from the village, including the trains on the Mount Washington R.R., and the Cherry Mountain Land Slide. Fine croquet lawns, lawn tennis courts, and spacious play-ground for children. A heating apparatus contributes to the comfort of those sojourning late in the season. The cuisine is of high character and the table is supplied from a farm of 100 acres which adjoins the grounds. Excellent livery and a stage belonging to the house is in attendance at the depot on arrival of trains.

Whitefield

The village of Whitefield is situated at the junction of the Jefferson and the White Mountain Division of the Concord Railroads, on both of which it has stations, and is becoming a populous place, owing to the extensive lumber mills it contains. It possesses Roman Catholic, Baptist, Methodist and Advent churches. It has three or four boarding-houses, the largest being situated on a plateau northeast of the village, the location commanding extensive views of both the White and Franconia Ranges.

Mountain View House, William F. Dodge & Son, accommodates 100 guests, at $2 per day and $8 to $12 per week. Situated on the high plateau referred to, two miles from the village, this house commands most extensive views of both the White Mountain and Franconia Ranges and is surmounted by an inclosed observatory, from which mountains are visible on every side. It has been remodeled and enlarged to meet the demand caused by its increasing popularity. The rooms are large, well-furnished and supplied with the best beds, while open fire-places have been placed in the public rooms. It has good livery and farm in connection, supplying fresh vegetables, milk, cream and butter, while the table is liberally provided and every attention paid to the comfort of guests.

Franconia

The village of Franconia is pleasantly situated upon the Gale River, a branch of the Ammonoosuc, and lies about equidistant from Bethlehem, Littleton, and the Profile House, being midway on the road between the latter places. It consists of a long street in which there are about half a dozen boarding-houses, with Sugar Hill to its west. There are Baptist, Advent and Congregational churches. It is five miles from the Littleton station of the White Mountains Division of the Concord R.R. and about the same distance from the stations of the branch railroads at Bethlehem and Profile House.

Forest Hills Hotel, Priest & Dudley, is situated on the crest of Pine Hill, 300 feet above the village of Franconia. It is equally distant from Bethlehem and the Profile House on the stage road between those places. It has the advantage of an unobstructed view in all directions, including the entire Presidential and Franconia Ranges, is surrounded by extensive graded lawns, with abundance of large pines for shade. It is modern in style of architecture, and all its appointments are first-class. Steam has been added throughout. Some of the best people who regularly visit the mountains are guests of this hotel, and during the season it is filled with a very select company.

Goodnow House, E. H. Goodnow and J. W. Peckett, Jr., in a most commanding position on Sugar Hill, accommodates 250 guests on reasonable terms. Situated 1,400 feet above the level of the sea, with wooded walks in the rear, this house possesses an uninterrupted view of the entire White Mountain and Franconia Ranges, while its peculiar location gives it immunity from malaria and hay-fever. Tennis and croquet lawns and superior livery.

Mount Lafayette House, Richardson Brothers, accommodates sixty guests, at $2 per day for transient board, $7 to $10 per week in July and August, and $1 per day in September and October. The house is pleasantly located between two rivers, at the forks of which is a beautiful grove, and commands a fine view of the Franconia and other ranges. The sleeping apartments have been furnished with double-deck spring beds and hair mattresses. The table is supplied with vegetables and milk from a large farm connected. Livery, bowling alley, telephonic communication, etc. First-class trout fishing within easy distance.

Sugar Hill

derives its name from a large grove of sugar maples on its summit, and is situated about two miles to the west of Franconia, and seven from Lisbon, its nearest station of the White Mountains Division of the Concord R.R. From its highest point is obtained a superb view, encompassing the entire horizon. Commencing at the northeast, many miles away, with Mount Starr King and its neighboring heights, the eye, wandering to the right until it has taken in every point of the compass, embraces in its vision the monarchs of the Presidential Range, Mount Lafayette and its neighbors and Moosilauke. Then, after crossing the Connecticut Valley it is impressed with a broad panoramic view of the Green Mountains of Vermont; and, extending a hundred miles along the horizon, the circuit of vision terminates with the Canadian Heights, observable in the dim distance. The scene, in its magnitude and grandeur, is unsurpassed by any in the White Mountain region. The little straggling village of Sugar Hill is situated on the western slope of the ridge, and contains one or two stores and Baptist and Advent churches. The places of interest within a drive are the Profile House, the Old Man of the Mountains, Mount Lafayette, Echo and Profile Lakes, the Flume, the Pool, the Basin and other beauties of the Franconia Notch; and nearer are Bridal Veil Falls, Mink and Schreber Ponds, Howland's Flume, etc., while it is but a pleasant afternoon's ride to Bethlehem and back.

Sunset Hill House and Cottage, Bowles & Hoskins, located on the very crest of the hill 1,650 feet above sea-level, accommodates 275 guests, at $3

The Hotel Lookoff in Sugar Hill.

per day for transient board and from $10 to $17.50 per week. This house and cottage have been built in the most thorough manner, and are supplied with all improvements now required in a first-class hotel—open fires, baths, telegraph office, etc.,—while the windows of every room command most delightful and extensive prospects. Improvements and additions made last year consist of an extension 40 × 80 feet containing a large drawing-room, three other parlors and billiard-room with open fireplaces; as well as 24 new sleeping apartments. The former drawing-room has been converted into a music-room with stage appointments, and the grounds have been improved. The latter contain over a dozen tennis courts, as well as croquet lawns. For this season the house has received a further addition of fifty feet, two stories high, so as to afford it increased kitchen accommodation. Carriages await the arrival of trains at Lisbon station. A new and extensive livery stable a short distance from the house.

Hotel Look-Off, Hiram Noyes & Sons, an entirely new house 1,900 feet above sea-level and commanding a grand and extensive panorama of mountain scenery, accommodates 200 guests. The rates are, for transient board, $3 per day; and per week, table board for each person, $7, with rooms ranging from $5 to $13. The hotel faces east, with Franconia Notch in full sight, and with every window commanding a fine outlook. Rooms, large and airy, well furnished, lighted with gas and supplied with electric bells. House warmed with steam heat and open fires. Scientific plumbing and every sanitary precaution. Twenty acres of lawn tennis courts and pleasure grounds, with fine maple and poplar groves a few rods distant. This house especially desirable for those enjoying autumnal scenery. Telephonic communication and two mails daily. Extensive livery. Nearest railroad station Lisbon, N.H.

Mount Moosilauke

is one of the outlying peaks of the great mountain family of New Hampshire, and commands from its summit, at an elevation of 4,811 feet, a grand panoramic view, not obtainable from any other height, including Lake Winnipesaukee, the Connecticut valley, with the Green and Adirondack mountains beyond, and the White Mountain ranges. An excellent carriage road leads to the summit from Warren, and there are paths from Benton on the north, and from North Woodstock on the east side of the mountain. There is telephonic communication between the Tip-Top House, at the summit, and the Warren Station of the White Mountains Division of the Concord R.R.

The Moosilauke, John F. Thayer, was erected in 1886, on the southern spur of Mount Moosilauke, at an elevation of 1,700 feet. It accommodates 100 guests, at $3 per day for transient board, and $9 to $18 per week. All the rooms command fine outlooks and are provided with electric bells. The house is heated by steam and open fires, is lighted by gas, and has on three sides piazzas twelve feet broad. Best sanitary condition is secured by scientific plumbing. Entire immunity from hay-fever. The air is pure and bracing, the supply of water from mountain springs inexhaustible, and a large maple grove near the house. The hotel faces the east, with Mounts Cushman, Kineo and Waternomee in front, summit of Mount Moosilauke, showing Tip-Top House to the north, and Mount Carr, Baker River Valley and distant peaks to the south. No region is more noted for its trout fishing. The summit is accessible by a two hours' drive. Post-office (Breezy Point, N.H.) in the house, and telephone connecting with summit and with railroad station in Warren, where carriages meet noon express trains and others by previous intimation by mail or telegraph. This is pre-eminently a family hotel, and is especially adapted to secure the comfort of early and late visitors, while the changing tints of the endless forests are unusually varied and extensive.

Tip-Top House, Miss S. F. Woodworth, accommodates forty guests; the rates being $3 per day and $14 per week. This house was enlarged in 1881, and visitors are assured that they will be made entirely comfortable while enjoying the vast panorama spread out before them. The views are those detailed in the preceding description of Mount Moosilauke. It is ten miles from the Warren station, and five miles from Breezy Point. Carriages meet the White Mountain Express, arriving at Warren from the north about noon and from the south about 2 P.M.

North Woodstock

is a charming village delightfully situated not far from the bend of the beautiful Pemigewasset Valley, about five miles below the point at which the river escapes from the rock-bound grasp of the Franconia Notch, and near to where its waters are united with those of the Eastern Branch. It lies at the northern terminus of the Pemigewasset Valley Railroad, the construction of which, a year or two ago, started into existence a new hamlet devoted to the accommodation of summer guests, who cannot fail to appreciate the scenic banquet here set before them by Dame Nature. In addition to its invigorating air, pure water and fine scenery, North Woodstock commands attention from its proximity to some of the most impressive features of the mountain region. On its west rise Mounts Moosilauke and Blue, the summit of the former being accessible by a feasible path seven miles in length, while Mount Russell looms up on the east. Five miles to the north lies the Gateway to Franconia Notch, with its Flume, its Pool, its Basin, its Profile and Echo Lakes, and the stern Old Man of the Mountain. These and many other objects, including Mount Lafayette and its neighboring peaks, Georgianna and other waterfalls, Agassiz Basin, Walker's Ice Cave, etc., are all easily accessible in a day or half-day excursion, while the ponds and streams in the vicinity afford ample sport to the wielder of the rod and line. There are Baptist and Free-Will Baptist churches near by. A stage line conveys travellers to the Profile Branch of the Profile and Franconia Notch Railroad, ten miles north, for Bethlehem, Mount Washington and the east side of the mountains.

Deer Park Hotel, Buchanan & Willis, was erected in 1887, was greatly enlarged last season, and now accommodates 200 guests; transient rate, $3.50 per day, and from $14 to $21 per week. This hotel has been furnished throughout regardless of expense, has office, hall and dining-room finished in oak, the parlors in whitewood, has open fire-places in side parlor and office, and is supplied with steam heat and gas. It also contains electric bells, bath-room, a good laundry, and billiard and pool tables, a plentiful supply of water from neighboring heights, with every safeguard against fire, and sanitary arrangements of most scientific character. First-class orchestra. Piazzas twelve feet wide surround the house, and command extensive views, while every window presents the same advantage. Large livery stables a hundred rods distant and well equipped with new carriages for mountain travel.

1904

Above the Birds

Bradford Torrey

From *Nature's Invitation*

IN THE COURSE of my seven days at the summit of Mount Washington I listed six species of birds. A few snowbirds—three or four—were to be found almost always in the neighborhood of the stables; a myrtle warbler was seen on the climb up the cone from the Lakes of the Clouds; twice I heard a goldfinch passing somewhere overhead; a sharp-shinned hawk, as I took it to be, showed itself one day, none too clearly, flying through the mist; and the next afternoon, as I sat in the rear of the old Tip-Top House waiting for the glories of the sunset, a sparrow hawk shot past me so near as to display not only his rusty tail, but the black bands on the side of his neck. Here are five species. The sixth was one that, rightly or wrongly, I should not have expected to find in so treeless a place. I speak of the red-breasted (or Canadian) nuthatch. On two mornings, as all hands were out upon the platform at sunrise, we heard the characteristic nasal calls of this northern forester, and saw two birds scrambling about the roofs of the buildings; and more than once at other times I noticed one or two on the wing. The species is very common this season in Franconia, —where it was extremely scarce a year ago,—and I was pleased at the summit when a lady standing near me remarked to her husband, "Why, that is the note we have been hearing so continually at the Rangeleys." It was so incessant there, she told me, as to be almost a trouble. Let us hope that this autumnal abundance in New Hampshire foreshadows a nuthatch winter in Massachusetts.

The all but total absence of birds at the summit was a most striking thing. It helped greatly to intensify the loneliness and silence, that won-

derful mountain silence—no leaf to rustle, no brook to murmur, no bird
to sing—which, wherever I walked, I was always stopping to listen to. I
should love to praise it, but language for such a purpose would need to be
found on the spot, the stillness itself suggesting the words; and I came
down from the summit more than a week ago. It must have been, I think,
something like that apocalyptic "silence in heaven."

As for the birds, I should have felt their absence more disagreeably but
for the fact that I had a novel and absorbing occupation with which to en-
liven my walks, and even to beguile effectually what otherwise might have
been idle odds and ends of the day. For the nonce I had turned entomological collector. My search was for rare Alpine insects. Not that I knew
anything about them; it would have been all one to me if most of what I
saw had been created out of nothing the day before; but I was in learned
company and needed no science of my own. My part was to carry a
"cyanide bottle" and put into it any beetle, moth, fly, or other insect—ants
and spiders excepted—on which I could lay my ignorant fingers. The possessor of the learning—enough and to spare for the two of us—has made
many collecting visits to the summit; her list of Mount Washington species
numbers more than sixteen hundred, if I remember the figures correctly,
and no inconsiderable proportion of them are honored with her name. A
proud lot they would be if they knew it. But the end is not yet; there are
many winged mountaineers still to be pinned, and in the prosecution of
such an enterprise, so she gave me to understand, two bottles are better
than one, no matter who carries the second one. Her language was rather
encouraging than complimentary, it might have seemed, but I did not
mind; and for seven days I was never without a bottle about my person except when I lay in bed.

If I went down to the Lakes of the Clouds, for example, the poison-
bottle went with me; and the looker-on, had there been one,—as luckily
there wasn't,—might have seen me on my knees, with hands outstretched
over the water, struggling to snatch from the surface a poor, unhappy,
"skater," or a "lucky bug" (it really was lucky, for it got away while the skater
perished), as a possible prize for my lady's cork-lined box. On all my jaunts
down the carriage-road (and they were many, longer or shorter, that route
offering the readiest means of escape from the frequent summit-capping
cloud) the same scientific vial was my companion. If a grasshopper jumped
(not the common one with banded legs, of which I saw a superfluity, but
a handsome, rare-looking green fellow, making me think of Leigh Hunt's
"green little vaulter in the sunny grass"), I stole murderously after him, and
with a reckless clutch at the stunted bush on which he had settled I gath-

ered him in and put him to sleep. (This was well done, for he was really of a wingless Alpine species, and only my employer's third specimen of this kind.) If a "daddy-long-legs," prayerless friend of my childhood, crawled across the way, he, too, hapless creature, with legs so superfluously numerous and elongated that he could not hurry, even to save his life, fell a victim to my uninstructed zeal. He died easily, for all his undevout habits, but the sacrifice was useless. He proved to be no longer among the entomologist's desiderata, though he also is Alpine, and it is not many years since she herself discovered him here, an insect till then unregistered by human science.

All caterpillars I was bidden to bring in alive; and so, of course, I did, rolling them up in scraps of soft paper and committing them tenderly in my pocket. My chief business, however, after I had breathed the air, eaten my fill of mountain blueberries ("Happy," said I, "is the mouth that feeds on much manna"), and looked my fill at the northern peaks,—for I was not employed by the day, but by the piece, and could steal an hour to myself now and then with a clear conscience,—my principal occupation, I say, was to pry under the boulders for beetles. "Leave no stone unturned," the entomologist had said, with her fine gift of laconic quotation; but she could not have intended the commission to be taken literally. The stones were too many, and human existence is too brief. She meant no more than that I should use a reasonable diligence; and so much I surely did, till the ends of my fingers were in danger of being skinned alive. Down on all fours I got, lifted a stone quickly, fastened an eagle eye upon the exposed hollow, and if a dark object, no matter how small or how large, was seen to be scurrying to its burrow, I thrust my fingers into the dirt in frantic efforts to seize it. I knew not which were common and which were rare; my only course was to let none escape. But many were too swift for me, with all my efforts, and of all that I captured in this manner I am not sure that one was "worth mounting." I quote those last two words partly by way of emphasis. They stood for the lowest round in the ladder of my entomological ambition. What I most of all desired was to discover a new species; next I coveted a species new to New England; after that a new species to Mount Washington; and last of all a specimen worth saving, or, as my employer said, "worth mounting"—in short, worth a pin.

My most productive field, like her own, was about the front of the hotel itself. In warm afternoons flies, beetles, moths and what not are known to drop out of the invisible, from nobody can tell where, upon the windows or the white clapboards of the house. Here, not once, but with something like regularity, insects have been captured, the like of which have never been seen elsewhere except in the West Indies or Mexico, in Greenland or among the Rocky Mountains. How such wanderers come, and why, are among the things that no man knoweth. Enough that they are known to come. And who could tell but one might have come for me? Here, at all events, was my golden opportunity. Let me not miss it. If by chance, therefore, the lady herself stepped inside for a minute or two, I hastened to take her place. Tourists by the dozen might be watching me curiously, or even derisively, my equanimity was undisturbed. Science is a shield. Vial in hand (my *vade-mecum* I called it, Latin being in the air), I walked along the platform, with my eyes upon the glass and the paint, and woe to the unlucky insect that was there taking the sun. The yawning mouth of a bottle was clapped over him, the world swam before his eyes, and long before he knew it he was on his way to be a specimen. Strange things happen to insects, though they are not the only ones who have found perdition in a bottle.

Sometimes I climbed the stairs to the upper floors of the observatory. No matter how high I went, the higher the better. In the warm hours of the day the air at the very top was almost a cloud of tiny wings. "Excelsior" is the insects' watchword. Once, in the upper room, I bottled carelessly a small black-and-white moth. Its appearance was ordinary enough; no doubt it was common; but it was an insect, and hit or miss I took it in. And in due course it went into the entomologist's hands with the rest of the catch. She emptied the vial, and passed an unexciting comment or two upon the few flies and beetles it contained; perhaps she remarked that one of them might be worth mounting—I do not remember precisely; it was a way she had of egging me on; but the next morning she said: "You didn't tell me anything about the lovely moth you took yesterday." I was obliged to stop and think. "Oh, that little black-and-white thing," I said. Yes, that was the one—"new to the summit." If I was not proud, then pride does not dwell in earthly minds. This, I confide, was not my only contribution to the fauna of our highest New England mountain; I seem to remember a short-winged beetle also; but the moth, being in the Lepidoptera, is my especial glory. I wish I could recall its name, that I might print it here for the reading of future generations.

With such pursuits did I improve the spare hours of my Mount Washington week. I have no thought of boasting. At least I would not seem to do so. It was little enough that I accomplished, or could hope to accomplish, hampered as I was by my ignorance. Probably I shall never have a beetle, much less a moth, named after me; but with that precious black-and-white rarity in mind I feel that even in the way of entomology I have not lived altogether in vain.

Scientific studies apart, the best hours of the week (after some spent along the carriage-road, resting here and there upon a boulder to enjoy the magnificent, ever-shifting prospect, and some—not hours, alas, but minutes—spent in eating the ambrosial, banana-savored, soul-satisfying berries of *Vaccinium coespitosum*)—my best hours, I say, were perhaps those of a certain wonderful evening. The air was warm, no breath stirring, the sky clear, and the half world below us, as we walked the hotel platform, lay covered with white clouds, on which the full moon was shining. The stillness, the mildness, the brightness, the sense of elevation, and the bewitching, unearthly scene, all this was like an evening in fairyland. For the time being, it is to be feared, even the rarest of moths would have seemed a matter of secondary importance. Such is the power of beauty. So truly was it born to make other things forgotten.

Logging the Forests

1893

The Vanishing Forests

From *Report of the New Hampshire Forestry Commission*

ONE OF THE GREATEST difficulties we have to encounter here in New Hampshire, in the effort to begin to take care of our mountain forests in some rational and practical way, is the fact that we have never had any real forestry in this country, anywhere, and therefore the whole subject is a matter of theory to our people. It is something to talk and write about, and to many minds it presents an attractive field for the invention of fantastic notions. We cannot point to any actual example of the practice of it in this country, and say, "It is like that." In European countries there are instances of it almost everywhere, and the young men from New Hampshire who traveled in France and Germany can see there exactly what forestry means, and how it is managed. It is a great disadvantage to have to describe anything of this kind without any accessible example to refer to as an object lesson or illustration. But there is at present no way of avoiding this inconvenience, and it is therefore all the more important that whoever writes for the public on this subject should be simple, definite, and plain in his method of treatment. This requirement has not always been regarded by writers on forestry subjects in this country, and there has been in consequence a considerable element of vagueness, unreality, and error in the popular idea of forestry.

But forestry is simply the management of wooded lands for profit, by treating the forest as a permanent crop. It is a branch or kind of agriculture; field culture in which trees are the crop produced; instead of corn or potatoes. Forestry is merely the art or method of handling or treating this crop, and the land on which it grows, in such a way that it will yield the best returns to the forest owner or manager, that is, that it shall be the most profitable. Because trees take so long to grow there can be no profit in forestry, can, indeed, be no forestry at all, except by keeping the land permanently wooded. Unlike most of our other crops, the forest—especially when planted by Nature, as all our forests have been—does not all mature or become ready for the harvest at the same time. Therefore, in real forestry, the crop is not all taken off at once. There are always some trees which are mature and ready to be cut, and every year those which have reached this condition should be carefully taken out, leaving the immature trees more room and a better chance to grow. If the mature trees are not cut they soon begin to decay and to decline in value. If this method of treatment is allowed a forest will go on improving for ages. It will produce more and more timber as the forest becomes older, and the quality of the product will steadily improve, because the soil of the forest is all the time growing richer and stronger. As in the case of every other product of the soil, the sensible forest grower chooses for this crop the land that appears the best adapted for its profitable production. He does not establish a forest on land that would yield a greater profit if used in growing corn or potatoes. This is about all there is of forestry that is essential or fundamental. Nature shows plainly to the people who have eyes and the power of thought, what land is suited to other crops, and what should be devoted to the growing of forests. There is no difficulty in knowing the difference here in New Hampshire. Our mountain lands are not susceptible of any other kind of agriculture than forest growth. This is the only profitable crop they will produce.

It would be hard to find a more wonderful instance of the complete adaptation of parts to each other and to the whole, of far-reaching relations, binding many separate interests and purposes together in a complex unity of result, than is shown in the dependence of all the arts of civilized life in New Hampshire upon the permanent and unimpaired performance of their natural functions and offices by the mountain forests of the State. Our situation at the present time is exactly this: We have not yet learned how to handle or manage our mountain forests in such a way as to allow them to continue to perform their natural and indispensable offices with unimpaired efficiency. Our methods of treatment have already resulted in a very considerable impairment and diminution of the efficiency of the mountain forests of the State, and it is plain that without some radical change in our management this impairment will be extended in a very destructive degree.

The first, or most obvious use or office of mountain forests is the production of timber. This constitutes the interest and value of these forests from the lumberman's point of view, and the profound importance of this

function is manifest in the fact that the permanent and abundant production of timber is necessary, not only to the comfort and convenience of
human beings inhabiting the earth, but also to their *existence* in a state of
civilization. It follows from these facts that the interest of the lumberman,
and all those who depend upon his business for the supply of timber, im-
peratively demands that forest conditions shall be permanently maintained on all the lands which will grow timber profitably, while they are
unsuited to the production of other crops. Self-interest on the part of the
lumberman, and of everybody else, requires this, but self-interest has not
been an enlightened or efficient guide in this instance. Up to the present
time, the lumberman's inadequate and short sighted way of looking at the
matter has prevailed entirely in the management of the mountain forests
of New Hampshire. No other idea of forest management has had a particle of influence on the treatment of the White Mountain forests. The
lumbermen have had full control in that magnificent forest region, with
no interference from any source whatever. The consequence is, that over a
large proportion of the whole region, they have permanently impaired the
value of this splendid property, and on some areas have entirely destroyed
its productive capacity forever.

The methods of lumbering, or cutting off the timber, and of the "handling" of the land after the butchery of the forest, which have been fol
lowed in some portions of the White Mountain region, have already been
fatally destructive of forest conditions on limited areas, and, if they were
generally applied, would in time bring about the entire extinction of the
lumber industry in all that territory, with every interest and investment
that depends upon it. The extirpation of the forest which has thus been
accomplished in a very short time in some small districts, is entirely un-
necessary. All the timber the region would ever have produced could have
been utilized without destroying forest conditions—or even impairing
their permanence—on a single square mile of the great mountain wilderness. There could be perpetual cutting, and everywhere the perpetual re-
production of the forest. This is the system already practiced by some of
the owners of large tracts of timber lands, especially by proprietors of wood
pulp manufactures, and if it had been generally adopted, with effective
safeguards against forest fires, there would, to-day, be no mountain forest
problem for the people of New Hampshire.

The treatment of the forests of the White Mountain region is not purely
or chiefly a matter of forestry in a special sense, with a broader meaning
than is usually attached to it in European usage. The peculiar character
and conformation of the White Mountain country, and its geographical

relation to the great centres of population of our Eastern States, render its forests much more important and valuable as essential features of the mountain scenery than as sources of supply for timber products. That is, the money value of the forests as scenery, if there were never another tree cut in the mountain region, would exceed the value of all the timber and timber products of every kind that the region would ever produce. Whatever may be the value and importance of the White Mountain forests as a source of supply for lumber, they are still more important and valuable as scenery; and we should so think of them, as the less is rightly to be subordinated to the greater.

But it is a remarkable and most interesting fact, that these two functions of the mountain forests, the production of timber for the market, and the adornment of the hills with a garment of perpetual beauty for the delight of our summer and autumn visitors, though distinct from each other, are not in the least degree, antagonistic when they are brought into true and right relations with each other. The scenery is the chief interest, the essential thing, and when it is so regarded, the preservation of the scenery involves and insures the perpetuity of the timber supply without impairment or diminution.

A strange misapprehension seems to possess the minds of many persons regarding the effect of the preservation of the scenery on the timber supply. They appear to think that if the lumber interests were subordinated to the scenery interest, the production of timber in northern New Hampshire would all die, or would immediately stop growing. On the contrary, as we have pointed out, if the scenery were regarded as the chief thing, and were properly cared for, the supply of timber would be perpetual, and it would steadily increase in quantity and improve in quality forever.

The people of New Hampshire are very far from having an adequate appreciation of the beauty and value of their own mountain scenery. This is because they do not know how peculiar and superior the scenery of the White Mountain region is, when compared with all other mountain scenery in our country. Whatever the Old World may have to show in the way of interesting and attractive scenery, there is no other region in the United States which in any considerable degree resembles this great possession of ours. The special interest of the White Mountain country consists in the great number of complete and beautiful landscapes contained in a small area. Nowhere else in our country can so many different, perfect, and interesting landscape pictures be found in a territory so limited in its entire aggregate extent. The White Mountain landscapes are extraordinarily beautiful. They have not the quality of grandeur, and it is an error to call our scenery grand; but grandeur is not restful, it is not a desirable quality for every-day companionship. The White Mountain landscapes are restful; they are satisfactory, in an eminent degree, to the people who love beautiful scenery. They are full of pleasant suggestion. Some of them have the element of dreamy softness and illusion which poets love, and which is so large a factor in the attractiveness and satisfactoriness of the finest mountain landscapes. This description does not apply to all the White Mountain landscapes now, but it did apply to them before the unthinking and regardless tree-fellers had invaded and laid waste these ancient sanctuaries of sylvan beauty and peace.

Another reason for our lack of appreciation of the value and attractiveness of our own scenery, is the fact that we who live among the hills have never experienced any need of the healthful and restorative influences of beautiful mountain scenery. Living here all year in the pure air of the country, or in our small towns, we have little perception of the peculiarly exhausted and devitalized condition which results from the crowded life of the cities. We do not know how people feel, nor what they need, after many months of living where they breathe each other's breath over and over again, till science itself is puzzled to find new names for their resulting maladies. We do not appreciate the value of our mountain scenery to the multitude of dwellers in the great towns; but we ought, at least, to have regard for the value to ourselves and our children of the revenues which our scenery brings to us from people who feel the need of it for themselves, and who appreciate its benefits so highly that they are willing to pay many millions of dollars every year for the opportunity of a few week's sojourn amid the freshness and beauty of our forest-clad hills.

Under the conditions of our modern life some such opportunity for summer rest, recreation, and change of place is of great importance to the people who live in the cities. It is already indispensable to many millions of such persons, and the number to whom the White Mountain region is naturally the most attractive and convenient summer resort in the world, is stupendous, and it is increasing every year. Our New Hampshire mountains are so near and so easily accessible to the great populations of Boston, New York, and Philadelphia, that the entire area of our mountain forest region is sure to be very soon required for their summer playground, if we take care of it and maintain its natural attractiveness. There is no other region of mountain scenery in the United States which is so nearly secure against all possible competition as the White Mountain region would be forever if the mountain forests were managed in a rational and practical way.

The White Mountain forest region should have been a perpetual source of inestimable benefits as a mountain summer resort, a region of infinite sylvan variety, beauty, and peace. What is it that the people of the cities need and desire when they seek a mountain region in summer? Let us use a little analysis here. First, they want contact with Nature, as the opposite of the too great obtrusiveness and pressure of the presence and action of other human beings upon them during the rest of the year. They want to be alone with Nature where she is interesting and beautiful.

In the early times of our country's history, when we had but a sparse population, which nearly all lived on farms or in small towns, summer vacations and excursions for rest, recreation, and the restoration of wasted energies, were not needed as they are now. But as our country has filled up and millions of our people have crowded into cities to live, there has arisen an absolute necessity for a change of conditions and methods of life in the hot season of the year for a great proportion of our whole population. People must get out of doors. They must lay aside business, and put off the burden of daily care for a while in order to be able to go on at all. It is not the impulse of poetical fancies, or of sentimental whims or caprices of any kind. It is a practical matter, a matter of the wisest and most necessary economy, of the economy of life itself, and of its highest forces.

Without such a pause in work, such a period of contact with Nature and the out-of-door world, as a means for the restoration of exhausted vitality, neither physical nor mental health can long be maintained. Life will not continue to be sane and efficient without an occasional visit to the sources of healing and strength in Nature's great sanitarium, the open air. It is true that there are multitudes of persons, especially of women, in our country, who never have such a vacation, for whom there never arrives "a lull in the hot race," to use Mr. Matthew Arnold's words, but they need it all the same; and it is a calamity, not only to them, but to all who are near them, that the hard conditions of their lives forbid their ever yielding to the imperative need for out-of-door rest and enjoyment.

Now unless there is to be a great and speedy change in the treatment of some portions of the White Mountain forests by the owners of them, the myriad's of people from the cities who have been coming year after year to this great mountain country of woods and waterfalls, and shaded, flashing streams, will soon begin to take down their maps of this region of their former unrestrained wandering and delight, and mark it here and there with big, black letters, "NO USE TO COME AGAIN." This great woodland heritage of the people is in danger of passing from them. Its beauty and delightsomeness are being gradually—and in some cases, rapidly—destroyed. In the old days visitors could wander where they pleased, and ever-varying beauty companioned their steps everywhere; and this power and freedom to go where they pleased without passing beyond the beauty and restfulness of the forest, was one of the chief sources of enjoyment for our summer guests, one of the principal attractions of the region for them. It is the wandering, the exploring, the going on, to "fresh woods and pastures new," which inspires "vital feelings of delight" in true lovers of the woods. Wordsworth's expression was chosen by a great poet's insight, and it describes perfectly the experience of hundreds of thousands of weary men and women in these abodes of beauty and freedom and peace in former days. The mountain forests gave them "vital feelings of delight."

But now, although when we look at it from a few miles away the forest still appears to be unbroken over a large portion of the White Mountain region, when we go about on foot, or drive along the roads, we find there has been almost everywhere a great deal of cutting, or where it has not yet begun, the lumbermen are, in most districts, preparing for extensive operations. This has already caused alarm among the hotel proprietors and their guests, as they note the vigor with which the slaughter of the forest is pushed forward in the vicinity of some of the great mountain houses.

Many persons from the large cities of our country, who long ago purchased sites for summer homes in the White Mountain region, and built houses on them which they have occupied every summer for many years, are complaining that the beautiful scenery which first attracted them to our State is being rapidly destroyed. They can, of course, protect their own grounds from the wood cutters, but with the great mountain slopes around them despoiled of their summer freshness, and the gorgeous autumnal robes of the hills changed to the debris and litter which the destroyers of the forest leave behind them over mile beyond mile of the mountain landscape, these owners of New Hampshire summer homes feel that the value of their investments here is very seriously impaired. The natural tendency or inclination of the friends of the earlier summer settlers in a beautiful mountain country to colonize around the homes of the pioneers everywhere, is, in this instance, most unfortunately interfered with, and to a great extent broken up.

All tourists remember the long and exquisite drives through various portions of the White Mountain forests in former years, the roads shaded and embosomed under a bower of greenery, mile after mile all the way. To what multitudes of people the enchanting coolness of these woods, and the murmurous music of their crystal waters, have given us rest and delight! Now, in many places, the scenery is ruined. Former visitors, remembering their delightful excursions, often start out to repeat them, but find that for a large part of the distance the woods along many of the roads have been cut off. The trunks of the white birches, which rose through the green leafage like slender shafts of silver, have been cut up into suitable lengths for the market, and the tops of the trees sprawl everywhere across the ground in most repulsive confusion and entanglement. In summer the sun glare is hot on the roads, and the air seems entirely changed. And yet the attractiveness of this region as a summer play-ground for the dwellers in the cities was its chief value to the State of New Hampshire. A considerable proportion of this value has already been destroyed, and what still remains of it is being diminished every year.

When we are weary with the life of men in the crowded cities it is not sympathy that we need from Nature. We do not want her to say that she pities us. It is her silent unconcern that heals and soothes us. The city people want the forest in summer; they wish to be able to feel the solitude of the woods around them whenever they choose to seek it. The mountains shorn of their forests would not have the slightest element of attraction remaining for the thronging thousands of summer tourists from the great towns. Nothing could be more repulsive to these seekers for rest and recreation in the enjoyment of sylvan beauty than the hideous tangle and disorder of tree tops which debases and smothers the mountain sides, and all their noble lines, in the track of the lumbermen. Every acre of our White Mountain region would have been needed in time if we had taken care of it. It would have amply repaid all expenditures required for making every part of it accessible by good and pleasant roads, and five or six million dollars which our people say they now receive from summer visitors would soon have been doubled again and again.

Then, too, we might have had some real forestry here in the State of New Hampshire, if we had been sufficiently advanced in the art of living, if we had had the interest in the public welfare, and the perception of our obligation to coming generations, which are necessary to the development and persistence of civilization. The entire White Mountain region should have been held permanently in the possession of the State. Then a real school of forestry could have been established somewhere in those great mountain forests, and young men could have trained in the knowledge and practice of this art, and they could have been employed in the care of the forests and woodlands of other portions of our country.

The timber could have been cut off as the trees matured, and, of course, should have been so cut off. Nothing could be more absurd, or farther from the truth, than the notion that under any system of forestry the timber would never be utilized, or the trees removed. Whenever a tree has come to its best estate it should be cut down and its wood applied to some useful purpose, so as to obtain its value, and in order to provide for a succession of generation of trees, and thus for the permanent life of the forest.

If the White Mountain forests had been thus intelligently managed and administered they would now have been for a long time yielding an increasing revenue to the people of the State. The whole population would have been greatly benefited by the reduction of taxation. Every man and woman in the State would have been richer to-day—would have had more of the means of subsistence, and of comfort and happiness, than at present. Every child in the state would have been born to a better inheritance, and into more favorable conditions than now. The mountain forests would have been better now than ever before, and they would have gone on increasing in value to the people of the State, with the increasing density of the population of our country in general, and on account of the exhaustion of the timber supply in regions fit for agriculture.

The White Mountain region is not fit for agriculture. In most of it, agriculture is impossible. No part of it is suitable for any other than forest conditions, and these should have been maintained forever. It is, indeed, impossible to disturb forest conditions there very extensively, or to remove the forests permanently, without destroying the region itself, and annihilating everything that makes it of any value. It is doubtful if an instance of more obvious and complete adaptation of an extensive region to a special and particular use can be found in the whole world. Nature made our great northern mountain territory for the permanent and everlasting growth of forests, and this sole and exclusive adaptation to a most important and necessary function should have been recognized and respected.

May 1895

Pullman, New Hampshire: A Lumber Camp

George H. Moses

From *The Granite Monthly*

PULLMAN, NEW HAMPSHIRE — you may not find it on your map; you may not mail a letter to that address and have it delivered; no enterprising scalper may sell you a reduced rate railroad ticket to that destination; yet it exists and there is some basis of fact for my fancy in thus titling the lumber town of Lincoln on the East Branch of the Pemigewasset.

On the first of September, 1892, the spot where now this village stands was a dense and virgin forest, which, in common with nearly all the country within sight from any adjacent coign of vantage, had just come into the possession of Messrs. J. E. Henry & Sons, whose gigantic lumber operations in the Zealand valley had reduced the supply of "raw material" there and had driven them to seek newer and more original fields. The title under which the Messrs. Henry took possession of the territory was at the time, and is now, the largest single transfer of forested property recorded in any New Hampshire registry, and the sum involved amounted to the half million mark, while the tract which changed hands aggregated approximately, one hundred thousand acres. This, together with the Messrs. Henry's former holdings, which lie contiguous and just to the north, gave them undisputed sway over nearly one hundred and twenty thousand acres of solid spruce forest which a newspaper writer has fairly characterized as "The Grand Duchy of Lincoln."

But this is digression. On the first of September, 1892, let me repeat, where now stands the lumber town of Lincoln was a dense, virgin forest.

A year later the village of Lincoln with school, store, dwellings, shops, and mills was in visible evidence to all. It had sprung up almost in a night through the boundless energy and unflagging courage of its owners, who in the face of a steadily falling market deepened their investment and increased their risk.

The owners of this Pullman of ours knew that they must have a railroad to make their village a success—and so they built one, afterward selling it to the Concord & Montreal, who now operate the mile and a half of track from North Woodstock to Lincoln. From Lincoln the East Branch & Lincoln railroad has been built now a distance of nearly ten miles into the woods. This road is owned by the Messrs. Henry, and is utilized for the transportation of lumber and supplies, though in summer excursion parties of summer boarders visiting the loggers' camps are frequent. For solidity of construction this railroad is the equal of any in the state if not in New England, and its equipment is of the most powerful and superb quality, for modern lumbering demands only the best.

At the village there is an air of the utmost vivacity. Across from the tiny station is the longest saw mill in New England, which when both sides are running with night and day gangs makes a daily record of something like two hundred thousand feet of sawn lumber. Scarcely a hand's breadth on the other side stands the car shop, where the dwarfish lumber cars are manufactured and repaired. Next door to that stands the smithy where the horses are shod, the car iron-work furnished, and the company jobbing done. Next to that comes the establishment of the company harness maker, and across the street from them all is the office, store, and postoffice, where one may mail a letter, telegraph a friend, secure a railroad pass over the L. & E. B., or buy anything from a goose-yoke to a second-hand pulpit.

These buildings line either side of the short street leading from the station to the main thoroughfare of the village, Sawdust Boulevard, so called from its paving, which is entirely of pungent spruce sawdust.

This avenue in one sense reminds one of the czar's railroad. You will remember how when a line was projected from Moscow to St. Petersburg the engineers brought a map to the emperor and asked him to designate the cities and towns on the way through which he wished the road to pass. Laying a rule upon the map, the czar drew a straight line from Moscow to St. Petersburg, "Build it there," he said. So of this avenue. Desiring to tap this country road at the most convenient point and also to secure entrance to their village by wagon, the Henrys cut a road from Lincoln to North Woodstock, straight as a die, directly through the woods, emerging upon the highway near the Deer Park Hotel. Along the further extremity of this

J. E. Henry's paper mill in Lincoln as photographed in 1898.

road, and facing the village of Lincoln, are ranged the cottages which have been erected for the mill men and mechanics.

Architecturally these are not imposing. Artistically they are not appealing. The garish ochre and umber of their colorings are strongly offensive on a hot summer's day. But they serve their purpose: they shelter the workmen of our Pullman, and yield the owners a handsome return on their cost.

The village of Lincoln is the outgrowth of their present system of lumber manufacture. It is not a perfect community by any means, yet it is superior in all its managerial features. This is a necessary fact because the town is designed to supply needs which were purely managerial. When the Messrs. Henry came into the possession of their present forest holdings they faced contingencies of which the lumber men of New Hampshire had known nothing, and to meet the demand at every point they were in fact compelled to create the village of Lincoln. The mountain could not go to Mahomet in this case; Mahomet could not go to the mountain; so he heaped up a mountain of his own. The government and discipline are, as one might suppose, intensely paternal and the administration is most rigid. The old town of Lincoln, what there is of it, lies off to the west from "The Grand Duchy," and the population is aligned along the highway leading northward to the Franconia Notch. The selectmen and other town officials are therefore chosen from among the older inhabitants, and "The Grand Duchy" is left almost wholly to its own devices, the Grand Dukes making and enforcing whatever regulations they deem necessary to the peace and dignity of their grand ducal estate. Prohibition is the rule in our Pullman, and it does prohibit. No man eats unless he works, on the true theory of Captain John Smith, and the lords of the realm themselves are most exemplary in their obedience. The labor accomplished daily by the Henrys, father and sons, comes nothing short of Herculean. "The old man" Henry, as he is known from the Pemigewasset to the St. Lawrence, has led a life of almost unremitting toil, and the dignity of labor is a family tenet with him. What he has accomplished by way of accumulated lands and fortunes is the result of his personal efforts and is not likely to diminish from lack of attention.

The real extent of the Grand Duchy of Lincoln is by no means indicated by its busy metropolis and may be approximated only by a trip over the railroad which has pushed its way up the East Branch to the junction of the Hancock Branch and is now winding up this latter stream, with a total length of nearly ten miles. Almost every rod of the way is busy. Here is a smaller mill set down on a spur where the surplus of the first is con-

Logging the East Branch country in 1904.

sumed, there are the charcoal kilns where with commendable economy a portion of the forest by-product is utilized, yonder is a "camp" where the men live, on this side is a stable sheltering the horses employed on the slopes, and all along are the landings with the worn trail leading away up on the mountain sides whence comes the almost constant ring of the axe, the occasional crash of the falling spruce, and the musical tingle of the team-bells as they make their way up and down. To carry on the operations of this plant requires the services of hundreds of men and animals and thousands of capital must be kept in almost continuous circulation as wage-money, for repairs, in buildings, in restocking, and for the thousand and one things which every day crop out in a business of such magnitude. And with the keenness of the present competition in the lumber market nothing but the highest degree of administrative capacity, with practically unlimited credit, and a close knowledge of men and affairs. These the owners are able to supply in such full measure that it cannot be charged to their inability to handle it that they have abandoned the manufacturing end of the work and, leasing their mills, content themselves with selling logs, cordwood, and charcoal.

The opportunities which the owners of this property possess are numberless in almost every direction, but I need not enumerate them all. When one recalls that the number of hands employed in this New Hampshire Pullman are many times as numerous as the entire body of original inhabitants and that they are dependent for everything upon the inclinations of the owners of the village, the possibilities by way of politics are highly suggestive. And when one thinks of the agitation for the preservation of the forests of the White Mountain region among whose foothills this forest lies, there is suggested the boundless opportunity which the Messrs. Henry have of demonstrating how to use and at the same time to preserve the valuable growth.

In politics the Grand Dukes of Lincoln are making no move, but in forestry they are doing something. At the present rate of cutting it will take the axemen thirty years to cover the entire tract of one hundred and twenty thousand acres. In other words they cannot expect a second crop in less than thirty years, an interval of ample duration to enable a profitable second harvesting, provided the first crop has been removed with sufficient discretion as to the choice of trees to be felled and care in the manner of felling them. The first element already enters into the proprietor's calculations and their intention is expressed to remove no tree of less than twelve inches in diameter at the stump. The second element is, I fear, entirely wanting, for, though loggers seek the forest opening for a tree to fall into, they are strangely careless of the character of the growth over which they let the victim fall. The restriction as to size is, however, of prime importance. In partial compensation for the reduced present profit the charcoal kiln has been set up, an apparatus which meets the foresters' liveliest approbation so long as its use is confined to legitimate channels and its capacious maw swallows up nothing but the tops and limbs which are too often left upon the ground in the lumbered forest to decay and become a menace in the presence of the ever recurring fear of fire. These are but feeble steps toward that pattern of perfection which our New Hampshire Pullman might become in the eyes of American lumbermen, but since they are in the right direction they deserve credit.

James Everell Henry

J. E. Henry II

From *An Account of the Life of James Everell Henry I and His Town of Lincoln, N.H.*

Fifty years after the death of White Mountain lumber baron James Everell Henry (on April 19, 1912), James E. Henry II of Clearwater, Florida, privately published a history of his grandfather's life and times in New Hampshire. A portion of that history is featured here. The elder Henry, whose logging practices earned him the title "wood butcher," probably had more impact on the eventual preservation of the White Mountains than any individual of his era. The following excerpt tells of Henry's "invasion" of the pristine New Zealand Valley in the 1880s and of his later move to Lincoln, where he would establish himself as the king of New Hampshire lumbermen.

IT WAS AT FABYANS that Grandfather had a store and office when he first began operating in the White Mountains, 40 miles from Woodsville, and it was there that my father, George, and my uncle, John, began to help with the business, the latter, mostly in the office, writing letters for grandfather, and tending to the store. Grandfather hated to write letters, so Uncle John once said, and Grandma told me that he was a very bad speller.

Mount Washington rears its 6,228 ft. head a few miles east of Fabyans, and the famous Mt. Washington Hotel, built in the early 1900s, near the Base Station of the cog railroad to the Summit, is located at what is called Bretton Woods (why that name I do not know). The building on the main highway that was, and probably still is, the Caddy House for the Bretton Woods Golf Course, was once the stable for the teams of horses with which the logs were hauled to the mill when Grandfather logged that area.

I believe that Charles Joy looked after the mill at Zealand and that A. T. Baldwin was the partner who attended to the Woodsville end of business, or maybe he was just a silent partner, I don't know which. Of course, Grandfather being the "senior partner" superintended the business operations as a whole. When the timber southeast of Fabyans was exhausted, work was begun on the Zealand Valley stand a bit to the southwest and logs were brought to the mill by some 30 teams of horses. Also, at Zealand from the earliest days there were kilns, where the hardwood that was cut, was turned into charcoal, replaced nowadays to a great extent by bituminous coal. It was only the soft wood, mostly spruce and hemlock, that was sawed into lumber.

In the early years of logging in the forest of the United States there was no idea of selective cutting to preserve our woodlands, such as is practiced nowadays, where only the mature trees are cut and the younger ones left to complete their growth, but everything was cut that was of a size to be used, thus leaving the mountains and valleys denuded of their primeval beauty. All that remained after a logging operation was a tangle of "slash," meaning the branches and tops of the trees that had been trimmed off before the logs were taken to the sawmill, and which provided excellent fuel for the matches of careless hunters and fishermen or a bolt of lightning, so that not only was the slash burned up, but the fire would run on into standing timber and hundreds of acres would be burned over and left valueless. Forest fire was, in dry summers, the constant worry of my father thru the years, as he had seen when a young man the destruction caused by such a holocaust in this same Zealand Notch region in 1888, when forest fire destroyed some 12,000 acres of standing timber. Twenty-five years later I saw the destruction left by that conflagration, which was still just a wasteland of desolation and second growth bushes, valueless except for wild blueberries, which the bears like anyway.

It may be well to explain how charcoal, mentioned above, was made, as best I can remember it, since there were such charcoal kilns in Lincoln when I was a small boy. They were made of brick and were in a long narrow building, with small rooms the whole length of it, made by brick partitions inside built from front to back. The kilns near Lincoln, about two miles up the logging railroad from town, were built on a hillside with a railroad siding at the back from which the loads of 4-foot pieces of hardwood could be transferred through openings at the top of the kilns, to be stacked inside on a sort of grating so that a fire could be built underneath, access to which was through cast iron doors located at ground level at the front. There was practically no air allowed to enter the kiln, as that would

James Everell Henry

have encouraged rapid combustion, with the result that the stacked wood was charred, not burned, and thus became charcoal, which brought a good price in those early days at Zealand. The charcoal kilns were profitably operated also for the first few years at Lincoln.

The lumber and charcoal business at Zealand prospered and a small settlement came into being there. Of course, the company store and office had to be transferred to Zealand and, tired of so much commuting to Woodsville, Grandfather built a house there for his family and the move to the new house was made in 1882. The house was situated between two lines of railroad, the Portland and Ogdensburg (afterward called the Maine Central), which . . . had been built up through Crawford Notch in 1875. The other line was, I believe, the Boston, Concord and Montreal. It was quite handy to be so near two railway lines, and Uncle Charles went to school at Twin Mountain by train each morning and back in the afternoon. . . .

Grandfather took time out from his business activities to celebrate with Grandma on April 5, 1879, their twenty-fifth wedding anniversary with gifts of silver and an evening of festivities, but for which, you may be sure, Grandma herself, with the help of Katie McCarthy, did the "catering." The evening was a success and was a red letter day in Grandma's life, and maybe Grandfather's also. Little did they think that they would also celebrate a Golden Wedding later in Lincoln.

When the store and office were moved to Zealand, Uncle John continued the work he had done at Fabyans, and my father was still busy with the outside activities, while also pinch-hitting as a harness maker, when necessary, as there was a lot of leather work needed to keep up the equipment of so many logging teams. In 1880 Grandfather and A. T. Baldwin bought the interest of Charles Joy, and the firm name became Henry & Baldwin, and then in 1882 Grandfather bought Baldwin's interest, so, when he moved to Zealand to live, he had become the sole owner of the business, which became in 1891, the J. E. Henry & Sons Co. An additional company was formed later, when paper began to be manufactured in Lincoln, which was called the Henry Paper Co., but the J. E. Henry & Sons Co. was still active till Lincoln and both businesses were sold in August 1917.

I have spoken of Tintah, Minnesota, so right here I'd better tell more about that phase of Grandfather's life. Late in the 1870s wheat farming in the prairie states was booming and there had been some bumper crops. Therefore, Grandfather and his partners decided to buy some land in western Minnesota. Several sections of land were bought at what was to be the town of Tintah (a section of 640 acres or one square mile) and Grandfather and Grandma went out there for three summers, 1880–81–82, I believe. This was at the time that Grandfather was buying out his partners and apparently he thought he might get some extra cash by raising wheat, but it was not a successful venture, as poor wheat years began at just that time. Ida and Hattie and their husbands had moved to Tintah to help, so Grandfather made a deal with the young couples to sell his holdings to them for $5,000 apiece, probably not cash, with the understanding that since he was offering them such a bargain, so much land at such a low price, they must expect nothing from him in the way of an inheritance, and he stuck to that agreement, unfair as it seems.

Here is a story about Grandma and her feeling about the would-be settlers of the far west, as she saw them when they went through Tintah with their wagons and household goods. One day when my Cousin Kate, as a child, was "rhapsodizing" (Kate's own expression) about the noble pioneers and their covered wagons, Grandma observed with one of her characteristic 'Hmphs,' "I saw pioneers aplenty and not one was worth a tinker's darn." I imagine there were some sorry, misfit specimens among them and those are the ones Grandma meant, as there were many who really became the builders of the west.

My own father spent at least one summer at Tintah, helping during those three years, and one story he used to tell me about an experience he had may prove amusing here. It was a frontier town, and looked like it even in 1905, when I saw it with ten-year-old eyes, as the store fronts resembled the ones with which movies and TV westerns have made later generations familiar. Father, then about nineteen years old, had read about gun-toting cowboys and pioneers, and wishing to emulate them, bought a revolver, which he wore when riding horseback, and tried practicing fast draws of his weapon. One Sunday, when work was not in order, he was taking a ride across the seemingly endless prairie, flat as a board for miles in every direction, with only here and there a small group of farm buildings and a few trees to break the monotony. In those days he said one often saw the bleached bones of some of the countless thousands of American bison, commonly called buffalo, which had been slaughtered, some for meat, but most of them for their hides, scattered over the plains. I might add that tons and tons of these bones were later shipped East to be calcined. People needing fuel for their cooking fires, and in the absence of firewood, were accustomed to utilize for the purpose, what was called "buffalo chips," but which was actually the dried excrement of the bison herds. That Sunday, looking for "adventure," Father saw what resembled a prairie wolf, and gave chase on his horse, but however fast he rode he could never seem to get near enough for a shot. This continued for some distance when Father noticed a settler's shack not far ahead and much to his surprise the wolf seemed to be heading for it. As he got nearer he began to realize that maybe his fleet quarry was not a wolf after all, but a dog, and he was sure of it when it went directly to the house and sat down quietly by the door with as near a grin on his face as a dog can have. By that time the farmer came to see what was afoot and so Father, feeling very sheepish, rode meekly up and asked the direction of Tintah, naturally not saying anything about the dog.

After that rather long transgression, to return to Zealand. When Grandfather bought Baldwin's interest in the company, he decided it would be better in every way to haul logs to the mill by means of a railroad, so a route was surveyed through Zealand Notch and construction started in the early 1880s. The only earth-moving equipment in those days consisted of men and wheelbarrows or horses and dumpcarts, the earth being dug out by hand with picks and shovels, and roots being cut by grub hoes. Dynamite was used to blast ledges and rocks, of course. Part of the railroad right-of-way was literally hewn out of the rocky flank of Whiteface [actually Whitewall] Mountain by these means. Trestles had to be built in many places to bridge mountain streams, but in spite of the difficulties, the railroad grew apace and began to be used about 1883.

The first locomotives used were an old Pony No. 1, brought from Whitefield and Jefferson R.R., a nearby short line, and a used Boston, Concord and Montreal engine which Grandfather named the "Tintah." These were later discarded, some time after the first new one, a 25-ton Baldwin, made in 1886 and purchased from the Baldwin Locomotive Works of Philadelphia, and named the "J. E. Henry No. 1," was put into service. The next two were also Baldwins, weighing 35 tons each. They all were, of course, wood-burning locomotives, having the tall, flaring-at-the-top smokestacks, with screens, which were supposed to catch the sparks. The rails used on the Zealand Valley R.R. were of wrought iron, weighing 30 lbs. to the yard, laid 4 feet, 8½ inches apart, called Standard Gauge. The rails used later at Lincoln weighed 60 lb. to the yard, as the 30 lb. had been found to be too light.

COURTESY DAVID SUNDMAN

An East Branch and Lincoln logging train passes
over a wooden trestle with a full load of timber.

During these years Grandfather had had some dealings with a man named George Van Dyke, the head of the Connecticut Lumber Co., and in 1885 Van Dyke leased the Zealand mill for five years, with a J. H. Locke as manager for him. Grandfather was to supply the logs for the mill via his new railroad. Not only dimension lumber was sawed out at the mill, but also lath and box boards. It must not be forgotten that the charcoal kilns were also producing a very saleable product all this time. And when the logs were being drawn to the mill by horses, the manure from the stables was sold by the carload for fertilizer, so nothing that promised a profit was overlooked. It might be well to add here that after the railroad was in operation, or about that time, Grandfather obtained a charter to extend the Zealand Valley R.R. southwest through the mountains to connect with the Pemigewasset Valley R.R., which ended at that time at North Woodstock. That project, however, was never completed, although the logging railroad, started in 1892 from Lincoln, after the company moved there, eventually was built to within a few miles of the old right of way of the Zealand Valley R.R., near what was called Shoal Pond, where the fire of 1888 had destroyed so much timber.

During these busy years Zealand had grown to quite a good-sized village and need was felt for a school for the children of the men employed in the woods and in the mill, so a public subscription was taken up and a small building erected for the purpose, Grandfather doubtless standing a large part of the expense. Then a teacher was needed and my mother, then Bertha Sarah Cowen, about 17 years old and just out of Plymouth (N.H.) Normal School was hired. (I wish I knew how much salary she received.) Now whether she and my father, George Henry, were interested in each other before that time, I very much doubt, but being second cousins, they did know one another, anyway. However, "romance bloomed" and on Grandfather's 60th birthday, April 21, 1891, they were married, and were always very happy and companionable during their years together before Mother's untimely death at the age of 37. I believe that Mother continued to teach at the Zealand School till the move to Lincoln was made in August, 1892.

The logging and mill business was highly successful for Grandfather, and Van Dyke renewed his lease of the mill in 1890, so "J. E.," as Grandfather had begun to be called (but not to his face), decided to buy, with George Van Dyke, the thousands of acres of virgin timber south of the Zealand Valley holdings, in the township of Lincoln. Grandfather, with Father and Uncle John, had once cruised this timber when the idea of acquiring was being turned over in his mind. I might explain that "cruising timber" means going through the standing trees systematically on foot and estimating the quality and quantity of logs available. It was a sketchy cruise that they made, but they saw enough to realize that purchase of the property would be well worth while, so about 1890 Grandfather and Van Dyke bought the tract, amounting to about 100,000 acres, for around $500,000. Of course, they went into debt for it, but they knew that the value was there and more too. Van Dyke wanted to hold it for resale, but Grandfather wanted to log it, so he made a deal with Van Dyke, and purchased the latter's interest early in 1892.

Grandfather's plan was that J. E. Henry & Sons Co. would move all their men and equipment over the rather primitive highways from Zealand south to Lincoln, going down through Franconia Notch by the "Old Man of the Mountain," the "Great Stone Face" of Hawthorne's tale, commonly called the Profile. It was a distance of some 25 miles, the roundabout route they had to travel, and in the days of only horse-drawn vehicles, was indeed quite a project. . . .

I think I can best give an idea of [the expedition from Zealand] by quoting the words of Jim Doherty, one of its members, as told to Robert Stanley, Editor of the Pycolog (Parker-Young Co. log) and published in the August, 1921 issue.

"That day in August, 1892, we drove over from the other side, down thru the Notch. There was quite a party of us. Mr. Henry and his sons, George, John, and Charley, Jim Ward. Jim Boyle, and his sons, Henry, Billy, Joe, Abe, Jack and Charley, and myself and perhaps some others whom I don't remember now. Then there was the women folks and the children." (There was also Louis, another Boyle boy, whom Jim forgot to mention.)

"When we got to Lincoln we found only four farmhouses, the Dearborn Place, the Parker Place, and the two Pollard farmhouses. These were located on the 'Back Road' and they are still standing with the exception of the Parker House. . . . What is now the village of Lincoln was then all woods. Main Street, Church Street, School Street, and the mill site were all cleared out of the forest. There was a small field in front of Mrs. J. E. Henry's house, extending from where the bungalow now stands as far as the 'Clothespin', but everything else was woods—nothing but standing timber and lots of that.

"Well the day after we got here we all went to work clearing land, building houses, and putting in the railroad. Jim Ward was woods boss, and Jim Boyle was section boss [of the railroad] and 'Old J. E.' was boss of us all. We all went to work at six o'clock in the morning and we worked till six o'clock at night, and when the night came we knew we had been busy. Pay brought us from $22 to $24 a month, besides our board.

"During the fall we had 100 to 150 men working and by winter we had finished six houses, a store, a barn, a blacksmith shop and a harness shop. Besides that we had cleared a lot of land, and made a start on the railroad, so that by March, two miles of track was finished and the logs started rolling into Lincoln. Then a portable saw mill was set up and the lumber sawed for more houses, which were built along Main Street, and for the big sawmill which in a few more months was completed and turning out a hundred thousand feet a day of sawed timber.

"During those first months the women and children stayed in the farmhouses and the rest of us stayed in tents or any other place we could find. The 'Old Man Himself' slept on a mattress on the floor of the harness shop. We had plenty to eat, much of the food being shipped in from the outside.

"It was a hard winter, that first one—four or five feet of snow and lots of cold weather. The houses were little more than shacks, but we were all packed in so tight that everyone managed to keep warm. There were no electrical lights and but a few of the conveniences which we now have, but everybody was happy, everybody was busy, and there wasn't much grumbling. They were great old days."

July 4, 1900

The Boa Constrictor of
the White Mountains, or
the Worst "Trust"
in the World

Rev. John E. Johnson

WHAT IS IT? The New Hampshire Land Company.

Where is it? Up among the granite hills of that state.

What is its object? To deforest and depopulate the region lying around the head waters of the Merrimack river in the heart of the White Mountains.

Its history and *modus operandi?* In the early days of the company it was allowed to acquire for a song all the public lands thereabouts, and later to "take over" all tax-titles, until finally there was no considerable tracts in that vicinity which it did not own.

It is not necessary to explain the process by which, after a long period of dormancy, the stock of the company passed into the hands of one man for next to nothing.

This was the first stage of the concern's career.

The next step was also a process of "refrigeration," and is still going on. It consisted of getting rid of the native population, a hardy stock, who had clung to the home wood lots belonging to the rough areas which they called their farms—for they were more lumbermen that agriculturalists. These must need be driven out to make way for deforesting operations on a large scale.

The method adopted was a very simple one—they were starved out.

The company refused to sell them any land. The farmers, exhausting their limited tracts of woodland and unable to buy more at any price, gradually found themselves without logs for their local mills—and almost every farmer had one.[1] Their sons, robbed of their winter employment, took no longer to the woods but to the cities, leaving the old folks to fall slowly but surely into the clutches of the company which took their farms from them or their heirs, in most cases for a dollar or two an acre. This process is now going on and may be seen in all its stages from valleys where it has just begun to those out of which the entire population has been driven.[2]

The land is thus made ready for the professional lumberman who purchases it in tracts of not less than 10,000 acres and begins operations; whose last terms are often written in charcoal. It frequently happens, however, that, owing to misrepresentations as to the amount of timber on them, the denuded tracts fall back, through two or three bankruptcies, into the hands of the company, which thereby succeeds in skinning not only the land but the lumbermen, who are its bitterest enemies.

The last move will doubtless be to get a bill through the state legislature to purchase these deforested areas for a public reservation at a price ten times as great as that originally paid for the lumber lots.

This expelled native population is displaced for a few years by sturdy French Canadian wood choppers, a number of whom settle down upon any of the old farms that can be captured, and the rest return to the Province of Quebec with their hard earned savings.

In this way the heart of the old granite state is being eaten out, or the

1. It is related that when the news of Bunker Hill was brought to John Stark, he was in the saw mill on his farm, lower down on the Merrimack where he now lies buried. (Has he turned in his grave?)

2. Take for a single instance the old Gordon mill up Moosilauke brook just above the Agassiz Basin two miles from the village of North Woodstock Besides the Gordons there were three or four other farmers that depended upon it. Monroe Gordon built that mill many years ago. It is now for sale for fire wood, or soon will be; the great family of boys scattered from here to the Indian Territory; his and the other farms trembling in the scales of the Land Company—Go up Thornton Gore and see the ruined farm houses and ask for the old mills up there. That beautiful Alpine valley is almost ready for the lumbermen.

Monroe Gordon was a specimen man of these mountains, of gigantic stature and Herculean strength, as upright morally as he was physically. One quarter of his blood in his veins might have been traced to Passaconaway and the other three quarters to John Stark. He fell last winter to the earth and now lies stretched along it like one of the few surviving "first growths" of our fast fading forests. The last boy who has stayed at home "to take care of the old man" may now sell out to the Company and leave for parts unknown. (Could he be blamed if he first carried his father's bones over the state line into Canada and buried them there?)

blood in its veins displaced with that of a race inimical to the traditions of the first settlers.

Summer visitors to this section of the White Mountains have noticed the many deserted farms and dilapidated buildings and have wondered at such scenes, not dreaming that the cause was to be found in the operations of a company *chartered to do it*; that this desolation was due to the gradual tightening of the coils of a boa constrictor *legalized* to crush the human life out of these regions, preparatory to stripping them of their forests; for depopulation here is not due to the causes which have led to the abandonment of farms elsewhere in the state. The inhabitants of this section never depended exclusively upon the scant returns from their rough farms for a living but rather upon their winter's work in the woods, a dependence that never would have been exhausted had they been left in possession, since their methods were those which are now advocated by scientific forestry. The farmer felled some of the largest trees in the woods every winter and hauling them out endwise injured nothing but rather left the rest better for it. His successor, the professional lumberman, cuts everything, rolls it down the mountain, crushing the saplings, and not content with that, often burns the refuse for charcoal. The Land Company has boasted that extensive lumber operations never could have been undertaken in this section without its assistance in preparing the way—an assistance which in one instance they say involved the preliminary acquisition of sixty different titles.

This White Mountain wilderness is the last considerable one in New Hampshire, the tide of agricultural improvement having long ago surged around it and swept northward leaving untouched, until the Land Company could get in its preliminary work upon it, this grand natural park out of whose heart gushes the Merrimack, which flows the whole length of the state and is the main artery of its economic life. This region is unrivalled for natural beauty this side of the Rockies, and may well be called the Switzerland of America.

The tide of travel to it for health and recreation is an ever increasing one, the governor of New Hampshire in a recent message estimating the annual expenditure of tourists to it at over five million dollars. In view of this fact and the further one that the Merrimack is gradually dwindling, to the great detriment of the manufactories that line its banks, it is amazing that the process of denuding this upper region of its forests in the most wasteful manner has not been arrested, or at least hindered, long ago, and it probably would have been but for the fact that the whole business is largely in the hands of an unscrupulous and merciless corporation—a

Trust of the most concentrated, ruthless and soulless character, which is bent on reducing the entire section to a blackened, hideous, howling wilderness.

Nor does the baleful influence of this typical trust stop here. Not content to go its own gait in its unhindered destruction of the forests, it puts its veto on all enterprises of every description in any region where it happens to be the largest land owner, on the ground that it is the majority and therefore sovereign. It hinders, for instance, in every possible way the summer boarding house business in which some of the natives have taken refuge. No roads are allowed to be opened through the company's lands to points of interest, such as waterfalls, lakes, etc., (and it owns in many neighborhoods all but the fringes of the streams and the village sites). Seekers after health and recreation are repelled and even driven away; deserted farms, with no lumber on them, are "bid up" against sons of the state who seriously accept and would gladly act on the widely circulated advertisements and invitations of public officials at the capital and try to purchase them for summer homes. If the individual competitor succeeds in capturing a mountain eyrie of a few acres and, camping out on it, invites tired out humanity (teachers, preachers, students, artists, *et id omne genus*) to come and share it with him he can never add to it for love nor money; on the other hand this company does not hesitate to buy a cordon around him, cut him off from the highway and by and by perhaps turn him over to a lumberman who will smoke him out unless he leaves. No physician can hope to purchase a site for a sanitarium from this company, which may partly explain the fact that there are at least six in the mountains of Pennsylvania alone. No hotel keeper, as experience has repeatedly shown, can enlarge his holdings, square a lot, or buy an acre of connecting land, no matter how wild and useless it may be, from this company. The answer is always at last, "We sell only in lots of not less than 10,000 acres and to lumbermen." Very recently a growing village in the heart of this region, threatened with typhoid fever and the loss of its rapidly increasing summer business, applied to the legislature for a charter for a waterworks which was reasonably sure to pay its way from the beginning but the land company opposed the application by means that can easily be imagined. What chance would a backwood community stand against such a trust before any legislature in the country? The opposition in this case was based on the fact that the company owned all of the real estate in town with the exception of a comparatively few acres and might suffer an increase in its tax rate if the waterworks failed to be self supporting. (The entire cost of the enterprise was $13,000 and the village which already had an opera house and many large hotels was a rapidly growing summer resort.) The only way out of this threatening alternative of death or desertion was at last found in an appeal to the railroad company, whose authority in that section of the state is the only one that is feared or effective and which ordered its attorney to withdraw its cooperation from the Land Company and give it to the town. (The more souls there are in a corporation the less likely it is to be soulless.) The interests of the railroad are permanently identified with those of the regions through which it runs, but this Land Company was organized expressly to ravage and lay waste the sections in which it operates, and is one of the most merciless and unadulterated despotisms imaginable. Its official head often talks about selling a whole town to a pulp company without any allusion whatever to its human population, as though they were so many serfs or slaves and went with the land as a matter of course—like a Southern plantation before the war—or worse still, as though they went with the wood for pulp.

Various individuals and organizations have applied to this corporation from time to time in the name of health, recreation, public interests and individual rights, but in vain. The final answer, after no end of palaver, is always an irrelevant and incomprehensible jumble, in letters, magazine articles and forestry reports (*sic*) made up of boastings about having facilitated great lumber operations that could never have gotten under way without them, and on the other hand, of never having cut a tree themselves.

The history of this trust furnishes one of the strongest arguments for the Single Tax law that could be adduced. Some trusts have been said to have their public advantages, but this one is an ideal infamy, an unalloyed outrage upon the rights of everybody without one single consideration to recommend it. Is there no way of abolishing or even regulating such a public nuisance? Has any state a right to charter a company to suck its own life out? And what is a state anyway? Is it a corrupt legislature steered by a Land Company which actually exclaims through its executive officer and owner, "I am the state?"

Can there be any wonder that Socialism, Henry George's land philosophy and the war on Trusts are rapidly coming to the front as political issues? It was such intolerable outrages upon the rights of the people in the name of the law that brought on the French Revolution, and they now threaten to bring on a new American Revolution that will free the bone and sinew of the land from the grinding despotism of Trusts and Corporations. Do the people exist for the laws or the laws for the people?

The "Forest Cantons" are the richest of any of the cantons in Switzerland for the reason that the woodlands there belong to the public; and one will frequently hear how much a town got for wood in a certain year. The "Mir," of Commune, in Russia holds all unimproved lands in common. Nowhere in the world perhaps, outside of this boasted land of the liberty, will you find a population abandoned by its rulers to such a remorseless despotism as this vampire of the White Mountains, the New Hampshire Land Company.

If Trusts and Corporations like this one can be legally intrenched under the protection of our Constitution, then the victims of them may exclaim with Madam Roland, "O, Liberty, what crimes are committed in thy name!" Life where they are is for common people a veritable Reign of Terror in the name of Freedom.

The writer of this paper has been for many years a missionary in the White Mountains, under a license from the Episcopal Bishop of New Hampshire, and the statements herein made have been either matters of his own personal experience and observations or have come to him directly from his friends and neighbors, and he will welcome any provocation which will afford him an opportunity to substantiate and supplement them.

What is the use of trying to accomplish anything in any philanthropic or public-spirited way, to say nothing about morality and religion, where the material and political conditions are so appalling? How can you expect people to be honest or virtuous when they are robbed of all collateral means of making a living on their rocky farms and jammed down on to a level of squalor little better than that of their cattle, their forests taken from them and the price of hemlock boards jumped from six or seven dollars a thousand up to seventeen? How can they build cheap boarding houses to save themselves? What wonder then that their houses and barns are dilapidated, and their morals also?

Governor Rollins sometime ago called attention to the moral degeneration of many rural regions in the state, but he failed to point out the fact that such degeneration is always associated with poverty and unfavorable physical conditions. What is the use of sending missionaries to communities ground under the heel of such a soulless and degrading Trust as the one in question? The place to evangelize New Hampshire is at Concord. Let the apostles of morality and religion begin at Jerusalem. The most noticeable and shameless back-sliding in the state is not to be found, after all, in remote rustic communities but rather at the seat of government. Give the hill towns better laws, more adequate protection for life and property, an exercise of justice worthy of the name. Take the taxes off the summer boarding house business, the last ditch of the lingering native. Take them off the rough farm, the hovel, the one cow, and put them on the great forests, the only accumulation of unearned wealth in these regions and upon which alone it is possible to "realize" easily and immediately. If the land companies own the towns outright as they claim to, let them pay the taxes on them instead of almost nothing as at present. Require corporations chartered in other states for the purpose of waging a war of extermination on the native population of New Hampshire, to make some report to the authorities of the state in which they operate, and drive them at least out of their attitude of opposition to the efforts of local government to hold onto its own people—or drive them out of the state entirely. Give the relics of a race which produced a John Stark (the most characteristic American that ever lived) as fair a chance as they would have in Russia (not to mention Switzerland). Say to the governor of New Hampshire, "What your people want is not more meeting houses but more meat." They need a Renaissance of domestic architecture and general physical wellbeing more than they need a "Revival" of religion. In the evolution of righteousness political economy precedes piety. The Law goes before Gospel.

Both political parties have incorporated a plank against Trusts into their platforms for the coming presidential election: will they at least unite in this state in an attempt to crush such an unmitigated outrage upon the rights of humanity as the New Hampshire Land Company.

June 19, 1986

The Weeks Act:
A 75th Anniversary
Appraisal

Sherman Adams

*In celebration of the 75th anniversary of the passage of the historic Weeks Act—
which authorized the creation of the first federal forest reserves in the East—
one-time woodsmen-turned-New Hampshire governor, Sherman Adams of
Lincoln, gave the keynote address at a June 19, 1986 ceremony held at the Mount
Washington Hotel at Bretton Woods. The text of that speech by Adams (1899–
1986), who would die just a few months later at the age of 87, is featured below.
Here, he tells the history behind the creation of the White Mountain National
Forest in 1911.*

WE ARE HERE TODAY to celebrate the seventy-fifth anniversary of the
Weeks Act and its offspring in New Hampshire, the White Mountain National Forest. It is, in every sense of the word, a *people's* forest. It came about
because private enterprise, nonprofit organizations and government em-
ployees worked in concert to save the White Mountains. The Weeks Act
of 1911 was prescient; it recognized this area as a national treasure, one held
in delicate balance by diverse groups of local, state, regional and national
interests. We are here, therefore, to praise that foresight and balance. Yet
in recognition of recent disagreement, we are also here to restore harmony—the kind of harmony so much in evidence seventy-five years ago.

The forests of New Hampshire have always had recognized value, but
only in the past hundred years or so have we been able to articulate that

value and recognize its full potential. The real "father" of New Hampshire forestry was Concord's James B. Walker. A lawyer by training, Walker spent the last three decades of the 19th century championing such causes as better care for the insane, "scientific" agriculture and good forestry.

Throughout the 1870s, Walker traveled the state, urging local farmers to take better care of their woodlots. Not only were trees a valuable "crop," but they protected the soil. In 1883, as a member of New Hampshire's first forestry commission, Walker gave the keynote address at the annual meeting of the New Hampshire Fish and Game League. By this time, his thinking on the subject of forestry had matured and moved beyond the farm. Walker was convinced that New Hampshire's entire environment—its soil, water and air—depended upon good forests. Beyond aesthetics, Walker stressed the economic advantages of good forests. Cut timber was only one of the advantages; good forests also attracted tourists and sportsmen.

Walker led a small group of citizens concerned for the welfare and future of New Hampshire forests. Rising property taxes, destructive fires and the sale of large tracts of state-owned forest land in the White Mountains were some of the threats. Bad forestry was another. To preserve New Hampshire's forests, Walker continued to appeal to the better instincts of private landowners. Yet by 1886, he realized something more was needed. He urged that the State of New Hampshire get into the act by conducting a survey of its forests, passing tougher laws to prevent forests fires, considering tax relief for timberland owners, and finally, purchasing forest preserves.

If Joseph B. Walker was responsible for sounding the alarm, it was Philip W. Ayres and John W. Weeks who led the charge, culminating in the passage of the Weeks Act a quarter of a century later in 1911.

The effort to "save" New Hampshire forests had many dimensions, but the man who transcended them all was Philip Ayres. A historian by training and a social worker by experience, Ayres was hired as chief executive officer of the Society for the Protection of New Hampshire Forests in 1902. The organization was only a year old. In spite of its broad base of membership, however, the Forest Society had started off badly. It hoped to save New Hampshire's forests through an ambitious offering of academic and sentimental arguments (the *Boston Transcript* said of the early SPNHF campaign: "It roars too much of the sucking-dove tone"). Ayres changed all that. He not only created an appealing educational program, but he gave the Forest Society sharp focus by campaigning for a federal reserve in the White Mountains.

The idea of creating a federal forest reserve was not radical—there had been federal forest reserves in the West since 1891—but the idea of purchasing private lands to create a reserve in the East was controversial. Efforts to create a federal reserve in the southern Appalachians had begun in the 1880s, but by 1900, the local efforts had largely disintegrated. What remained was in the hands of U.S. Chief Forester Gifford Pinchot, but his attempts to win federal approval for a federal reserve in the southern Appalachians met with failure.

Philip Ayres had studied the southern campaign. Whereas the southern effort had suffered from political ineptitude and broad support, Ayres put together a politically astute plan. He assembled a coalition made up of diverse elements—loggers and pulp manufacturers, nature lovers, hotel owners, political leaders, literary figures and just about anyone else who could see the economic and environmental advantages to saving the White Mountains. Groups like the Appalachian Mountain Club, the New Hampshire Federation of Women's Clubs, the Massachusetts Forestry Association and the New Hampshire Grange joined the fight as well. Finally, Ayres rose above the early objections of Gifford Pinchot and joined the effort to save the White Mountains with that to save the southern Appalachians. Ayres argued that the White Mountains were a *national* treasure, and as such, should be protected by federal law. An individual state like New Hampshire might purchase smaller state parks. Only the federal government had the resources to purchase and manage whole mountain ranges.

Had Massachusetts Congressman and New Hampshire native John W. Weeks not entered the picture, the legislative history of the Weeks Act might well have been "a tale full of sound and fury, signifying nothing." Between 1903 and 1909, there were repeated futile attempts to get a northeastern reserve through Congress. The main obstacle was Speaker Joe Cannon, bolstered by objections from congressmen representing other parts of the country claiming that it was a state, not a federal, issue. Even the nature of the legislation changed. In order to broaden the economic impact of the proposed reserve, and to override constitutional objections, proponents switched from "timber" to "water," claiming that the proposed reserve would insure the "navigability" of navigable waterways.

In 1908, Speaker Cannon surprised everyone by placing John W. Weeks on the all-important House Committee on Agriculture. Weeks was a businessman, and Cannon respected him. In spite of opposition from the Corps of Engineers and the Weather Bureau, Weeks came out in favor of forest reserves in the East. His now famous bill was introduced on July 23,

The Owl's Head forest fire of 1907, one of the fiercest in White Mountain history, didn't hurt ongoing efforts to convince the U.S. Congress that an Eastern Forest Preserve was needed.

1909, and was signed into law by President Taft on March 1, 1911. The Weeks Act called for state-federal legislation in fighting fires, and it allowed for other forest reserves outside of the White Mountains and southern Appalachians. A combination of businesses, nonprofit organizations, concerned citizens, and public officials had made it possible.

That the Weeks Act was an outstanding achievement in national forest conservation is axiomatic. But it was both, and more and less than that. Less, in the sense that it was quite narrow in its national scope. Its impact was restricted to the headwaters of navigable waterways (which happened to be just fine in New Hampshire but not very helpful in many other areas of the country). This limiting aspect of the legislation was the result of necessary political compromise and some assumed constitutional obstacles.

And it was much more. More even than the description given it in a 1936 *Journal of Forestry* editorial: "... the principal landmark on the pathway of natural progress in forestry."

As the highest summit of these white hills, Mt. Washington stands proudly and permanently above its companions. So the Weeks Act, at the Silver Jubilee celebration held in this very room on September 13, 1936, was seen standing like a giant peak, surrounded by the lesser hills of other conservation legislation.

Its lofty stature derives from two critical elements of its evolution; two factors which were essential to its passage and successful implementation. I will return to these in conclusion when I look ahead to the 100th anniversary celebration.

First, the act was ultimately, and in the finest sense, a people's proposition. It was not born of the U.S. Forest Service or Gifford Pinchot or Philip Ayres and his Society. It was rather a coalescence of the public interest in natural resource protection and management, the public concern over forest depletion, and the public appreciation for the unique array of goods and services which emanate from the forest.

It was the first measure of a nation passing beyond the frontier attitude that the only forest land necessary to protect was already in the public domain. It signified, in a maturing nation, a public recognition that all forest land, even that in private ownership, contributed to the public good and was worthy of the application thereto of newly defined principles of conservation.

The second essential element was the vision of the act's supporters of a "working forest." They, especially the New Englanders, recognized that the new national forests must fit within, and must complement, the existing mosaic of land uses. This meant from the very start that the forests must be managed under what we now term "multiple use" principles. Recreation, timber production, soil, water and wildlife protection and enhancement—all have their rightful place and all must be considered in management decisions.

It was this mix of uses that initially garnered and continued to hold together the broad coalition of individuals and interest groups without whose support the eastern national forest system would never have become a reality.

No discussion of multiple uses would be complete without mention of recreation—a use that has had a profound influence on every other use and user.

Outdoor recreation in these hills had its origins some ninety years prior to the enactment of the Weeks Act by way of the slow development of bridle paths to various summits, later becoming foot trails or routes for other means of locomotion, such as the Mt. Washington Carriage Road and, later, the Cog Railway.

By 1936, footpaths had been extended throughout the forest by enterprising hiking organizations, the Appalachian Mountain Club, being the oldest and largest, and by the Civilian Conservation Corps program which had established a number of camps throughout the forest. The young men of the CCC were busily building new trails and Adirondack shelters, constructing picnic areas and campgrounds, and clearing ski trails.

The AMC, under the leadership of Joe Dodge, its legendary huts manager in Pinkham Notch, had completed a system of mountain shelters by 1932. Thus the CCC and the AMC combined had opened up the more remote areas of the White Mountains to hiking and camping, all this a prelude for things to come.

The 50th anniversary of the Weeks Act coincided with the recreation explosion which had been building through the 1950s. The facilities constructed in the '30s, idled during World War II, now provided the framework upon which this growth found place and nourishment. The Outdoor Recreation Resources Review Commission's Report in 1958 made dramatic and potent recommendations for the future. Congress acted by establishing the Land and Water Conservation Fund and the Bureau of Outdoor Recreation.

State and national forests and parks benefited from comprehensive planning efforts, and then qualified for capital funds to expand existing facilities and create new ones. The WMNF benefited from enlarged recreation budgets, resulting in improved campgrounds, trails, forest roads and picnic areas.

Meanwhile, the AMC had not been idle and had established a huts construction committee to plan and oversee an improvement and expansion program. The summer of 1961, coincident with the issuance of a *National Geographic* Magazine story about the hut system by Justice William O. Douglas, proved to be the busiest summer in the history of the huts.

All over the forest, recreation pursuits were intensifying, from the new-to-the-scene snowmobile trailriders to the technical climbers on rock and ice. With the completion of the Kancamagus Highway in 1959, non-hikers could view the heart of the WMNF by traversing the thirty-four-mile highway between Conway and Lincoln, thus opening up this hitherto wild area to greater numbers of the public.

At the fiftieth anniversary of the Weeks Act, the WMNF was feeling the increasing impact of recreationists on a year-round basis. Forest administrators, cooperators and users all, were well aware that the rush was just beginning; the question was, how great will be the crush of recreationists in the years ahead and what will be the land use and management consequences?

Pride and confidence set the tone and substance of the fiftieth anniversary celebration held at the Crawford House in 1961. The coalition of interests that had supported the forest and its steward, the U.S. Forest Service, for five decades was strong and building with the involvement now of other groups—Audubon Society of New Hampshire, snowmobilers and others. Earlier, Forest Supervisor Clifford Graham, recognizing the growing potential for conflict along with the increasing numbers of groups with a role to play in forest planning, had established a formal citizens' advisory committee.

And if the burgeoning recreational use, coupled with the traditional lumbering and other activities, were the only issues that had to be resolved, the next twenty-five years could have gone as smoothly as the atmosphere at the Crawford House would have predicted.

But this was not to be. For quietly, without public debate, the U.S. Forest Service adopted evenaged silviculture with clearcutting as its principal means of harvesting throughout the country. This occurred almost simultaneously with the Crawford House celebration. After decades of using locally-modified selective and selection cutting programs, the Forest Service had by 1962 incorporated in a wholesale, indiscriminate manner this aesthetically disruptive and, in forest conditions such as those prevalent in the White Mountains, scientifically questionable system.

Throughout most of the following semi-quinquennial, the Forest Service ignored the carefully but over-cautiously couched findings of its own research staff. They had determined in experiment after experiment that desirable silvicultural results in northern hardwoods could be obtained through individual and group selection systems. Perhaps even worse, the Forest Service ignored the pubic displeasure over clearcuts on scenic slopes and along highly visible trails and roadways. Strong criticism of clearcutting was heard from traditional friends including the SPNHF but the bureaucratic momentum was too great. Regional or local differences would not be accommodated.

This myopic mission, with all its misuses and abuses, was justified because it was cheaper and easier to control and administer. In their defense, the Forest Service had just been through several years of tight-budgeting for timber sales preparations. Funds for silvicultural niceties were virtually impossible to come by. They were, in addition, dealing with a forest that had been shaped by the poor harvesting practices of the past. Thus, the conclusion that clearcutting and starting all over again with a fresh forest was appealing.

Nevertheless, the net result was clearcutting. In the eyes of many, the only difference between logging practices of the 1890s and the current version was the increased efficiency of the modern heavy machinery.

Thus, for the first time since 1911, the public confidence in the U.S. Forest Service was seriously shaken. After decades of exhibiting their outstanding professionalism and integrity of purpose to the tenets of forest conservation that all its friends could share, the Forest Service staff was forced into defending the indefensible. Because of an ill-advised national edict the very qualities we had long admired (and still do) of steadfastness and loyalty caused a friction between the service and its natural allies.

The direct consequence of this on the White Mountains and elsewhere was an alienation of affection. The movement for a national wilderness system gained professional approval in 1964. This legislation was both timely and appropriate. Unfortunately it was aided in its passage and subsequently pressed into implementation by those who saw wilderness designation as the only certain means by which their favorite niche of a national forest could be protected against the very public agency that had been assigned to guard and manage it.

I suspect (or at least hope) there is not one person in this room who does not share my belief that we must have *wildness* (with a lower case "w" in Thoreau's meaning when he said "In wildness is the preservation of the world") as well as *Wilderness* (with a capital "W" as in the congressional designated Wilderness with its prohibitions against many burcaucratically-enumerated nonconforming uses including timber harvesting and recreation for anyone but the physically unimpaired). But I trust that most of you will also share my concern that the heavy-handed big "W" wilderness may be overused and abused. Especially in New England, where we have both the tradition of multiple use and the pressure of nearly one-fifth of the nation's population on less than 5 percent of the nation's land mass, we need to make this meager land base accommodate the optimum variety of uses. The European experience serves as a fine example. They have been able to adapt their silviculture and their land management to a socio-environmental ethic that transcends the artificial reliance on big "W" designation. I will shortly propose the silvicultural part of the solution that will lead to such a Nirvana.

While the public's dissatisfaction and old-time friend's disappointment over insensitive silviculture highlight the disturbing threat to our New England tradition of consensus building among users of the White Mountains, the danger to the forest has other roots as well. Using a large tract of public land as an ideological battleground and the dedicated professional public servants who manage it as whipping boys is a reflection of a national trend toward divisiveness in public debates brought about by the special purpose groups with single-minded goals. The carefully forged White Mountain Wilderness Compromise of 1984 was prepared by a broad coalition of New England organizations and interests. It was nearly torn apart when Washington groups, led by The Wilderness Society, unrelentingly attacked the legislation. Fortunately, the narrow interest dissidents lost out, but not before local organizations (principally SPNHF and AMC) spent tens of thousands of dollars in countering their tactics and propaganda. Locally, where once a handful of parties could hammer out a consensus position, the list of special interest private groups, public bodies and individuals involved in White Mountain affairs now runs into the hundreds.

In the early days of this century there were strong ties between the political and economic decision-makers in New Hampshire and Massachusetts. These alliances helped immensely to bring about both the Weeks Act and the many subsequent legislative measures that expanded and improved it. Now primarily the AMC, with its headquarters in Boston but a permanent staff, facility and membership base in New Hampshire, exhibits the political and social maturity that good neighbors interested in common good must share. Other from Massachusetts and beyond have little or no stake in the effect of their actions on the local residents or economy of White Mountain communities. The results of their activities all too often prove it.

New Hampshire has changed also. The recent explosive growth in the southern counties has placed the balance of political and economic power as far from the White Mountains as it possibly can be within the Granite State.

The White Mountain National Forest itself has changed as it has matured. At its seventy-fifth birthday, it contains hundreds of thousands of acres of forest also reaching maturity. Now, under the protective management of the U.S. Forest Service, vast areas of formerly cut-off, burnt-over lands that were left behind after the heavy cutting at the century's turn are ready to be harvested. But with harvesting comes roads and a popularly perceived dramatic change in wilderness values.

All this adds up to the very real likelihood that the community of interests that has worked so well together will have a most difficult time indeed in maintaining a positive and progressive approach to public policy issues. The traditional New England town meeting attitude of mutual respect is now threatened by newcomers whose first move is to call a press conference, whose means is not consensus but confrontation.

Now, that is the bad news or at least a candid appraisal of the causes and possible consequences of the changes that have taken place since the halcyon days of 1961.

Before I look ahead at what could (and I hope should) be the themes more happily recalled when the 100th anniversary is celebrated, let us regain a measure of well-earned pride by recounting just two recent and significant achievements.

Already the most complete of all Weeks Act forests, the WMNF continues to grow both within and beyond its original proclamation lines. In addition to the steady, programmed acquisition of inholdings, twice since 1975 the forests' traditional allies have successfully won large congressional appropriations to secure tens of thousands of acres. These lands were either originally excluded from the forest by virtue of their ownership by the large hotels at the time (the Waumbek, Crawford House and the Mt. Washington) or, like Sandwich Notch, whose appropriate protection was seen through annexation to the forest. Within the past two months, two critical missing links have been negotiated—the western slopes of the Pilot Range and the beautiful valley of the Peabody River north of the Auto Road to Gorham.

Earlier I likened the process of consensus building on this forest to the respectful give-and-take of a New England town meeting. Town meetings themselves play a vital role as well. No land may be acquired for this forest outside its proclamation lines without local approval. Without our strong tradition of balanced use and without the expectation that local interests, including lumbering, snowmobiling and developed recreation will get a fair shake in land use decisions, the local communities will promptly shut down any further expansion. The single-use wilderness zealots or those on the other extreme conveniently ignore the fact that people live and must find livelihood along every boundary of this forest. It is not an island to be carved up for competing and exclusionary uses. In this sense, too, it is a people's forest.

A comprehensive management plan for the forest, many years under debate and public review, was released this spring. It will guide the course of this forest for the next ten years. Its genesis involved literally hundreds of public meetings and information sessions with thousands of participants. The plan is remarkable for more than its substance, which I should add, I heartily endorse. The process of planning on this forest brings out the best in the Forest Service personnel and sometimes the worst in the public they serve. The patient professionalism and integrity of purpose exhibited by the staff on this forest has been shown again in their resolve to listen and to attempt to achieve a consensus of all the uses that make sense for the natural resources they are pledged to protect and make available for human benefit.

That the plan will be appealed by several dissident groups merely illustrates the point made earlier that selfishness and narrow interests, unchecked by the requirement of local accountability, are putting severe strain on this forest and its ability to continue its traditional multi-purpose role.

If I could write the outline for a speech to be given at the 100th anniversary celebration in 2011, I would hope to start off with two themes mentioned earlier as crucial to the initial passage and successful implementation of the Weeks Act: the working forest (as Joseph B. Walker advocated) and the broad-based public support (Philip Ayres' notion).

Walker linked good forestry to other issues of the general environment and economic welfare. In the 100 years that have passed, the science of forestry has progressed in this country to the point where we know not only that Walker was right but how to do it. In order to maintain a working forest on the WMNF, we must practice quality silviculture. By this I mean unevenaged management with individual tree selection or group selection systems of harvesting. Since most of you in the audience are neither silviculturists nor foresters, I will henceforth use the term quality silviculture and save you from the details of forestry nomenclature.

What Walker seemed to know inherently, we have had to learn the hard way. Quality silviculture fits lightly on the land and is less manipulative of nature. Quality silviculture will produce quality trees which will create a quality forest. All of the species which are presently commercially important can be grown, including those light-loving species such as white birch.

The definition of quality silviculture can and should be extended to include special treatments including small clear cuts where, for example, aspen regeneration is needed for wildlife.

The new forest plan calls for about 30 percent of the forest to be managed under what I am calling quality silviculture. This is an important step in the right direction but it is not enough. If we are to recapture, hold and build on the broad public support that has slipped away in recent years, we must make a total commitment. And as I will suggest in just a moment, we will not be able to remove the institutional and budgetary barriers to such a major change unless we do have that broad public support.

The Weeks Act manifested the concept that Philip Ayres advocated, a people's forest that protected and produced the goods and services desired by the broadest possible range of our society, all within the ultimate restraint that the basic productivity of the land not be diminished. This is not to suggest that every acre on this forest should be equally devoted to every use. We long ago realized that certain areas should have dominant uses, whether for wilderness, recreation, wildlife or timber. We now have a forest where roughly half is managed primarily or exclusively for recreation and scenic values and upon which there is no timber harvesting. The other half, where timber production is an important element in the mix of uses, is where the future debates and battles will take place. Quality silviculture will significantly lessen the conflict between harvesting and other uses.

If we are to see this forest become less of a battleground and more of a common ground, we must resolve to take on, with the skill and fervor equal to that of Weeks and his contemporaries, the budgetary barrier to quality silviculture and improved recreation management. For it is the inconsistency and inadequacy of the Forest Service appropriations that blocks the way to making this an exemplary working forest. Quality silviculture and a quality forest will cost more money. Adding additional lands to this forest will cost money. Now seems hardly the propitious time to make such a proposal. But it is precisely now that we must. For without a noble and far-reaching goal we will not be able to rally the support necessary to accomplish our objective. Without that broad pubic support, the factions which are now seeking to carve the forest up into special interest domains will succeed.

We have been blessed here by the kindness of nature in the creation of these White Mountains. The ingenuity of man, personified by Walker, Ayres and Weeks and their inspired conception and carefully crafted coalitions; the integrity of the U.S. Forest Service; have all combined to place on this natural gift a means by which we may protect and use it.

We today have the obligation to secure past progress and to build on it a forest for the future—an exemplary forest that sets a national example, by practice and policy, for the public needs in 2011.

Mountain Explorations

April 12, 1876

The East Branch
of the Pemigewasset

Warren Upham

From *Appalachia*

THE DRAINAGE BASIN of the East Branch forms part of one of the largest tracts of wilderness in New Hampshire. This includes the central and southern portions of the White Mountain region, and is wholly occupied by alternate mountains and valleys, and covered by a pathless forest. The traveller who would drive found this area by the shortest circuit of highway, must go through Sandwich Notch, Franconia Notch, Bethlehem, the White Mountain Notch, Conway and Tamworth, — a distance of one hundred and ten miles. This territory, still untraversed by roads, lies near the geographical centre of New Hampshire. The distance from Massachusetts line to the mouth of the East Branch is ninety miles, or almost exactly half the length of the State.

This stream is the first considerable tributary to the river which is almost invariably called Pemigewasset for the first fifty-two miles of its course, to Franklin, where it receives the waters from Winnipiseogee lake; below which place it is the Merrimack, whose falls have created Manchester, Lowell, and Lawrence. This application of two different names to the same river seems to have been a trouble to Philip Carrigain, and publisher of the State Map in 1816. He gives Pemigewasset as a name for the upper portion, but places Merrimack first in preference; and when we come to the East Branch the name "Merrimack river" is applied to it, and the stream from the north is designated as the "Middle Branch." Where they unite, nine miles south from Profile lake, the stream of the main val-

ley is indeed smaller than its tributary from the east. The drainage area of
the former is short and narrow, being included between the Lafayette and
Kinsman ranges, while the basin of the East Branch is fifteen miles long
and ten miles wide. It can scarcely be considered the main stream, however, because it is not the continuance of the straight valley.

The mountains which bound the basin of the East Branch, beginning
at the northwest, are the Lafayette range; Haystack Mt.; the Twin Mt.
Range, which extends south nearly to the East Branch, terminating in Mt.
Bond; the Willey Mt. Range; the range including Mts. Nancy, Anderson,
Lowell, Carrigain, and Hancock; and, on the south side of Hancock
Branch, Mt. Kancamagus, and the range which curves northwest from
Osceola to Loon Pond Mt.

The rocks of this region are all eruptive, being granites of several kinds,
with small areas of porphyry. They are probably of Cambrian age, the date
of their upheaval being after the formation of most of the White Mountain rocks.

The principal tributaries to the East Branch on the north are Franconia Branch and the outlet from New Zealand Pond; and on the south, the
outlet from Howe's Pond, Cedar Brook, which comes in from between
Carrigain and Hancock Mts., and the Hancock Branch, the largest of
these, which joins the East Branch about five miles above its mouth, coming from the south side of Hancock Mt. and the northern slopes of the
Osceola range.

The work of lumbering has been attempted in this wilderness, and the
marks of blasting may be seen where the lumbermen have tried to clear
the Hancock Branch from some of its boulders for the purpose of floating
logs on its spring floods, but neither this stream nor the East Branch are
equal to this task. They are small streams, by no means capable of floating
a log, except when in flood, and their whole course is of comparatively
rapid descent and everywhere obstructed by boulders. The wood and lumber would be very valuable if it was situated in southern New Hampshire
or eastern Massachusetts; but without a railroad, which will probably
sometime be built for this purpose, it does not repay the cost of getting it
to the market.

The source of the East Branch is a considerable pond at the southwest base of Mt. Willey, which has an altitude of about two thousand
seven hundred feet above the sea, being some one hundred feet lower than
the lowest point of water-shed between it and Saco river, on the south
side of Mt. Willey. This is Ethan's Pond, named from Ethan Allen Crawford, the "giant of the mountains." It is more than one-fourth mile verti-

cally above the Willey House, which is only some two miles distant, and residents there speak of going to the top of the mountain to fish in this pond.

One of the principal objects of interest of the upper portion of the East Branch are the falls named in honor of Thoreau, about four miles below its source, where, in a short distance, the stream falls more than one hundred and fifty feet in picturesque cascades. The foot of these falls is about two thousand one hundred feet above sea. Of other interesting cascades may be mentioned the falls on Franconia Branch, about one third of a mile above its mouth, where, as on so many of these mountain torrents, the power of water to wear the rocks is well seen; and the cascades on the little rivulet that descends from Loon Pond.

The height at the mouth of Franconia Branch is probably about 1200 feet, and the height of the mouth of the East Branch is, by levelling, 710 feet, or 242 feet above the Pemigewasset river at Plymouth, eighteen miles farther south. The lowest points in the watershed of the East Branch basin are, on the south, the notch at Greeley Ponds, which are tributary to Mad River, 1815 feet above sea; and on the north, at New Zealand Pond, 2123 feet above sea, according to barometric measurement.

The work of geological exploration in this wilderness was undertaken in August, 1871, by a small party of students, under the direction of the State Geologist. A temporary camp was located about a mile up the Franconia Branch, some eight miles from Mr. Pollard's, the last house on the East Branch, from which we transported our provisions, with blankets, an axe, the requisite hammer, &c. on our backs. I will finish with a description of two journeys taken from this camp. The first was to Mts. Bond and Guyot. Our route was north to the fork of the Franconia Branch, where the Lafayette and Redrock brooks unite. There we climbed the steep north and south ridge which lies between these brooks, being about 1500 feet above them, and separated by them by a hollow at its north end from the surrounding high mountain ranges. From the wooded summit of this ridge we looked east to the high south end of the Twin Mt. Range, which towered temptingly above us, two or three miles distant. The day was beautiful, and the air very clear, with scarcely a cloud in the sky. Here we divided our party, two continuing north to explore the ridge on which we were, and two crossing east to the south end of the Twin range. The east side of the ridge on which we were is very abrupt, but consists of broken ledges, nowhere presenting a naked wall of rock. The brook in the valley which we crossed has been called Redrock, from the ledges of red felsite, at first called jasper, which were discovered on its east side two or three miles farther north. Pebbles from this source abound in the channels of the streams as far as to the mouth of East Branch.

At starting we noticed a little open space in the valley below, and by chance our route took us to it. It was a small swampy patch of perhaps half an acre, which for some cause not very apparent was destitute of trees. This is mentioned because the forest is everywhere, with the temporary exception of burnt spots, well remembered by all who have clambered over their charred logs, and the rare places where a gale may have opened a "windfall." Such spots must be shunned, if possible, in your journey. But the highest summits often surround themselves, especially on the north or west sides, with an almost impenetrable dwarf forest, even more difficult, and which sometimes cannot be avoided by the mountain climber. This was the case with the mountain before us. In passing through or over these thickets, uprightness must be sacrificed, and one must go under, through, or over the stout spreading branches and tops, just as the least difficult way appears to be.

At length we came again in sight of the almost perpendicular face of rock, like some castle wall, 100 feet or so in height, at the top of the south peak on its northwest side, which we had specially noticed from the lower ridge west of Redrock brook. This precipitous ledge supplied a name for this summit during our explorations, to serve for convenience of designation till a better title should be assigned. A name afterward proposed for this point was Mt. Percival, in honor of the poet and geologist of Connecticut. Somewhat later, when the subject of nomenclature was discussed by this Club, the names Bond and Guyot where found in the list of those who had rendered service in mapping and describing the geography of these mountains. Their labors had been nearly equal, and greater in importance than those of any others in this field, and it was thought appropriate that their names should be applied to some two conspicuous summits near together, which should commemorate their work. The south end of the Twin Mt. range was the only place where two such peaks still remained without established names, and it was thought best to adopt these titles for them. Mt. Bond is the one farthest south, being a little east of the northwest side of which are the precipitous crags. Mt. Guyot is about three-fourths of a mile distant, being a little east of north from Mt. Bond, with an intervening hollow of about 100 feet. Both these summits are without trees, and have the characteristic arctic plants which are found in temperate regions only on bleak mountain tops; both are mainly solid ledge, with here and there small spaces of earth and alpine flowers. In the intervening hollow there are quite abundant patches of dwarf spruce, but these may be avoided in going across.

The northern summit, Mt. Guyot, is higher than Mt. Bond by about 100 feet; thence northward, the massive ridge continues nearly the same for about three miles, only slightly lower than the points known as the South and North Twin Mts., with which the range ends. The greatest depressions in this distance do not probably exceed 200 feet. As seen from Mt. Lafayette, this long ridge appears to be very nearly of uniform height. The Twin Mts. have an altitude of 4900 feet, or 350 feet less than Lafayette, and Mts. Guyot and Bond are probably about 4800 and 4700 feet in height.

From these summits, especially from Mt. Bond, which best overlooks the East Branch valley, the prospect is extensive and grand. As far as the view extends, we see only mountains and valleys and forest. There is no appearance of any of the works of man, except that we discern the houses on the summit of Mt. Washington, fifteen miles distant. All is silent untrodden forest, and all around are the lofty foreheads of our highest mountains. The sharp crest of Lafayette is our neighbor on the west, and Mt. Willey, somewhat farther distant on the east. South of the East Branch valley, Mts. Carrigain and Hancock appear from this point of view, as rounded, massive summits, nearly alike in shape and height. The whole view shows, more completely than that from any other point, the mountain wilderness of the East Branch. A path ought to be made for ascending the Twin Mts. from Carroll, when visitors will do well to follow the high range south and see this valley from Mt. Bond.

A second journey was from the same camp to the summit of Mt. Carrigain, following the nearly straight course of the East Branch to the mouth of Cedar brook. Thence we went up this brook a mile or so to a fork, at which place we began the ascent of the mountain. This was the northwest side, and we apprehended trouble from the usual growth of dwarf spruce, but, on the contrary, the ascent was the easiest found in all our mountain journeys. The slope is very regular, just steep enough to make one satisfied that he is fast getting towards the top, the path being through a rather open forest with no underbrush, and for the most of the way over a carpet of green moss, decked with abundance of the pink-striped Oxalis of our northern woods. On the northwest slope the surface is almost wholly of glacial drift, which extends to the summit where we first met outcropping ledges. The height of this mountain is by barometer 4678 feet, about 250 feet higher than Hancock Mt., which lifts its huge north and south ridge at a distance of two or three miles to the west. Carrigain Mt., though higher, is less massive, descending steeply on all sides from the crest, which extends three-fourths of a mile to the northeast from the point reached by us, terminating in Vose's Spur. We found here trees twenty-five to thirty feet high, and so stout that one may stand with perfect security in the top of a tree, with half the body above its highest twigs, and take magnetic bearings and make sketches quite at leisure. This summit will probably soon be cleared to afford visitors a view, standing on the solid earth.

The route which I have described for climbing this mountain is that which would be taken in going up from the East Branch. Most visitors to it will start from the Saco, following Sawyer's river and Carrigain brook, by which route the ascent and return may be accomplished in one day. Two days must be taken for a trip to either Mts. Bond and Guyot, or Mt. Carrigain, if the journey is from Pemigewasset river.

March 14, 1883

The Twin Mountain Range

A. E. Scott

From *Appalachia*

The so-called Scott-Ricker expedition of 1882, in which three men and three women undertook a rugged seven-day journey through the White Mountain wilderness, stands as one of the most remarkable undertakings in New Hampshire hiking annals. Led by Augustus E. Scott of Boston, the ambitious Councilor of Improvements for the Appalachian Mountain Club, the trek featured a grueling traverse of the then trailless Twin-Bond Range, plus a walk through the virgin forest of the Pemigewasset Wilderness. Scott originally planned to cross the Twin-Bond Range in the company of a single woodsman, but when word got out of his planned excursion, journalist Charlotte Ricker asked to be a part of the expedition team. Eventually two other women—whose identities have unfortunately been lost to history—were invited to participate, along with two woodsmen, one being Allen Thompson of Bethlehem, a well-known local guide.

THE TWIN MOUNTAIN RANGE has long been regarded by Appalachians as an interesting field for exploration. Many times we have looked longingly from high summits, especially from Lafayette, upon its bare ledges and wooded ridges, and resolved at an early day to make their more intimate acquaintance; but the summits are so distant from the clearings, and the reports to those who had attempted to reach them and failed were so discouraging, that it was difficult to find any one who cared to join the undertaking. In August last I determined to make the attempt, accompanied by a single woodsman, who might be of service in an emergency and who would assist in carrying the packs.

The Range stretches from the valley of the Ammonoosuc on the north, to the valley of the East Branch of the Pemigewasset on the south, and consists of a long, broad ridge, with a number of elevations from one to four hundred feet above the general level, four of which have received the names respectively of North and South Twin, Guyot, and Bond. It is surrounded on all sides by vast wooded tracts, lumbered only a short distance at the northerly end, and otherwise very little explored. It was my plan to enter the forest on the north, force my way to the summit of the North Peak; thence, crossing the whole ridge and descending into the East Branch region, to make my exit from the forest as circumstances required.

While making the arrangements, I was surprised to receive a letter from a gentleman somewhat prominent at Bethlehem, where the plan had become known through the woodsman whom I had engaged, which ran as follows: "If any ladies are to join you in making the Twin Mountain exploration, Miss X., who has had much experience among the mountains, asks the privilege of being on of the party."

I replied at once that I had failed to find any man who wished to undertake it, and it had not occurred to me as among the possibilities that any woman would desire to do so. "But," I added, half in jest, "whenever I hear of a woman who desires to explore wild places, and to see the old forests as they exist far away from ordinary routes of travel, I am filled with an equal desire to assist her in doing so. If Miss X. is capable of enduring long-continued and fatiguing work; can endure thirst perhaps for hours; can sleep without blanket, or possibly without shelter of any sort; can force her way through shrub of the most fearful kind, where the clothes may be torn to shreds; can endure extremes of heat and perhaps of cold; can go all day in a storm, drenched to the skin,—if she can endure these things, and —after my assurance that these and even greater hardships are probable on the proposed trip—still wishes to attempt, I will invite the only lady I know for whom the undertaking is feasible, to accompany her."

By the returning mail I was informed that, notwithstanding all my discouragements, Miss X. was exceedingly anxious to go on the exploration. While reading this last letter in the presence of another lady-member of the Club, she at once enthusiastically asked to join the party. I was fairly caught. I had painted the probable difficulties of the proposed exploration in glowing colors, and had rather disdainfully expressed a willingness to invite ladies to accompany me if they dared attempt it; and here were three ladies who not only dared, but were eager to go. I would not retract, although I had many misgivings, and some doubts of their reaching even the first summit.

Another packman is engaged, and an early day appointed for starting. At the time appointed we meet on the highway, about two miles north of the Twin Mountain House; the provisions and the few necessary articles we are to carry are securely packed, and the journey is begun.

We cross the Ammonoosuc by the railroad bridge, traverse the cleared field beyond, and soon enter the forest. As we wind along the old logging-road in single file, the two packmen take the lead: one an old man of sixty, who claims to know something about the region,—the other a young man, whose chief recommendations are his pleasant face and broad shoulders. They present a picturesque appearance in their new, embroidered shirts, with their heads protruding through their meal-bag packs. The ladies follow: one an M.D., who is happy in escaping for a few days a wearisome city practice; one a student of medicine, only too ready to leave pills and powders for a mountain climb,—both these members of the Appalachian Mountain Club; the third, a special correspondent, somewhat nervous in this her first forest experience. I bring up the rear with a huge pack, carried easily on an Appalachian frame.

The road runs parallel with and some distance from Little River for two miles. We pass an extensive logging-camp, known as Tarbell's; another, a short distance beyond, called Day's, and soon after turn abruptly from the road down to the noisy stream. The day is warm; there is no fixed point which we must reach before night. The old man is happy with his fishpole, wading in the middle of the stream, and lingering by the frequent cascades and in the cool shades; we press slowly on, sometimes jumping from bowlder to bowlder, and sometimes finding an easy way in the forest along the river's banks. By the middle of the afternoon we have passed around the great foot-hill, which lies northerly from the north summit, and is sometimes pointed out as one of the Twins, and reach the stream which flows from the intervening ravine. This stream flows into Little River at the foot of quite remarkable falls, deserving of a name and more than this passing notice. From this point the valley grows narrow,—the long ridge, which stretches easterly from the North Summit, rising rapidly from the stream on one side, and the Little River Range even more rapidly on the other. We leave the stream and bear southwesterly up this shoulder, until the declining sun warns us to select a camping ground. We have been climbing diagonally, so that we are close to the ravine on the southerly side of the ridge. Descending a short distance, we come upon a cold stream, find a favorable spot, and build our camp.

We have plenty of time to build a somewhat elaborate one in the usual fashion. Two crotched sticks are placed the required distance apart for uprights; a pole is stretched across, and others placed on this for rafters, which extend back to the ground; the roof is covered with bark; the sides are protected with branches of fir and spruce; the front open, and the floor covered with boughs. A mountain-ash is cut for a backlog, and smaller logs of maple and birch for fuel. A fire is kindled, the old man displays the treasures of his basket, and soon a score or two of speckled trout are sputtering over the coals. We have merely lunched on the way, and are in good condition to enjoy our sumptuous repast of oatmeal, hard bread, and trout. There is no array of fine linen or china, or attendants to serve us; but we have a log for a table,—covered with a network of lichens and mosses more delicate than the tracery on the finest damask,—birch bark for plates and napkins, fingers or pointed sticks for forks, and a frying-pan common to all. We talk over the events of the day. The ladies are elated at the success of the first day's tramp, and have no fears for the morrow. The repast over, we stretch back upon the fragrant boughs. For a while we are merry with jest and song and story, and the forest resounds with shouts of laughter; but anon the silence is only broken by the nasal utterances of the old man,—who sleeps outside with his back against a stump,—the crackling of the flames, and the brawling of the stream beyond. It is a novel experience to some of the party; and, in the morning, the reddened eyes and stiffened limbs indicate that they have had the usual experience of a first night in camp.

Breakfast over, the journalist and the packmen are eager to be off, and as we are merely to climb the shoulder on the slope of which we have camped,—so that there is little danger of becoming separated,—they start off ahead, agreeing to wait for us on the summit. We caution them against drinking freely in the early part of the day, for we anticipate a waterless summit. An hour later we follow, bearing northwesterly until we are out of the ravine, and then westerly to the summit. It is a fine forest and we enjoy the climb, although the ascent is rapid. The day is warm, and we soon pass beyond the limits of water. At about eleven o'clock the forest proper seems to end very abruptly, and a quite different growth begins. We have reached the line of scrub spruces, and are soon floundering helplessly. We are familiar with scrub as it appears on Adams, Carrigain, and other summits, but the worst places on those summits seem to us like pleasure-grounds compared to this. Twin Mountain scrub is unique; it is indescribable. We walk upon the tree-tops, only to disappear at last; we crawl prone beneath the lowest branches; we cut our way through with the hatchet; we try first one way, then another, and always feel that some other way must be better. We imagine our friends waiting for us on the summit, and despair of reaching them; when, as we climb upon an out-cropping rock and get a view of the immense sea of scrub stretching in all directions, we descry in the distance their heads just above the level. To feel that we are not alone in our misery revives our courage, and we press on inch by inch, until about one o'clock we reach the bare ledges that crop out on the northwesterly side of the summit. Our companions soon arrive, and we throw ourselves upon the ground,—heedless for awhile of the magnificent view stretched out before us. We are all suffering from thirst, but the packmen have not heeded the advice of the morning and are in a deplorable condition. There is almost a mutiny for the possession of the pint canteen of water which one of the ladies has brought safely through; but we dole out a half-gill only to each person, reserving the remainder for a greater emergency which we fear may arise.

We are suddenly aroused by brilliant flashes which come to us from Bethlehem, and we eagerly respond with a bit of glass brought for the purpose. Some friends knew that we hoped to reach this summit at about this time, and they are inquiring for us. We have not the code sufficiently at command to exchange messages; but it is interesting to communicate even in this mute way with friends so far below us and so widely separated, and it arouses a chain of pleasant thought.

The summit of the North Twin is rounded, the slope being gradual for a considerable distance toward the east and south and rapid on the north and west. It is covered with scrub, with the exception of a small space on the northwesterly side. We get extended views from this point toward the west and north, and from ledges which rise above the scrub a short distance from the real summit, toward the east and south. The summit of the South Twin, apparently higher than the North, is hardly a mile distant, and the col between is very slight.

A shower threatens, and we hope for a heavy rain that we may quench our thirst; but only sufficient water falls to wet the scrub, and we are drenched to the skin by contact with the wet branches. This growth is not so thick on the southerly side, and we do not have great difficulty in the descent; but we find no water, and dare not attempt the climb of the South Peak without it.

From the col the descent is rapid into the great ravine between the immense shoulders which extend easterly from both summits. We bear down into this ravine, and soon come upon the track of a slide two or three rods wide, and extending far as we can see down the mountain-side. The centre of the slide is evidently the bed of a stream now dry. We follow it down, and at last find water trickling drop by drop through a crevice in the rocks.

It is too late in the afternoon to begin another ascent, and we conclude to go into camp. We search in vain for a level spot, and are forced to build our camp among the rocks, filling up the spaces between as well as we can with moss. We are at such an altitude that it is difficult to get sufficient bark to cover our shelter; but fuel is abundant, and we care more for warmth than for a covering. We do not dine as sumptuously as we did last night, but are quite content with hard bread and hot oatmeal. We are in a wretched plight, wet and torn, but all jolly,—the journalist only showing slight symptoms of discouragement. We spend some time in repairing the ravages of the scrub; but there are few jokes and stories, and the camp is still at an early hour.

We have a refreshing sleep, fitted in among the rocks, and are off at an early hour in the morning, determined to advance farther on our way than yesterday. We are in the same ravine in which we camped the preceding night, only higher up on the head wall. As on the previous day, the journalist starts off in advance with the packmen. The men carry, for our mutual benefit, a half-gallon of tea.

The climb is exceedingly steep and treacherous, and we strike the scrub nearly a half-mile from the summit; but we patiently work through it and reach the summit in the middle of the forenoon. We have not seen our companions, have been without water, and expect to find them with their can of tea on the summit; but they are nowhere to be seen, and do not make their appearance until nearly two hours later. They are nearly exhausted; the men have disposed of the last drop of tea, and again make demands on the small canteen which the ladies are carrying for an emergency.

We find about an acre of bare ledges, so that the view is unobstructed in all directions. It is grand beyond description. We are especially interested in the range we are exploring and the mountains which are near to us. From this south peak the two summits seem to be of about equal height. From other elevations it is impossible to form any conception of the great ridges that extend east and west from the various summits of this range, and the immense ravines between them. Two of these ravines open into the valley of the Little River.

On the easterly side of this valley rise abruptly the Little River Mountains and we have ample opportunity to study this range, about which little seems to be known. It extends from Mt. Hale, on the north, nearly to the East Branch region on the south. At the head of the Little River Valley it seems to be separated by a slight depression from the ridge which extends northeasterly from the summit now called Guyot.

Beyond the Little River Mountains we trace distinctly the valley of the

New Zealand River, and two or three ranges of hills between the New Zealand Notch and the northerly part of the Field-Willey Range. On the west we have an equally good opportunity to study Garfield, the unnamed ridge south of it, the eastern slopes of the Franconia Range, and the great valleys between. The ridge south of Garfield lies between the two branches of the Franconia River. At its southerly end are large cliffs, which the old man calls Owl's Head. A long ridge, with three distinct summits, curves around southwesterly, ending abruptly opposite these cliffs. Between these two slopes flows Red Rock Brook.

Directly south of us, a mile distant, with two or three intervening elevations, rises a pointed summit, wooded to the top, and nearly as high as the Twins. Southwesterly from this summit, closely connected with it and only slightly lower, are two broad, bare, and picturesque plateaus, with a slight depression between them. We are of the opinion that this summit, with these plateaus, should be known as Guyot. Still farther south, separated from the farthest plateau by a narrow col, a hundred feet below the latter, rises sharply another summit, somewhat higher than the last, wooded to the top; and stretching southwesterly, also, from this is a long narrow ridge, at the end of which rise the enormous cliffs which have been called Bond. The last summit has been called by some, Guyot. There seems to be no good reason why the cliffs, which are so evidently a part of and so near to this summit, should receive a separate name, especially when there are so many prominent peaks in the range without names; and we suggest that the whole of this part of the mountain mass should be known as Bond, — Guyot being applied to the portion north of it, as previously suggested.

We remain on the South Twin for two hours, enjoying the view and carefully jotting in our note-books the new points we discover, but thirst compels an advance. We resolve to reach the col beyond the ledgy plateaus by night, and conclude to leave the intervening scrubby hills on our right, bearing low enough into the ravine on the left to find water. In the middle of the afternoon, soon after we have got through the scrub, and not far from the centre of the col south of the summit, we discover a beautiful spring — the only water we find on the whole range within a reasonable distance of the ridge. The season was very dry, and we believe this spring will never fail. The packmen and our journalist bear evident signs of demoralization, — the new, embroidered shirts have long ceased to be attractive, and the flannel dress of the latter is torn to shreds; but the other ladies are fresh, and three of us decide to press on that we may have a longer time to remain on the summit beyond, leaving the others to follow when rested. They promise to follow our trail, which is very distinct, and to reach us before night.

As we bear up toward the summit, we find the scrub worse than any we have yet seen, and many times we are almost conquered; but we reach the summit, and press down to the plateau below. We are thrilled with delight. We are surrounded on all sides by mountain peaks which shut out all signs of civilization, save the buildings on Washington. The sun is setting behind Lafayette, the shadows are filling the deep ravines, and a profound stillness prevails. Darkness is rapidly approaching, and our friends have not appeared. It is useless to try to find them; so we gather a pile of dry wood, kindle a bright fire, and make ourselves comfortable on the dry moss. At last the old man emerges from the scrub, alone. He reports that the others entirely gave out after we left; that they have gone down into the ravine for water, and have sent him to overtake us and bring us back. It is quite dark, but we start at once. We cannot retrace out steps through the spruces, but we hurry across the ledges and descend by the rocks—which fortunately extend below the scrub—to the col beyond, and along the top of the head wall of the great ravine, down the side of which they have gone. It is very steep, and so dark that we have to feel our way with the greatest care. We are following down the bed of a stream, and distinctly hear the water gurgling under our feet, but it is so far beneath the rocks, that we cannot reach it. We continually shout to our companions, but get no response. We give up all hope of finding them for the night, but continue to descend and grope about, on hands and knees, between the rocks in our search for water. We hear it rippling tantalizingly beneath,—sometimes, apparently, near to us,—but always beyond our reach, until, al last, after an hour's search, it gushes out, cool and clear, beneath the huge bowlder that blocks the way.

We have not lunched since breakfast. On inquiry we find that all the provisions have been left with the rest of the party; and we have nothing to eat, save two small sticks of prepared chocolate. We have our kettle with us. We boil two quarts of water and stir in the chocolate; there is enough for all, and we are quite satisfied with our evening repast. The old man attempts to cut wood for the fire, but falls asleep with his axe in hand, and we cannot arouse him. We grope about and gather a considerable pile of dead wood for the night's supply, and then fit ourselves in among the rocks for pleasant dreams. I certainly have them, and do not wake till morning, when I find, to my chagrin, that the Doctor has spent much of the night in tending the fire; but she declares it was a delightful experience, and both ladies are merry and enthusiastic.

We have nothing to eat, and while we are sitting around the remnants of our fire, in doubt as to what shall be done, we hear a faint shout from far down the ravine. The old man answers. They find our direction, and in half an hour our lost companions are with us. They have had a good fire, plenty to eat, and a good night's sleep. We hastily breakfast, and climb back to the col from which we descended the night before.

The last peak in the range, which we have suggested should be called Bond, rises rapidly from this col. We determine to keep below the scrub-line, by flanking this summit to the right; but we soon find ourselves in difficulty, and think the better way is to aim directly for the top. This side is very steep, in some places precipitous. We are forced at last to bear up the mountain, and come out, about noon, not far from the summit, near a huge bowlder which is a noticeable feature from distant points. From this point the great cliffs are a mile away. It is not difficult to reach the col by following the rocks which appear above the scrub on the southerly slope, or to ascend the cliffs beyond.

These cliffs are several acres in extent, bare of vegetation, and stretch out southwesterly, extending nearer to the Franconia River than to the East Branch. On the northwesterly side they jut into the gulf, and rise almost vertically from the valley below, like the ruins of some enormous castle. A long ridge extends westerly from the summit, ending in a high, wooded bluff, which also falls off abruptly toward the Franconia River, and on the side towards the cliffs. The great gulf, between the cliffs and this wooded bluff, seems more stupendous than those in the sides of Washington. A narrow gateway leads through the Cliffs down the head-wall of this ravine, similar to that leading into King's Ravine.

It seemed to us that it would be easy to reach these cliffs by following up the Franconia Branch to the stream which flows in on the right, about one mile from its junction with the East Branch, — then following this stream through the ravine and ascending the wall through this gateway. Another long, wooded ridge slopes southerly from the bowlder to which I have referred, clear to the East Branch. Between this and the cliffs, on the easterly side, there is another immense gorge.

We had felt the views from the South Twin and from the plateaus of Guyot were grand and beautiful, but the view from this crag surpasses everything we have ever beheld. Never before have we realized the extent of the Pemigewasset Forest, or the grandeur of the mountains which rise in and around it. We have found no water since leaving camp; as usual, the men have on the way disposed of all the tea they started with, and we are suffering intensely from thirst. Our lips crack and the skin peels from the roofs of our mouths. The old man declares he never will attempt another trip like this, the young man would give a thousand dollars (which he does not possess) to be at home, and the journalist begins to discuss the easiest way of emerging from the valley below; but the rest are unmindful of their discomforts, and—although it is the day when the mercury rises the highest in the lowlands, and we cannot escape the merciless rays of the sun which are pouring vertically upon us—we linger an hour entranced by the wonderful beauty of the scene.

The belt of scrub surrounding this crag is narrow, but we get through it only after a severe battle. We descend rapidly the steep wall of the ravine, on the southeasterly side of the cliff, and in a couple of hours strike the head-waters of Bear Brook. We are so exhausted that we are ready to go into camp at an early hour. The timber is large, the bark peels readily, and we construct a luxurious camp close to the noisy stream.

The next morning we start early and follow down this stream through a constantly widening valley, heavily wooded, with enormous pines scattered here and there, until, at last, we reach the longed-for river. The old man is at once in the middle of the stream with fishpole in hand, and in half an hour a pan of delicious trout is set before us. We are so delighted to reach an abundance of water that we delay here for three hours in the cool shades among the rocks. The old man goes ahead up the river, and when we finally reach him, near the Forks, he has strings of upwards of two hundred trout. The Forks are supposed to be twelve miles from the mouth of the river. The views of Hancock and Carrigain at this point are very wild and beautiful. The southerly branch of the river, rising in Howe's Pond near the Saco Valley, is fed by streams which flow from the Nancy-Carrigain Range; while the northerly branch, rising in Willey Pond and in the swamps on the side of Mt. Field, is fed by larger streams flowing from New Zealand Notch, and from the deep gorges which extend up into the southerly end of the Little River and Twin Mountains. Between these two branches there is a long line of wooded hills, one of which, lying close to Thoreau Falls, is of considerable height.

We follow the northerly branch, hoping to reach a camp built last year, on another exploration made by some of the party; but the distance is greater than we suppose, and darkness overtakes us before the camp is reached. We find a charming spot in a cluster of pines close to the edge of the river, where we build our camp-fire. The frying-pan is filled and re-filled many times with trout, for we have broken our three days' fasting on oatmeal and stale bread, and it seems as though we can never get enough. We have no shelter, and soon after dark the clouds gather and the rain begins to fall, threatening an uncomfortable night; but later on the moon shines forth, and camp-fire blazes brightly, and we are dry and happy.

A change has come over the old man; he has forgotten the discomforts of the mountains, and—so long as fish abound—he cares not for home. He regales us with stories of the woods, in which he is the principal actor, and our camp is not silent until a late hour.

Our journalist is still anxious to reach home. It seems possible for her either to follow down the stream and reach North Woodstock by way of Pollard's; or, continuing up the stream, to follow the branch which flows from Willey Pond, thence by the trail and the Appalachian path to the Willey House. She decides upon the latter course, and it is arranged that she and the young man shall start as soon as it is light, hoping to reach the Willey House before night. Soon after their departure the old man starts up the stream with rod in hand, agreeing to wait dinner for us on the rocks above Thoreau Falls. The morning is beautiful, and we do not hasten from our charming nook among the pines. We sometimes clamber along the banks in the old forest; at others wade in the middle of the stream, taking little heed of time. We reach Thoreau Falls, and spend an hour in climbing about the rocks. It is a wild spot. The river tumbles over the ledges between high bluffs in many picturesque leaps. A short distance below the foot of the falls, the stream which flows from New Zealand Pond comes in from the north. A half-mile up this stream the valley is very narrow, the mountains on either side rising rapidly. This is the only place in this valley, or in the valley of the New Zealand River, which can properly be called a notch.

It is four o'clock when we reach the top of the falls. We find upon the rocks the frying-pan full of trout, and the old man fast asleep on the bank above. He informs us that two hours before, the young man appeared in breathless haste, stating that the journalist had entirely given out and was anxiously waiting two miles beyond for the doctors to come up. We hasten on, but do not find matters in the serious condition we feared. She had despaired of getting out, and had thought it wise to wait where we should reach her before night. During the afternoon the clouds have been gathering and the wind rising, and the rain is now falling. We work rapidly and build a camp, but are drenched before it is completed; and the rain drives with such fury that it affords us slight protection; yet we get considerable comfort from our smouldering camp-fire, and cannot help enjoying the wilderness of the night.

The stream, in which we were wading a few hours before, becomes a maddened torrent carrying everything before it. The great trees sway and creak; the thunder rolls heavily, and the lightning crashes in the forest all around us; but about midnight the stars suddenly appear. We renew our camp-fire, and before morning we are dry and comfortable. Again the journalist arranges an early start, — and this time with both men, that she may be sure of success. She has shown a wonderful perseverance under very adverse circumstances, but is much pleased with the prospect of returning home. They are to go out by Willey Pond, and we propose to explore the main stream to its source on Mt. Field. They meet with no difficulty, and are out by the middle of the afternoon.

We follow slowly, reluctant to leave the old forest and the wild stream. The forest is full of well-trodden paths of deer, and we frequently see their delicate footprints and occasionally fresh tracks of a bear, but we get few glimpses of animal life.

From the mouth of the river, nearly to Thoreau's Falls, the ascent is very gradual, presenting few obstacles to a roadway. This gradual rise continues up the stream, which flows in below the falls, to the height of the land at New Zealand Pond. The New Zealand River rises near the pond, and the descent through its valley to the Ammonoosuc is also gradual. The lumber in the whole region is valuable, and we may expect, at an early day, to be able to go through this forest—from the Ammonoosuc to the upper waters of the Pemigewasset—by regular conveyance.

For a mile or two above the falls the rise is gradual; but above Willey Pond Brook the ledges constantly crop out, and the stream becomes very rapid. A mile above the brook we reach the wild gorge referred to in an account of an exploration made last year. The water dashes down high cliffs in a succession of cascades, forming a picture of wonderful beauty. At the foot of the cascades, in the middle of the stream, rises a high rock, making a natural seat for the study of the picture. A short distance above the cascades we reach a swampy plateau sparsely covered with trees, in which the stream divides and is soon lost among the rocks and debris on the steep mountain-side.

We build a fire by a cool spring, dine on our last cup of oatmeal and our last stick of chocolate, hang our skillet high up on a tree for use another year, and begin the climb. We are directly under the steep western slopes of Mt. Field. Above us we see the immense ledges glistening in the sunlight.

The swampy plateau seems to extend a considerable distance to the north; and beyond the precipices there is a depression in the ridge, over which it seems to us there may be an easy exit to the Crawford House. But we are not sure of our bearings in that direction. Our supplies are entirely exhausted, and we cannot risk another night in the forest; so we bear southeasterly, to avoid the ledges and to strike the ridge between Mts. Field and Willey.

The climb is difficult; there is no soil,—nothing but immense fragments of rocks, covered with moss which treacherously conceals the pitfalls; and we are an hour and a half in reaching the ridge. We follow the ridge to the summit with little difficulty. The view is fine, especially down the Notch, and by clearing a small space we think it would equal that from Mt. Willey, in all directions. It is more direct to descend by way of Mt. Avalon, or the ravines on either side of it; but our time is limited, and we conclude to descend by way of Mt. Willard and the carriage road. It is very steep and ledgy, but we are expert after our seven day's climbing. We let ourselves down rapidly by the small birches and poplars in the rock crevices, cross the col, and climb the ledges of Willard. We are in a sorry plight to meet the hundred visitors who happen to be on the summit for a sunset view; but just as we are congratulating ourselves that we have escaped notice, we are recognized, and would soon have been the centre of a curious crowd, had we not excused ourselves with hasty explanation. Before starting we had taken the precaution to send some luggage to the Crawford House. In a half-hour there is a marked change in our garb, and we are on our way to Boston.

Exploring with the Appalachian Mountain Club

Excerpted from *Appalachia*

During the early years of the Appalachian Mountain Club's existence, most every issue of Appalachia *included reports by club members on their excursions in the White Mountains. Among those whose reports are featured below are former club president Charles Fay (1846–1931), and William H. Pickering (1858–1938), author of the 1882 book,* Walking Guide to the Mt. Washington Range.

Exploration of a Gorge on Mt. Lincoln

by Charles E. Fay
(May 1881)

In making the ascent of Mt. Lafayette, on the 12th of September, 1880, Professor Cross and myself, during our halt for lunch just beyond the lakes, noticed, as we looked across the broad intervening ravine, a narrow, dark shadow running for some distance down the precipitous northerly slope of the great west spur of Mt. Lincoln. It began perhaps a hundred feet, measured on a vertical, below the crest, and somewhat to the right of a noticeable protuberance of rock on the ridge-line—just to the right also of the upper part of the broad expanse of precipitous ledges that form so prominent a feature of the northwest slope of this mountain. It extended perhaps half-way down the remaining distance to the ravine bottom. A good opera-glass failing to determine its nature, we decided to explore it, and to return to the Profile House by the untried way of the ravine. This plan we successfully accomplished.

We found the mysterious shadow to be caused by a sunless gorge, which, if not so remarkable a natural feature as we had hoped to find, seems to us worthy of a visit from such sure-footed pedestrians as should find themselves on Mt. Lincoln. A half-hour would afford time to obtain a general idea of its character and return to the summit, but for a thorough exploration (such as we were unable to make) one should be provided with a long rope, and allow more than an hour. Time will also be saved if, when ascending Mt. Lafayette, one carefully notes the point on the crest-line below which the shadow begins. Descending too soon, we were forced to make our way several hundred feet through dense scrub growing on a treacherous and precipitous slope.

Reaching finally the proper point, we found a very steep, irregular, rocky gully, down which, during rains, a considerable quantity of water doubtless finds it way to the brook below, and where the drainings of the previous day's rain were still trickling. We undertook to make our way down it, but found this by no means an easy task. At one point our simplest course was to remove some large stones that had lodged in a broad crevice which began abruptly at the base of a steep rock, and to let ourselves down through the hole thus made to its steeply inclined bottom some six or seven feet below, thence out under the sky again. A few rods farther brought us to a place beyond which it seemed imprudent to venture without proper appliances. From here, so far as we could discover, there was an almost vertical decent of perhaps seventy-five feet. Much caution was requisite in abandoning our chosen path, as it was necessary to take advantage of a few widely separated projections of the rocky wall as foot-holds, and to choose discreetly upon which of the shrubs rooted in the wet, mossy soil we could rely for our grasp. On reaching higher growth, we made our way rapidly down to the rocky bed of the main stream.

We had intended to make our way to the lower end of the gully, and investigate it from below, but our time was quite too short. We had left the summit of Lincoln at 4.45; it was now, at least, 5.30, and this stream must be followed to its end, if possible, before dark. With our most earnest endeavors, this did not prove possible. The brook offered no essential variation from the usual type in these regions, not even in its quality of interminableness. In the upper portion, where the descent of the stream was rapid, our progress was necessarily slow over the great water-worn fragments of rock that filled its bed, and the slippery coating of moss which grew in profusion in the smoother ledgy portions of its course.

Fortunately, darkness did not overtake us until we had passed the worst portion of our way, and were within perhaps a quarter of a mile of the stage-road. From here on, unable to discern each other, or what lay at our feet, we proceeded, feeling our way foot by foot, cautiously discovering windfalls with our shins, until our patience was rewarded at the end of an hour by suddenly coming out upon the highway, at 8.05. Our course had been easily kept by remaining always within hearing of the brook on our right. We were surprised to find how practically useless the low rising moon was on lighting our way. Even where its rays fell into the woods about us, they served only to reveal the trunks of the trees above our heads.

Hedgehog Chasm

William H. Pickering
(June 1879)

Late in the summer of 1877, while staying at Campton Village, I heard of a great cleft, which was said to exist in a little mountain not eight miles away, and known as Mt. Hedgehog. This cleft had been discovered by three men independently, at different times, on each occasion the discoverer himself being lost. Two of the men had subsequently tried in vain to return to it. I obtained a description of its general appearance from the third man, and at length induced him to go with me in search of it. Our party left Campton early in the morning of Sept. 10, for Elkins's, which is the last house on the Mill Brook road. Here we met our guide, and were soon on our way up the steep slopes of Mt. Hedgehog. After an hour's fruitless search we heard a shout from one of the party, and running forward found him standing on a broad ledge of bare rock, down the very middle of which extended a long broad crevice. This was immediately identified by the guide as the place found by him some twenty years before. At one end he said grew two slender saplings; here we now found two sturdy full grown trees. I was let down into the chasm at one end, by means of a branch of a tree, and traversed its full length. It was very dark, and nothing but a narrow strip of light behind me indicated the opening. Near the entrance I found quantities of "daddy-long-legs," which had probably never before been disturbed by man or beast since the chasm was formed. So narrow is it at the bottom, that I had to climb over one of my companions in order to pass him, and we called to the rest not to come in till we had got out. Measurements were made with a cord brought for the purpose. We found it to be 90 ft. in length, 55 in depth, and one to two in breadth, at the top, and about six inches at the bottom.

Like the flume, it has a large boulder suspended between its walls, four or five feet in diameter. There is also another and smaller boulder suspended higher up. The best way to reach this spot in future, would be to strike the long ridge running westerly from Mt. Hedgehog, rather more than half way up, and then follow it up to the chasm. The latter is on the very edge of the ridge, and one could not miss it. Its position is marked by a solitary blazed pine tree which was then about eight feet in height. One side of the opening is three or four feet higher than the other, and one should move carefully, to avoid stepping into the chasm before seeing it.

A Three-Days' Trip over the Hancock-Carrigain Range

Webster Wells
(July 1880)

On Wednesday, Aug. 27, 1879, two members of the Appalachian Club, accompanied by two experienced woodsmen to act as porters, left Greeley's, Waterville, equipped with rations for four days, and bent on exploring the hidden recesses of this great central range of the Pemigewasset forest. We passed rapidly over the five miles of well-constructed path leading to the Greeley Ponds, and then plunged into the trackless wilderness which is watered by the Hancock Branch and its tributaries. We skirted the western slopes of Mt. Huntington, and finally, at about one o'clock, struck the Hancock Branch about half a mile east of its great south bend. After a hearty dinner at this point, we journeyed up the bed of the stream; preferring the rough rocks of the channel to the intricate snarl of underbrush and fallen timber which encumbered the mountain slopes on either side.

About two miles from our noon resting-place, we came to a place where the stream divides; one branch coming directly down the side of Hancock, the other flowing out of the notch between Hancock and Huntington. From this point, we followed the left-hand branch, and in a few minutes came upon a beautiful cascade; the water pouring in sheets over a rock formation which resembled a gigantic staircase. By six o'clock, we had followed the brook so far that a few pools were all that remained of it, and we decided to camp for the night. We were apparently at the base of the first of these mountains which we intended to explore,—Mt. Hancock; all around us towered the vast peaks and spurs of the mountain; and amid these grand surroundings, with a camp-fire in front of our rudely constructed cabin which burned several cords of wood in the course of the night, we slept soundly, storing up strength for the arduous labors of the morrow.

The next day, we rose at sun-rise, ate our breakfast, and got the dishes done in time to start at seven o'clock for the ascent of the mountain. We climbed directly up the slope, and in an hour reached the crest of the ridge which joins the two principal peaks, where we got a fine view of Carrigain towering two or three miles away, and presenting a remarkably massive appearance. We then followed the ridge line to the summit, which we reached at 8:30 a.m. The peak is covered with black and second-growth in about equal proportions, the line of demarcation traversing the very highest point in a direction from northwest to southeast; the second-growth being on the southwest side of this line. From all points of the low second-growth there is a good outlook, and a prospect embracing the whole mountain district may be obtained by climbing a tree. The view is grand, but does not equal that from Carrigain in comprehensiveness; the view of the latter peak, however, from Hancock, is very fine. We were unable to obtain a satisfactory view of the great East Branch valley, owing to the huge spurs which the mountain thrusts out to the north.

After two hours on the summit, we started down the mountain on the east side, intending to make a bee-line for Carrigain. We crossed a deep ravine and climbed to the summit of a tremendously steep and craggy ridge which lies between the two mountains. From its east side we got fine views of Carrigain, only a mile away, and on its slope, a quarter-way up, we noticed a little pond, hidden away in a deep recess, and surrounded by unbroken forests. We decided to make for it and dine on its shores. We reached it without difficulty, and found it to be about twelve acres in extent; its sandy beaches were completely covered with deer tracks, some of which our men said had been made within an hour. No traces of axe-marks or fires could be found in the vicinity, and it is doubtful if any human beings have ever before visited the locality.

After an hour and a half in this charming spot, we easily climbed to the summit of Carrigain in an hour, and, after a short stay, descended by the Club path and camped for the night at the point where the logging road to Livermore Mills crosses Carrigain Brook.

Our programme for the next day included a visit to Carrigain Notch, and the ascents of Mts. Anderson and Lowell. By great good luck, though none of us had ever been there before, we managed to pick out of the intricate maze of logging roads the proper route for the Notch, and after a tramp of an hour and a half we reached the divide. A few minutes' walk around the northerly slope of Lowell, on a level with the height of land in the Notch, brought us to a brook, crossing which we stood on the flanks of Mt. Anderson, and an easy climb of three quarters of an hour placed us on the peak. This mountain is wooded nearly over the whole summit, but a projecting ledge on the southwest side affords a grand view, comprising all the peaks of the mountain district from the Northern Kearsarge around by the south and west to Mt. Hale. The view of Carrigain is good, though not to be compared with that from Lowell; but the East Branch valley is shown far more satisfactorily than from the latter peak, and forms the most charming element in the prospect.

After an hour on Anderson, we struck through the woods to Mt. Lowell, which we reached in half an hour of easy walking. Lowell, like Anderson, is wooded on the highest peak, but a horseshoe-shaped clearing extends around the north side of the peak, by moving around which a view of nearly the whole horizon may be obtained, the only peaks invisible being those between Chocorua and Passaconaway. From a projecting ledge on the northwest side the best prospect is to be had, and the view of Carrigain from this point, looming over the profound depths of the Carrigain Notch, is one of the grandest sights among the mountains. The view of other mountains, too, is quite satisfactory, all the principal peaks of the White Mountain district being visible. We spent two hours on the ledge, and then descended the precipitous west side of the mountain into the Notch; a most arduous trip, and one which, owing to its dangerous character, I would not advise any one to undertake. Three quarters of an hour from the peak we crossed Carrigain Brook, soon found our friendly logging road, and half an hour later reached our camp of the previous night.

We packed up our things, started towards Livermore Mills, and when within half a mile of them crossed Sawyer's River, and headed for Waterville by way of the new path. Thunder had been muttering in the northwest for some time; and just as we reached the Waterville path, a heavy storm broke upon us. We pushed on through the rain and mud, and in about half an hour reached a dry shelter in the shape of a deserted log cabin. As this contained an iron stove and plenty of dry fuel, we were soon drying our wet clothes before a roaring fire; and after a good supper of trout and fried potatoes, we passed a quiet night.

Saturday, we returned to Waterville by way of the new path, where we arrived in good condition at 10 A.M. thoroughly satisfied with our trip, and resolved that it should not be our last expedition into this great stronghold of Nature.

1890

The Ascent of Mount Lafayette

Rev. Julius H. Ward

From *The White Mountains: A Guide to Their Interpretation*

IF THE ONLY AIM in climbing a mountain is to test one's legs, the passing and repassing over a stone wall will do nearly as well. There are some who think the glory of mountain climbing is in ascending as many peaks as possible. It is the number rather than the character of the peaks that constitutes the praise-worthiness of the act. The true aim in travel among the mountains is to make them such wise and intimate friends that they shall impart their secrets to us and respond to our demands for a life larger than our own. Every mountain has its own individuality as truly as every man. It may be large or small, but no hill is like another hill. It is this individuality that you feel on becoming better acquainted with them. The bridle path is never the same on the different peaks. The rocks are not the same; the springs are not in the same places; the timber-line varies with the height of each; the view from each, even in the same range, is as new as if the other peaks did not exist. This notation of differences grows upon one the more he enters into the life and atmosphere of the mountains, until he feels instinctively the characteristics of each one of the familiar peaks. Then there is something in the way that these peaks impress the imagination. You see them once and feel as you turn homeward that you can never take your last look of the magnificent sweep of the horizon which they lift up to the eye, and the imagery which is treasured in the memory is such that the imagination kindles it into life again and again in the quiet moments when mind and heart are unoccupied. This is the reward that all study of natural scenery brings to those who know how to observe. A friend of mine, who has travelled widely, can call up at a moment's notice perhaps a hundred pictures that have been so impressed upon his imagination and memory as to have become a permanent possession. It is these pictures, these impressions, these awakenings of the inner nature, these renewals of life by trying to comprehend a larger and different life, that constitute the abiding charm that the mountains have for imaginative and susceptible minds.

It is with these views of what one is to find in climbing mountains that I set out alone one morning to climb Mount Lafayette. A singular feeling comes over one who goes off on such an expedition alone. There are some things that are best done alone. You tell your secret to your lady-love alone. You best pray alone. You best think alone. You summon up courage best alone. No one ever thinks of dying otherwise than alone. I had never climbed a mountain before alone. It is the thing to do, and yet it is not always quite safe, unless you are more than sure of your bearings. I had been up the bridle path the year before and knew the route, but suppose I had slipped on a rock and sprained my ankle—or suppose a thousand and one other possibilities became realities—what might be my plight all alone on the peak? These thoughts always come to one, no matter what may have been his experience. Nearly all the deaths arising from exposure on the White Hills have resulted from going about alone. It is the remark of one who has been over these hills for the last thirty years that he never dared to undertake a route with which he was not familiar without a competent guide. If he is not needed to pioneer the way, he may be needed for an emergency that is almost sure to arise. This is specially the case on Mount Washington, and it is hardly less the case on Mount Lafayette, which is only about a thousand feet lower. However, I was glad to take the risks and go alone. It was also Hobson's choice. There was no one else to go. To have visited the Franconia Notch and not to have seen the top of Lafayette would have been like seeing Hamlet played with the character of Hamlet left out.

There is genuine refreshment in starting out from the hotel at an early hour to make the ascent of Lafayette. It is a three hours' climb along a tortuous path now so disused that many trees have fallen across it, and wherever there was once an apology for gravel that apology no longer exists. It winds first up under Eagle Cliff, and then passes through the gorge between the cliff and a spur of Mount Lafayette. It looks as if the mountain had been left unfinished at this point. Here is the natural home of wolves and bears, the great caves made by the confusion of rocks showing open-

Scenic Mount Lafayette rises up steeply
out of well-traveled Franconia Notch.

ings at every turn. A little way further up the peak is one of the coolest mountain springs I have ever drank from. Then comes the real tug of the ascent, but is it worth telling? Are not all ascents alike in their weariness for the flesh, even if they increase the buoyancy of the spirit? Well, it depends upon what you have trained yourself to see.

Half a mile farther up the mountain I found myself near one of the sources of the Ammonoosuc River, which was roaring from the depths of the chasm that lay a thousand feet below where I was ascending. The overhanging spurs of Mount Lafayette glistened in the morning sunshine, where the springs had moistened the lichened crags, and no vegetation hid their nakedness. The path now began to show the severity of the climate. The timber line grew less and less, and the stunted spruces and the courageous birches began to hand over their sway to the hardier vegetation. Next the scrub spruces showed their scraggy heads, as much as to say, "We have a hard time of it, too, but we never give up." By this time I had risen above the spur which reaches out to the Notch and overhangs the carriage road that passes through it. I could now see where I was. The Pemigewasset Valley stretched out below like a part of paradise, and the half-clothed peaks of Lafayette and its adjoining mountains commanded the horizon.

Mount Cannon, with its summit like a man's face covered with scabs, lifted up its huge front, but did not conceal the other peaks rising up in its ear. Away beyond its reach to the southwest rose the apparently round-topped Moosilauke, concealing the Connecticut Valley over which it stands sentinel. Snugly ensconced in the embrace of the spurs of Mount Cannon lay Lonesome Lake, looking as if it were the child of the wilderness, as indeed it is. Climbing up through the scrub, you come out upon the bare peak, where the Greenland sandwort makes the spaces between the rocks look like an Alpine garden. Here the ruggedness of the mountain is every moment more impressive. You go up a few rods and look back only to find that the world is constantly growing larger behind you.

At last you come up to the tiny spring that oozes out from the last cliff below the crown of the peak. Water is precious here. One can have only a cupful at a time. I remember how precious this water was once before to a dozen hungry mortals who sat down around it and partook of a luncheon that was miserably inadequate to the purpose for which it had been prepared. The spring was like an oasis in the desert. Water never tasted better.

Presently I resumed my course to the brow of the mountain. The view for the day was not the best that one could have desired, but you have to be satisfied with what you can get when you make these ventures. The mountains have no resource for displays to order. You take them as you find them, and it is this or nothing. But the view is simply grand, even when you can not see Mount Washington, and Mount Mansfield is hidden in the haze. Mount Lafayette is a second Mount Washington. You are not up so high, but the sense of isolated majesty, that is always the impression of the White Hills when seen from their sovereign peak, is repeated. Except toward Franconia and down the Pemigewasset Valley, there is nothing but the unbroken wilderness in sight. The view is unique. It is as if you were on the outskirts of the mountains and had taken just a good look over into their confines. The great furrows are seen, though not so regularly as from the top of Moosilauke, and the eye travels restlessly from summit to summit along the peaks to catch outlines that are familiar. Nothing is so clearly defined as Mount Washington; the Conway Kearsarge and Chocorua are sentinels to the east and south; the Green Mountains shut in the sky to the west; and the Canada hills loom up to the north.

It is not the least of the pleasures to be derived from the view to note how the peaks change with the variations of the atmosphere. They advance or recede, and grow larger or smaller, as the atmosphere is more or less dense. The clouds also have their share of importance. It is rare that the sky is here perfectly clear, and when it is you feel as if you had lost something from the view. The clouds are to the sky what light and shade are to the landscape, and they imprint upon the peaks and wooded hillsides the reflected glories of the sky. It is a sight worth seeing to watch the peak of Mount Washington as the clouds sweep around its summit and sport along its sides, and in this play of the sky and earth all the mountains seem to dance and sing, as the hills of Lebanon did to the imagination of the poet David. There is no end to the fancies that come to one when he is the sole occupant of a mountain top. Thoreau had all he could master in his little cabin on the edge of Walden Pond at Concord, but here they come in troops and crowds. Here old father Adam might have stood and seen precisely what I saw. How the mind travels backward through the ages at such a suggestion!

The geologist, Dr. T. Sterry Hunt, was explaining to me one day how the unity of the agents that have had a share in the growth of the earth into its present form is to be traced by following the changes in such rocks as compose the foundations of these mountains, and I could not help the impression that there is in the unfoldings of geology an evolution which corresponds to the other evolution that Darwin has traced in the vegetable and animal kingdom, and to that still further evolution of which Mr. John Fiske caught a glimpse as he passed, in his Destiny of Man, from the physical to the historical life of man as a member of universal society. On the top of a mountain one feels more than he can express, and this is what I dimly felt. I wish the mountains were not so inaccessible. What an advantage it would be if you could take in one of these mountain views as you take a horseback ride before breakfast! I found the attraction of Lafayette growing upon me the longer I stayed. Again and again I tried to turn from the scene, closing my eyes as soon as I had taken in the whole panorama, but my feet refused to turn homeward. There is a singular fascination in being up so high in the world all alone. The silence is delightful. There is a flowing together of impressions that you can not put into definite shape. The usual points of comparison do not serve. This is also seen in the sketches of Alpine travel. Men lose the adjectives, and seek in vain for the superlatives they want.

The descent of a mountain may be compared to the gradual diminution of the glory of a beautiful summer day. You lose your points of view one by one. There is a slow coming on of the commonness of things. Finally, you are chiefly anxious to reach the house and know how much has been left over from the dinner, or how soon supper will be ready. There is nothing that will make a man hungrier than the climbing of mountains, unless it is the waiting for the close of an old-fashioned ordination, while the "true blues" among the clergy make the candidate for settlement over the parish run the gauntlet of theological questioning till their ingenuity is exhausted. It might not be so well for the landlord at the Profile House if his guests should take to climbing the spur of Mount Lafayette, but I am sure that if both the men and the women could be induced to enter into the life of the mountains in this way, they would return to their homes in the cities with stronger muscles, better appetites, and more thorough preparation to endure the constant wear and strain of city life.

1893

Following a Lost Trail

Frank Bolles

From *At the North of Bearcamp Water*

*From his summer home on Lake Chocorua, literary naturalist Frank Bolles
(1856–1894) had a near perfect place from which to venture out into the woods
and mountains of his beloved Chocorua country. Bolles, a native of Winchester,
Mass., and for several years Secretary of Harvard University in Cambridge,
Mass., was first introduced to the scenic beauty of the southeastern White Mountains in the summer of 1883. By the end of the decade he'd taken up summer
residence at Lake Chocorua in a home often referred to in his writings as the
"red-roofed cottage." Though he died prematurely at age 39, Bolles managed to
see three books of his published, the best known of these being* At the North of
Bearcamp Water, *published in 1893. His other works included* Land of the
Lingering Snow *(1891) and* From Blomidon to Smoky *(1894). Chocorua's
Tenants, a collection of 14 Bolles' poems about the birds of Mt. Chocorua and
vicinity, was also published posthumously in 1895.*

OF THE MANY ROADS which start northward from Bearcamp Water,
every one is either warded off by the Sandwich range into the Saco or into
the Pemigewasset valley, or else smothered in the dark forest-clad ravines
between the mountain ridges. From Conway on the east to Campton and
Thornton on the west, there is no rift in the mountain wall through which
travel flows. There was a time, however, before the Civil War, when near
the middle of the great barrier the human current found an outlet southward from the upper end of Swift River intervale to the Bearcamp Valley.
Sitting by the fireside of a sturdy Albany farmer as the December moonlight gleamed upon the level snows of the intervale, I heard stories of the

lumbermen's journeys through those dark and narrow passes. Great spars and masts, the farmer said, had been hauled out of the valley under the frowning cliffs of Paugus, and carried safely to the level fields of Sandwich. Then there arose a storm such as old men know but once in a lifetime, and the passes were filled with tangled masses of wrecked forest. All the axes in Albany and Tamworth could not have cut a way through the snarl without many weeks of exhausting labor. So at least thought the lumbermen who attempted to pass the abattis raised by the storm. Years elapsed and the road became only a matter of vague tradition. Those who climbed the peak of Passaconaway or the lofty ledges of Paugus saw below them a panorama of ruin. Bleached bones of the great spruce forest lay there piled in magnificent confusion. Over the debris, springing from its midst, a dense growth of mountain ash, wild cherry, and hobble-bush made the chaos more chaotic. No trace of the lost trail was visible even to the most fanciful eye.

Between Paugus and Chocorua the hurricane had not done its worst work. There one could see four miles of narrow ravine reaching from the Tamworth fields directly northward to a steep ridge connecting Paugus with Chocorua at their northern slopes. On the other side of the barrier lay the Swift River intervale. If that ridge were out of the way, if it could be easily surmounted, or if a rift could be found in it, the journey of nearly thirty miles from the southern spurs of Paugus, round through Conway to the northern spurs, would be reduced to eight or nine miles. The people living at the upper end of Swift River valley, instead of having to travel sixteen miles to a post-office, doctor, minister, or store, could touch civilization by driving about eleven miles.

At half past four on the morning of Saturday, July 30, I drove rapidly away from my red-roofed cottage towards the southern foot of Paugus. Long days of parching heat had been brought to an end by a series of three heavy thunderstorms, which had drenched the country during the preceding evening. Nature had revived. The sky was bluer, the forest greener, the gold of the goldenrod more intense. Every particle of dust had been washed out of the air and off the many-tinted garments of the earth. For nearly a fortnight the mercury had been among the nineties as often as the clock struck noon. To face a cool breeze, to see everything sparkling with moisture, to have the air feel and appear thin and clear, was inspiring and exhilarating. To find the lost trail into the Swift River valley was now a matter of delightful interest.

At the southern foot of Paugus is a ruined mill and an old lumber camp. A good road leads thither from the highway, and the house at the point

where the lumber road begins is the home of Nat. Berry, farmer, lumberman, hunter, trapper, surveyor, carpenter, and public-spirited citizen. I felt
that if any man on the southern side of the mountains knew a way through
them, that man was Berry. Two years before, while wandering over the
ridges of Chocorua, I had been caught in one of Berry's forty-pound steel
bear traps. The springs of the trap were weak and it was deeply buried in
the moss, so that before its cruel jaws had closed firmly upon my ankle,
I thrust the stock of my gun between them and withdrew my foot. Berry's
greeting, as we drove up to his house, showed that he had not forgotten
my adventure, for he shouted, "Come at last, have you, to let me cut off
them ears? Can't c'lect my bounty on you without 'em." A few words told
Berry of my errand, and he at once showed interest in the quest.

"Thirty-seven years ago," he said, "when I was only twelve year old, a
road was run through from this house to the back settlements. It was a
winter road, but I recollect that a man and his wife drove over it in a pung.
They went in where you are a-going, with a railroad surveyor, and he said
there was only five hundred feet rising between here and the height of
land. There used to be another road between Toadback and Passaconaway,
but that's all choked up now by the harricane. This road is between Toadback and Conway, and I know that four miles of it is about as good going
now as ever it was."

It required little urging to induce Berry to join us, and our horse's head
was turned northward into the lumber road leading to the lost trail. As we
drove away from fields, roads, and the surroundings of habitations, animal
life grew less and less abundant, and plant life less varied. Around the
farms robins, sparrows, and swallows are to be seen or heard at every hour
in the day. Woodpeckers and chickadees abound in the orchards, and even
hawks spent more time in sight of hen-yards than they do in the gloomy
solitudes of the mountains. By the roadside goldenrod was in its glory,
while St. John's-wort was growing rusty. The pink of hardhack and this-
tles large and small, the yellow of the mullein, the reds of fireweed, pasture lily, and the sumac fruit, the purple of vervain, early asters, and the
persistent brunella, and the white of the exquisite dalibarda, of immor-
telles, arrowhead, and the graceful spiranthes in turn caught the eye as the
wagon rolled by pasture and sandbank, meadow, copse, and swamp.

From Berry's house we drove a long mile before the true primeval forest was reached. There, in a clearing of an acre or more, were the ruins of
a saw-mill, two or three slab houses, and a collapsed stable where the lumbermen's oxen had been kept in the winter nights, years ago. In the mill's
time sawdust had covered everything; but now the strong, quarrelsome

blackberry had mastered the sawdust. Our guide pointed to a break in the solid wall of woods surrounding the mill, so we struggled through the blackberry jungle and left the sunlight behind us. As we entered the forest, bird music ceased, few flowers decked the ground, — the pallid Indian pipe seeming more akin to the fungi than to flowers, — and not a squirrel disturbed the quiet of the endless aisles. Here and there small brightly colored toadstools and the fruit of bunchberry or clintonia lent a bit of vermilion, orange, yellow, or lustrous metallic blue to the dull brown carpet of the woods; or a branch of maple, prematurely robbed of its chlorophyll, gleamed in the far-off sunlight among the tree-tops. If by chance the eye caught a glimpse of the flowers of the rattlesnake plantain, or of some of the greenish wood orchids, it found in them less color than in the toadstools and less perfume than in the needles of the balsam.

There extended before us a clearly marked passageway between the giant trunks of ancient trees. It was the beginning of the old trail. Stout young saplings had grown up within it, and the long interlacing stems of the hobblebush, or "tangle-foot" as Berry called it, concealed its many inequalities. We proceeded slowly, cutting away bushes as we went, and the horse followed with the wagon, which rose and fell over logs and boulders as though tossed on the waves of the sea. At the end of half a mile, we decided to leave the horse with all of our impedimenta except axes and luncheon. A space was accordingly cleared, and Kitty, tied to a large tree, was fenced in on two sides to prevent her from walking around the tree, and so choking herself.

The trees which formed the forest were of many kinds, making it much more interesting than the monotonous spruce growth of the higher slopes. Those which were to all appearance the oldest were the yellow birches, hundreds of them having trunks over ten feet in circumference at a point two feet from the ground. Some of the giant hemlocks were larger, but they are, I believe, trees of more rapid growth than the yellow birch and so probably less venerable. There was a large representation of ancient beech-trees with trunks which looked as hard as granite, yet which made me think of wrestlers with swollen muscles strained and knotted under the tightly drawn skin. Some of the beeches seemed to have begun life in mid-air, for their trunks rested upon tripods or polypods or naked and spreading roots, which held them two or even three feet from the surface of the soil. In other cases these polypods clasped great boulders in their unyielding embrace, showing that the beech in its infancy had taken root upon the top of the rock, and year by year extended its thirsty tentacles lower and lower down the sides of its mossy foundation until the soil was reached. Then the hungry sapling, fed for so long on meagre supplies of food and water, must have expanded with sudden vigor, while its roots grew strong and gripped the rock in tighter and tighter embrace. The only way of accounting for the empty polypods seemed to be to suppose the trees to have sprouted upon stumps prone to decay, or upon rocks capable of rapid disintegration. Many of the glimpses through these beech woods reminded me of the grotesque forest pictures which are produced so frequently in German woodcuts.

Huge maples, with bark resembling that of ancient oaks, formed an important part of the forest, and so did canoe birches of various ages, solitary white pines of immense height, and old-growth spruces, the last named becoming more and more numerous as our road gained higher levels. Dozens of these trees had been struck by lightning and more or less injured. One had been completely shattered and surrounded by a spiral abattis of huge splinters stuck firmly into the ground.

The twilight and silence of the forest made it restful at first, but as the day wore on, rare glimpses of distance and of sunlight were as welcome to us as to men confined between prison walls.

We had gone rather more than three miles from Berry's house when our guide paused and said: "There, the old road is missing for a piece beyond this, and the best we can do is to head north and spot the trees as we go."

To that point there had been evident, to eyes accustomed to forest travel, a difference between the continuity of large timber and the strip once cleared of this timber in order to form the road. Looking back, we could see the passage; looking forward, there seemed to be no trace of it. The greater part of Paugus had been passed on our left, and on our right the peak of Chocorua, which at Berry's had been northeast, was not a little south of east from us. Before us the valley narrowed somewhat, and far ahead a continuation of the ridge of Paugus seemed to cross the northern sky line and approach the northern spurs of Chocorua. Blazing the trees as we walked by them, both on our left and on our right, on the south side of the trunks and on their north sides also, we pushed forward due north. Ever since leaving the ruined mill our way had lain close to the foot of Paugus, the width of the valley being between us and the foot of Chocorua. Nearly a mile was traversed before we touched the wall of Paugus barring the north and forcing us to bend eastward. Entering a narrow ravine, none too wide for a single road at its bottom, we came once more upon the lost trail. Marks of the axe were frequent, but the great hemlocks which it had felled were mere moss-covered pulp, and from their stumps viburnum or young trees had sprouted. Berry found spots on the trees which he re-

membered to have made when he guided the engineer through the pass
fifteen years before. The walls of the ravine grew steeper, and across it
fallen trees occasionally blocked the way. Presently it bent sharply to the
left, so that we were once more headed northward, and then it widened
into an amphitheatre half a mile in width, wholly surrounded by steep and
rocky sides. The old trail was again lost, and Berry declared that out of this
pocket there was no outlet save over the towering ridge at the north. The
story of the man and woman in a sleigh, who had once crossed this frowning barrier, alone sustained our hopes of finding a pass which could be
opened to wheels.

My watch said that it was 10:30 A.M. As we had begun our first meal at
four A.M., a second one seemed appropriate; so in the face of our frowning crisis we lay upon the moss and made way with the larger part of our
knapsack's contents. A red squirrel, inquisitive, petulant Chickaree, came
down from the ridge and chattered to us. Far above in the treetops two
birds called loudly to each other. Their notes were new to me, and so shy
were they that I secured only a distant glimpse of them through my glass.
They seemed to prefer the highest tips of dead trees, from which they
darted now and then into the air after insects. It did not require much
knowledge of birds to assign this noisy couple to the family of the tyrant
flycatchers, and their size was so great as to make them one of three
species,—kingbirds, great crested flycatchers, or olive-sided flycatchers.
As I knew the first two well, from daily chances to watch their habits, I felt
practically certain that these keepers of the pass were the wild, wayward,
and noisy olive-sided flycatchers of which I had heard so often, but never
before met on their breeding-grounds. Luncheon over, we faced the barrier, and selecting a shallow ravine in its side, began the ascent. While
struggling over huge boulders and winding around fallen trees we did not
feel as though wheels were ever likely to go where legs were having so hard
a time. Still the ascent was made in less than ten minutes, and to a practical road-builder the slope, cleared of its surface debris, would present few
serious obstacles.

On reaching the top we gained a view of the peak of Chocorua well to
the south of east, and of the ramparts of Paugus, half spruce hung and half
bald rock, bounding the long valley through which our morning tramp had
taken us. The peak of Chocorua had lost its horn-like contour and resembled more a combing wave dashing northward. It was the only part of the
mountain proper to be seen, as in the foreground a massive spur projecting northwestward completely concealed the principal mass. Looking towards the north, the prospect was disheartening. The ridge on which we

stood had been a battleground of the elements. It was, in the language of this region, a "harricane," and woe to the man who ventures into a "harricane." We advanced cautiously, choosing our ground, and cutting a narrow path through the small spruces, cherry saplings, and mountain maples which had overgrown the fallen forest. Every few steps we came upon stumps which bore the axe mark instead of that of the storm. We surmised that we had stuck a belt which had been "lumbered" before the hurricane had completed its destruction. Fighting on yard by yard, we crossed the top of the ridge and gained its northern edge. There the signs of timber cutting were plainer, and presently I noticed a curious ribbon of saplings reaching down the slope in front of us. The young trees in it were higher than the wreck on each side of it, yet the ribbon was the road and the wreck was all that remained of the forest through which the road had been cut long years ago. The broken thread of the lost trail had been found. Behind us a blazed path reached into the Bearcamp valley; before us the lumber road wound downward a short two miles to the Swift River road, now plainly visible over the sloping tree-tops.

We followed the lumber road down about a mile, searching for a hut which Berry remembered to have seen. As we descended, the "harricane" was left behind, and our ribbon of saplings led into the forest, its massed stems contrasting oddly with the wide-paced trunks of the primeval growth. Coming to the hut, which Berry said had been built twenty years before, we found it remarkably well preserved. Straw still remained in the lumbermen's bunks, pieces of the stove lay on the floor, and although the roof had been sprung by snow resting heavily upon it, the hut was as dry and habitable as ever. It even retained the "stuffy" smell of a dirty and ill-ventilated house. It was inhabited, too, not by men, but by hedgehogs, as the American porcupine is universally called in New Hampshire. They had been under it, through it, and over it. Every piece of stair, joist, or floor, upon which salt of grease had fallen, had been gnawed away by them. They had slept in the bunks both upstairs and down, and the stairs bore traces of their constant use.

In front of the hut stood a watering-trough. It was a huge log hollowed by the axe into two tanks, a small one at the upper end for man's use, and a larger one below for the cattle. Small logs had been neatly grooved as spouts to lead the water from the brook to the trough. Moss grew upon them now and the summer sunlight shone upon them, but it was easy to imagine the snow piled high upon the hills, smothering the brooks and burying the rough spouts, and to fancy that over the trampled snow the wooly and steaming oxen came to drink of the water, while a sturdy French

Canadian broke the ice with his axe and drank at the spot where from under the snow the spouts led the water into his end of the dugout. The cattle are dead, the axe has rusted, the Canadian has been killed in a brawl, or has gone back to his River St. Lawrence to spend his old age under the shadow of the cross, but the brook still murmurs over its pebbles, and when snow falls by the trough and the hut it is cleaner and purer than the foot of the lumberman left it.

Woe to the man who ventures into a "harricane"! Not content with the road which we had made and found over the ridge, we sought, as we turned homewards, to see whether another lumber road, which came into ours from the southeast, did not cross the ridge by an easier grade. Following it upward higher and higher, we came at last to an open ledge from which a beautiful view was gained. Northward of us frowned Bear Mountain, dark in its spruces. To its left were Lowell, Nancy, Anderson, and the rest of the proud retinue of Carrigain. Deep shadows lay in Carrigain Notch. Bluer and fairer, higher and more distant, the heads of Bond, Willey, and the Franconia Mountains rested against the sky. To the westward, above the long rampart of Paugus with its flat, gray cliffs capped by black spruce, towered the cone of Passaconaway, wooded to its very tip. Southward, just across a deep ravine and behind a heavily timbered spur, was Chocorua, its great tooth cutting into the blue heavens. Though we enjoyed the picture of the distance, we were filled with something like despair at the foreground. On three sides of us the "harricane" extended as far as the nature of the ground permitted us to see. Westward, along the ridge, in the direction in which lay our trail of the morning, it reached for half a mile at least, and through it we must go, unless, indeed, we preferred to retrace our steps into the Swift River valley and regain our path by such an ignominious circuit. Seen from above, the half-mile of forest wreck looked like a jack-straw table of the gods. Thousands of trees, averaging sixty or seventy feet in height, had been uprooted and flung together "every which way." They were flat upon the ground, piled in parallel lines, crossed at right angles, head to head, root to root, twisted as though by a whirlwind, or matted together as they might have been had a sea of water swept them from hill-crest to valley. Boulders of various sizes lay under the wreck, and, to make its confusion more distracting, saplings, briers, and vines flourished upon the ground shaded and enriched by the wasting ruin.

It took more than an hour to climb and tumble over half a mile of this tangle. Any one who has watched an ant laboriously traversing a stumble-field or a handful of hay, crawling along one straw, across some, under another, and anon climbing to a height to consult the distance, will know how we made our journey. Men go through great battles without a scratch, but they could not penetrate a "harricane" with any such fortunate results.

The spots on our blazed trees seemed as friendly as home on a winter's night, when at last we reached them and began the southward march. As we had been two hours without water, the first brook drew us to its side and held us entranced by its tiny cascades. In the pool from which I drank, half a dozen caddisworm cases lay upon the sand at the bottom. They were sand, yet not of the sand, for mind had rescued them from the monotony of their matter and made them significant of life. They had faithfully guarded their little builders while dormant, and now those awakened tenants had risen from the water, dried their gauzy wings in the sun and vanished in airy wanderings. Near the brook lay a dead tree, and upon it were fastened a number of brightly colored fungi. Their lower surfaces and margins were creamy white, then a band of orange vermilion passed around them, while the upper and principal part was greenish gray marked with dark brown wavelike lines. They reminded me, by their color and surface, of the tinted clay images or costume figures which are made by peasants in several parts of southern Europe, and in Japan. Anything more in contrast with the gloom of a northern forest would be hard to discover. Much of the ground near the brook was covered by yew bushes, on which, brilliant as jewels, gleamed their pendent and slightly attached red berries. The mosses and lichens were the glory of the wood. Never parched by thirst in these perpetual shades, they grew luxuriantly on boulders, fallen logs, standing trees, the faces of ledges, and over the moist brook banks and beds of leaf mould. What the great forest was to us, that the mosses must be to the minute insects which live among them.

So thoroughly had we spotted the trees in the morning, that as we followed our trail back there was not a moment when our eyes hesitated as to the direction of the path.

Four days passed, and on the morning of the fifth a gay column wound its way through the forest following the regained trail. Nearly a score of axes, hatchets, and savage machettas resounded upon the trees and shrubs which encroached upon the road. Behind the axemen came several horses, each bearing a rider as courageous as she was fair. If branches menaced the comfort of these riders, they were speedily hewn away; if the hobble-bush hid hollows or boulders in the road, it was cut off at the root; if the ford or a bog offered uncertain footing to the snorting horses, strong hands grasped their bridles and they were led through to surer ground. When the difficulties of the road became serious, the horses were left behind and the column pressed forward on foot. The ridge was met and stormed, the "harricane" was safely pierced, and hedgehog's hut was visited and passed, and the old lumber road was followed swiftly down to the grass-land and high-way of the Albany intervale. If one woman in days long past had traversed the winter road in a sleigh, others of her sex had now overcome greater difficulties and broken the stubborn barrier of the Sandwich range.

December 1916

Snow-Bound
in September

Robert Whitehill

From *Appalachia*

IT IS THE common lament of most of us mortals, who never wander very far from our own firesides, that "nothing ever happens to us." To minds which have to depend upon the adventures of Jack London's creations or the perils of the motion picture heroine for the thrills which are needed to quicken the circulation, it does indeed seem that existence is all too tame. Little do we realize that at any time we are likely to encounter some situation which will give us more real thrills than fall to the lot of the heroine in the jungle scene, protected as she is by an invisible wire screen and a half-dozen sharp-shooters. Yet the exciting evening's entertainment or the thrilling adventures on the printed page have one decided advantage over the other kind: one can end the story when he has had enough, and go to sleep in his own bed before the clock strikes twelve.

The great storm of September, 1915, furnished the unexpected "stage properties" for the scenario about to be unfolded, and furnished the amateur actors with more than they had bargained for in registering the various emotions while the crank was being turned.

This storm, lasting several days, made its fury felt from Canada to the Gulf of Mexico. It was especially severe in the White Mountain region, where the terrible gale devastated forests as no storm has done for many years. In the Franconia and Crawford Notches roads were rendered impassable by the fallen trees, while in some places heavy growths of timber for a mile or more were cut off, as if by the stroke of a giant scythe. The good old Peak House on Mount Chocorua, which has sheltered many happy trampers during more than a quarter of a century, strained at its moorings for the last time, and the place of its anchorage knew it no more. On Mt. Washington old stage-barns, which have stood more windy buffetings than almost any buildings on this continent, had finally to submit to broken roof-chains, blown-away doors, and one, to the bursting of its entire side. The Halfway House, four miles below on the carriage road, suffered only the blowing in of a door and a window. The stage-office on the summit withstood the storm without the loss of a single one of its architectural beauties, save the breaking of one of its roof chains. It did, however, have one of the roughest voyages in its history as it rose and fell to the music of the spheres. That its passengers were not lost, in their desire to gain terra firma, was due only to the presence of mind of the skipper, who guarded the exit with an axe. Down below, in the erstwhile peaceful vales, on the worst night of the storm, some of the more prudent of the good people kept their clothes on all night, ready to board up broken windows or to make a try for the cyclone cellar if all else failed. Such was the setting that was being arranged for the amateur actors "on that pleasant morn in the early fall" when this story really begins.

It was, indeed, a beautiful autumn morning, such as only those who know the crisp tang of mountain air can appreciate. Knapsacks had been packed, a fine breakfast dispatched, and the big seven passenger car stood chugging at the door in front of the Wilson Cottages in the lovely town of Jackson. Five eager passengers climbed aboard and stowed away their dunnage, ready for the start. First came the "Veteran," so called because climbing Mt. Washington was no new thing to him. In fact, half a century and more had passed since, as a boy, he first saw its glories in company with his father. During the later years he had been content with the lesser climbs, as a variation from his literary labors. It is whispered that the Veteran is writing a book. Next came Ottilie, a lady prominent in the society and club life of famous Milwaukee. To her the Canadian Rockies and most American mountains are as old friends, while she knows the White Mountains as thoroughly as a California school teacher knows Boston after a week's visit. Next in line is Parker, alias "the Timber Cruiser," so called because he has learned the lumber business, from the logging camp to the finished product, his more recent years having been spent in British Columbia near the lofty peak of Mt. Robson. Next comes his sister, "Mrs. Bob," a vivacious young matron, who believes in having something doing every minute. Last of all is Bob, who has no distinction other than being the husband of Mrs. Bob.

Just as the car is about to start someone sees the wistful look on the face of David, the eight year old son of the Bobs, and asks why he cannot come too; so he gleefully climbs in, to have the ride to the foot of the trail and come home with the driver. To be sure he hasn't had his breakfast, but there are sandwiches in the knapsack, and what is breakfast compared with a ride in the big car on such a morning? Away they go, with the farewell cheers of the chaffing guests giving the party a proper send-off.

Down the steep hill, through the village, across the Glen Ellis river and along the smooth and winding Glen Road the big car swiftly travels. The ten miles to the foot of the mountain is made in but a fraction of the time it used to take with the plodding horses. Arrived at the foot of the Tuckerman Ravine trail the party alights, with instructions to the driver to come to the Glen House for them Monday night at five o'clock, the plan being to spend Saturday night at the Lakes of the Clouds and Sunday night at the Madison Hut.

David's parents kiss him a fond good-bye, knapsacks are shouldered and the procession starts. As they leave the road the Ravine shows up before them with startling clearness, a peculiar gray appearance of the rocks through the clear air causing the party's pessimist to make mental observations that this beautiful weather is good for one day only. He doesn't dare to say so aloud, however. Into the woods the trail leads, until in a few minutes a little bridge is crossed, from which is viewed the beautiful Crystal Cascade. The perfect waterfall is worth going miles to see, and a stop of a few minutes is made, as it is unusually good on this particular morning.

The call sounds to "hoist packs" and the march begins at a moderate pace, as everyone wishes to have the Veteran take it easy and enjoy this trip, which is his first ascent of the mountain by the Tuckerman route. As all who know this trail will remember, the first part is through real forest, at a fairly steep grade, with most delightful streams crossing the path. Each one of these streams is an invitation to stop and have one little drink of the delicious water, noting with interest that the water is a little cooler at each stopping place, until one feels sure there must be ice somewhere in the vicinity.

Reaching Hermit Lake Camp, a little rest is taken while Ottilie photographs the group. The camp, which is nothing but a bark-covered log shelter, is clean and cozy withal, and it is noted that there are the materials for a fire, and enough odds and ends of food stuffs to keep a stormbound traveler from starvation for a day or two. The great boulder before the open side of the camp, against which the fires are made, could tell great stories of the campfire tales it has heard these many years. It is a wild and picturesque location, surrounded by scrubby forest, which somewhat screens but does not hide the frowning ramparts on three sides of the hut. The walls tower perhaps fifteen hundred feet above the spectator in rugged perpendicular fashion, which makes the novice wonder if there is any possible safe ascent.

On leaving the camp the party divides, as Ottilie and Parker are planning to make the still more strenuous ascent of Huntington's Ravine, the trail to which is a short distance below the camp. During their ascent they have several thrills, and on meeting the rest of the party at the summit, tell of fighting their way against a terrific wind between the headwall and the top of the mountain. Meanwhile the Veteran and the Bobs make progress at a moderate rate up Tuckerman's. Mrs. Bob's youthful enthusiasm finally gets the better of her, and she goes on ahead to the top of the head-wall near the Fall of the Thousand Streams, where she impatiently waits for the plodders.

On the way along the narrow ledge near the top of the Ravine, Bob is interested to observe the spot where he nearly went over the edge some years previous, when making the climb alone. At that time he was trying the stunt which proved fatal to Lot's wife, that is, looking backward. He saw out of the tail of his eye some perfectly good looking grass on the narrow path. As it happened, the grass had no soil under it but was growing out over the edge, so, of course, as he stepped on it, over the edge went he; and he might have kept on going, had not his bare right elbow caught in time to allow him to hang there and think over his sinful life, as he tried to climb back to safety.

At the top of the head-wall Mrs. Bob starts out at a lively pace on the climb up the rocky cone to the summit. The plodders still plod, and reach the top a good half hour later than she. In her joy at finally seeing them she knocks out a pane of glass from the stage-office window, and the keeper of the house, placated with half a dollar, immediately begins to put in another pane. It is well that he does, too, for the poor old stage-office will need whole windows for the next few days, if ever.

The party here is re-united and makes a rush for the new Summit House, which is just being closed for the season. Through the kindness of some of the guests still inside, in spite of the inhospitality of the management, the doors are unlocked and the hungry travelers are enabled to have their belated lunch and much hot coffee. After a comfortable rest in front of the big fireplace, they sally forth to go down via the Crawford Bridle Path to the Appalachian Club's new stone hut at the Lakes of the Clouds, where they are planning to spend the night. Little do they imagine for how many nights they are destined to be grateful to the shelter of its walls from the raging of the elements!

To shorten the distance to the hut a cut-off is taken, which leads straight down over the great masses of broken rocks on the cone, and here the ever-increasing wind strikes them with such fury that jumping from rock to rock is something of a feat. The three speedsters leave the Veteran in the rear with Bob, and the latter wonders at times whether his senior partner is going to make the ticklish steps without being blown over. This is no joke, for a misstep may mean broken bones.

As they are half way down the cone they see a fleet-footed, antelope sort of chap coming up the treacherous rocks on the run. This proves to be the care-taker of the Lakes of the Clouds hut with a knapsack on his back, on his way to the top for provisions—provisions which never came, and which might have served to make the long sojourn more endurable had they been available. Before the plodders have reached the trail at the foot of the cone, the redoubtable George, for such is his name, passes them on his way down, and still on the run.

As the hut comes more plainly into view, a figure capped with an oil-skin "sou'wester" can be seen pacing about in front of the stone house near the little lakes. This gentleman, later known as "The Scientist," is to play an important part in our drama, and to make the others glad that the fates sent him along to share their joys and sorrows. The Scientist has just come up via the trail from Crawfords, laden with a knapsack, two cameras and various other impedimenta, some of which proves very useful to the party during the next few days.

By about five o'clock the six travelers are inside the house enjoying the warm of the cookstove, and the prospects of a good supper by and by. The house, the particular pride of the Appalachian Club, is the last word in shelters of its kind. It was opened on August 7, 1915, at which time printed announcements of the opening where distributed, stating that it was built by voluntary subscriptions and dedicated to the use of "those who enjoy the higher altitudes." It is a fine structure of stone, capable of accommodating thirty-six persons with sleeping quarters. It is divided into two rooms; one with twenty-four folding bunks for men, and one with twelve for women. One feature of the house which is very attractive in fine weather, is the view to be obtained from the unusually large windows. Some of these are from five to seven feet high, and nine or ten feet long. From one, a magnificent view of the hotels and golf links at Bretton Woods may be had, also the Base Station on the cog railroad, the trestle known as Jacob's Ladder, and beautiful distant views of the town of Jefferson.

Lakes of the Clouds hut.

On this Saturday night the sunset was a gorgeous sight, and everybody enjoyed the beautiful views and explored the surroundings, though the high wind was too chilly to make long stops out of doors comfortable. Aside from the exposed situation the location of the hut is admirable, for the little lakes are but a few rods distant. From them the narrow stream which supplies the camp with drinking water pours down the beautiful Ammonoosuc Ravine, to emerge later as the well-known Ammonoosuc River. Near at hand the peak of Mt. Monroe rises several hundred feet above the camp and adds greatly to the picturesqueness of the scene. The daylight does not linger long, and the chief entertainment for awhile is in watching George, the care-taker, get supper ready. It is a real supper too, and one that is recalled in the lean days that are to follow, for there is real bread and real butter and real potatoes, things that later are as scarce as icicles in a boiler-room.

That first night in the new camp was a jolly one. In spite of the high wind prevailing, everyone was re-assured by the brilliant red sunset and had the feeling that the morrow might be fine. The proposed trip over the Northern Peaks—Clay, Jefferson and Adams—to the Madison Huts was eagerly anticipated; so at a fairly early hour George let down the folding bunks, arranged the blankets and everyone prepared to turn in. Owing to the fact that the ladies' dormitory was shut off from the heat of the fire and seemed rather cold and cheerless, the two ladies of the party elected to take a section of the larger room.

For a party of seven the night was a very quiet and restful one, aside from the roar of the wind rushing up the Ravine outside the house. Such few snores as could be heard were of a very refined and considerate sort, and all awakened with a feeling of gratitude to their fellow voyagers for not "making night hideous." Breakfast was had in good season, and plans were discussed. Sunday had not dawned as pleasantly as could be wished —far from it. A stiff wind was blowing, about all that one could stand against, and clouds were scudding low and thick. The more optimistic and venturesome members of the party were in favor of starting anyway, but one old croaker protested, and asseverated that a big storm was brewing, one which might last four or five days. He urged everyone to sit tight and enjoy the beauties of a rainy day in camp, with the hope of getting out by Friday. The croaker was promptly voted a nuisance, especially by the ladies, who dubbed him a "calamity howler." The calm and imperturbable Scientist came to his rescue, however, and read a few extracts from the "Appalachian Guide Book" as to the dangers of the Gulfside Trail in bad weather. This seemed to have the desired effect, and everybody calmed down and made the best of the situation. Rain was soon beating against the exposed windows and the wind steadily increased in velocity, keeping at it with violence until late in the afternoon, when the clouds suddenly parted and spirits rose. The sun attempted to come through and things looked decidedly better.

In spite of the fierce wind, somebody dared somebody else to take a run up Mt. Monroe, which is only a fifteen or twenty minute climb from the camp. All hands voted in favor of it and started up the east side of the peak, which was the lee side as the wind was blowing. Ottilie, who was the featherweight of the party, was firmly grasped by George, the guide, or she might have been blown away. As she neared the top, the wind seized her tightly tied veil and tore it from her head, carrying it straight up for several hundred feet, and then chased it at the rate of a mile a minute over Boott Spur in the direction of Jackson. A minute later, when she gained the summit, the gale might have made her follow suit, had not George rescued her. The Bobs, who were following, for once thanked their *embonpoint*, which was sufficient to keep them from going skyward. On the summit no one could safely stand, and all beat a hasty retreat toward the hut. They were not a minute too soon; for, by the time they were safely housed, a real storm began, a storm which raged without cessation until Thursday morning.

It was on this night that the Chocorua Peak House disappeared and that the greatest damage was done throughout the entire mountain region. The care-taker at the stage office on the summit of Washington estimated the wind velocity on that night at one hundred seventy-five miles an hour, and this does not seem incredible, as the United States Weather Bureau recorded one hundred eighty-six miles an hour at the time it maintained a station there, and this storm of 1915 was said to be the worst for thirty-five years.

Suffice it to say, that one who has not experienced such a storm can have no conception of what it means to be where the wind is traveling from two to three miles in a single minute. Had not the Lakes of the Clouds Hut been mostly strongly built, the uneasiness of its occupants would have been much greater. As it was apprehension prevailed, for the huge windows offered a splendid target for the fury of the gale. The steel window sash with its quarter inch panes was firmly embedded in masonry, but a tendency to bend and buckle could be noted with half an eye, as the savage gusts crashed against the glass barrier with the force of surf breaking on the rocks by the sea-shore. These ominous crashes served to make everyone reflect upon the consequences, should the windows give way. With windows gone there would be more real shelter in the lee of the masonry on the outside of the hut than there could possibly be within. Fortunately these forebodings were not realized, and in spite of doubts and fears all turned in at a seasonable hour. For the most, it was afterwards confessed, there was little sleep. Aside from the regular crashes of the gale there was a vibration of the entire stone structure, which required no seismograph to record, as it could be plainly felt by the would be sleeper lying in his narrow bunk.

Monday morning came at last, with the hurricane still doing its worst. To add to the general discomfort, the temperature had dropped greatly during the night, and investigation showed that the thermometer on the sheltered side of the house registered eighteen degrees above zero. Within it was not much warmer, before the fire was built; while, later in the day, an indoor temperature of thirty-eight degrees was the standard at a short distance of the stove. One of the most comfortable features of the situation was the ample supply of charcoal fuel. The food supply, however, caused serious thought of the future, should the storm continue, as now seemed probable. A consultation on this important subject, and an inventory of the scantily stocked larder, made it appear that a decree prohibiting more than two meals a day must be issued. It was done forthwith. Breakfast, thereafter, was changed to "brunch," a modern title, ascribed to Gelett Burgess, to designate a meal in which breakfast and lunch are combined.

It began to appear that the most comfortable place to spend the day, as well as the night, was in bed; so most of the boarders of the hostelry, kept under cover of the heavy blankets, and whiled away the hours by reading the few magazines which some thoughtful people had left in the camp. To hold a paper for more than a few minutes one wanted his gloves on, while the frosted breath of the occupants and the heavily frosted windows lent an Arctic air to the scent. The Veteran, who rather spurned the comfort of his couch in the daytime, felt the need of exercise to warm his feet on the chill concrete floor. Many miles he paced up and down the avenues be-tween the bunks—a picturesque figure, with his blue stocking cap pulled down over his ears, a blanket pinned tightly about his shoulders, and on his hands a pair of large and fuzzy gloves.

As the day wore on, gloom settled upon some of the party, as they realized what anxiety might be felt for them by their families. This was the day that they were due to be at the Glen House at "5 P.M." and failure to be there to meet the automobile would at once cause all sorts of fears as to their safety. They knew, of course, that the home folks could not tell whether they had been overcome by the storm on the trail over the Northern Peaks, or whether they were still safe in the shelter of the hut. Nothing could be done about it, as the only means of communication with the outside world, a wireless telegraph outfit (which had, been in use for a short time at the opening of the hut) had been dismantled. To attempt to escape through the raging gale seemed but to invite certain death.

At times the gloom gave place to gaiety, when some lively little inci-dent or some humorous story enlivened the whole party. The hawk-eyed George, for instance, captured a mouse which he tossed to Mrs. Bob, thinking to frighten her. To his surprise, she proceeded to make a pet of it, and George was obliged to make some holes in a baking-powder tin to serve as a cage where Mr. Mouse could live in comfort with a supply of cheese to feast upon.

Monday passed with no change in the weather. Such bits of out of doors as could be seen within a few rods of the house were thick with snow and the beautiful frost-feathers. It was quite possible to run, for exercise, for a couple of minutes outside on the sheltered side of the house; but let one venture beyond the corners and the gale would knock him flat. Somehow George and the hardy Parker at times managed to crawl to the stream for water. On one occasion Parker started with a full pail but the wind sucked

COURTESY DAVE GOVATSKI

The interior of AMC's Lakes of the Clouds hut, circa 1915.

out the contents, except for enough to cover the bottom, giving him a drenching that required hugging the stove for some time.

The generous providers of the furnishings of the hut had been wise enough to equip the place with eighty-five blankets, and it was well that they did, for by Monday night they were all called into requisition. Some, of course, were placed as mattresses and some for pillows, while each person was covered with a mountain of them; but, in spite of the fact that all slept with their clothes on, no one was too warm. The searching wind made such unhindered progress through the hut as to make it necessary for most of the guests to sleep with a cap on or to cover their heads with a blanket.

On Tuesday morning Bob wakened with the recollection of a dream freshly in mind. In his vision he had seen the front page of the *Boston American* with the words "Peary Volunteers" in huge headlines. On reading further, it developed that the enterprising sheet had started a relief expedition led by the intrepid explorer; while, not to be out-done, two other national heroes, General Funston and Ex-President Roosevelt had wired that they were on the way. This dream served to create some amusement; so, that whenever an unusual noise was heart outside, someone was sure to shout "There's Peary!"

Tuesday was much like Monday, only the food supply was getting lower. At this juncture the Scientist recalled a box of food which was pressed upon him as he came up the Crawford Trail on Saturday by Dr. Blake of Boston and his party, who were on their way down. As luck would have it, it contained some sliced chicken, which the ladies fried. They also made a peculiar but edible kind of bread from some package flour. This was eaten with some spoonfuls of melted bacon fat left over from the cooking, and the second and last meal of the day was voted a success. The Veteran was unkind enough to smuggle some samples of this bread into his knapsack, which he later took home and exhibited as geological curiosities.

Throughout all this time, let it not be forgotten, the storm was raging in earnest; though the fact that the windows had held thus far gave assurance of safety, that enabled the prisoners to feel more calm. The continued roar of the wind, however, had a wearing effect on the nerves, and the worry over the anxiety of those left at home was ever present. Lack of exercise, in itself, is enough to upset the equanimity of most individuals, while a poor and scanty diet goes far toward keeping the circulation subnormal. At times the cold seemed to get into one's bones in a paralyzing fashion, so the party formed a ring and marched around, each slapping the shoulders of his neighbor in front until all were again thoroughly warm.

The bed-time hour was an interesting time for George, who certainly earned his salary in arranging the many blankets and tucking everybody in. In this he was quite expert, as he folded them in such fashion as to make a sleeping-bag effect and keep out the chill breezes to the best possible advantage. It was voted many times by the party that the camp was fortunate in having such a versatile and well qualified care-taker. In the first place, George was a native of the mountain country and familiar with it from boyhood. He had also had great experience in the woods, both as a lumberjack and as a licensed guide. These were only a few of his accomplishments, as he was a licensed chauffeur, a motorman, a carpenter and a blazer of trails, having done trail work for the Appalachian Club for several years. In addition he was a good cook—when he had the necessary raw materials to cook.

Monday and Tuesday were long days, but Wednesday stretched its length even further, as the shelves containing the supplies were now nearly empty, and uneasiness was rampant. Plans were discussed as to what might be done in case the wind abated; but it was finally agreed that no move would be made until the weather was such that all could go and the party be preserved as a unit. The ladies busied themselves in cutting the remnants of an old blanket into strips where-with to make puttees, for they knew the snow would be deep on the trail and no one was equipped for Arctic travel.

During the day when the wind lulled a bit, the ladies, who were anxious to see whether travel in the storm might be possible, sallied out a few rods from the house toward the Crawford Trail. In an instant they were lost in the thick scudding clouds. One of the others inside had an inspiration and seized a cow-bell, which was kept for the purpose of signalling. This he rang violently in the doorway, and in a few minutes the adventurous girls returned. They afterwards confessed that they were hopelessly lost, although only a stone's throw from the camp. Wednesday night at 11 o'clock the last night-owl had retired. The storm was still raging with no sign of abatement.

At 5:15 on Thursday morning the first slumberer to awaken gave a shout of joy, which caused every sleepy head to emerge from its cocoon. A miracle had happened. The wind had ceased. The sky was clear. Instantly everyone was out of bed in a rush to the door. The imperturbable Scientist for a moment forgot his calm demeanor and dashed out into the snow in his stocking feet. The chorus of "Oh's" and "Ah's," which arose as the magnificent scene began to be comprehended, might have been heard a mile away in the clear air.

In the eyes of some tears of joy could well be imagined. Perhaps they were even there. The heavens overhead were a fleckless dome, the valleys below showed a glorious green, save for here and there a dainty cloud of purple chiffon. Rising lofty and impressive above the Lakes of the Clouds the great cone of Washington appeared in spotless white, resembling a huge frosted cake made for the king of all the giants. On the weather side of the stone hut marvelous frost-feathers covered the walls in wonderful patterns to the depth of a foot or more, while every rock to which these could attach had its Indian head-dress of eagle plumes in perfect white. In many cases their wonderful formations stood out to a length of several feet. As the rising sun began to approach the horizon, a roseate glow crowned the summits of Lafayette and the more distant Adirondacks, while far to the north the mountains of Canada were easily discernible. With all this display of magnificence it was difficult for the overjoyed party to eat the necessary breakfast and make the preparations for the flight from their erstwhile prison.

At seven o'clock all were ready for the march. It was decided to go up the cone to Washington summit, thence down the carriage road to Glen House. George volunteered to pilot the party. It was well that he did, too; for, while one might go almost anywhere over the snow, it was almost impossible for one but slightly familiar with the trail to follow it closely, with all the landmarks in a similar disguise of feathers.

A notice was left on the door, giving the roster of the party and information as to where they had gone. This was read a couple hours later by the rescue party sent to find the Scientist, and they gave up their search — otherwise a party of twenty volunteers, which had been organized, would have been called upon to take affairs in hand. The climb to the summit was wonderful, affording as it did every instant some new and undiscovered glory. As the ocean, gleaming in gold at Portland, came into view, cheers were given to show the grateful feelings of the party, not only at being discharged from their dungeon, but in being liberated on a morning in ten thousand. Words fail to describe the happiness of that climb, and the descent on the other side of the summit. Though feet were cold in wading the drifts in canvas sneakers, as some of the party did, hearts were warm enough to make up for it.

Arrived at the summit, mirrors were flashed, to signal news of safety to anxious friends in Jackson. The response was amazing; not only from Jackson but from beyond and from either side answering flashes were noticed. It seemed as if all New Hampshire must be watching the fairy scene on that perfect morning.

The story of the thawing of chilly bare feet in a shovel of snow at the stage-office, the description of the view from the summit, the bidding good bye to George, the meeting of the rescue party near the Halfway House — all these things might be forgiven if one were writing a book; but this is just a little tale of what happened to people of humdrum lives, "even as you and I."

1990

Journal from the
Appalachian Trail

Buddy Newell

*In early April 1989, Hilton "Buddy" Newell (1934–) stepped foot on the Appa-
lachian Trail on Springer Mountain in Georgia and began walking north
toward Mount Katahdin in Maine. The retired Bethlehem, N.H. postmaster
spent the next five months on the trail, getting as far as Vermont before calling it
quits for the season. The following year, Newell walked the final several hundred
miles to the AT's northern terminus atop Baxter Peak on Katahdin. The AT
experience was an extraordinary one for Newell and his family, for a variety of
reasons. His decision to attempt the thru-hike was inspired by his son, Randy, an
avid hiker who had often talked of traversing the AT himself someday. Unfortunately, Randy was diagnosed with multiple sclerosis during his final high school
years and shortly after graduating was confined to a wheelchair. "That's when I
made the decision to attempt the thru-hike," says Buddy, "as a surrogate hiker for
my son." During the 1989 portion of his thru-hike, two of Newell's other family
members took an active role in the 2,100-mile journey. His youngest daughter,
Dianne, and his grand-daughter, Nicole, joined Buddy for various stretches of
trail walking. Each night they'd tape record their impressions of the day, and
then send the tapes back home to Randy whenever the trampers reached a post
office. Tragically, about a year after Newell finished the AT, his daughter, Dianne, was killed in a car accident. The following year, Randy also passed away
from complications associated with his MS. The following entry from Newell's
AT journal tells of the trials and tribulations of hiking across the rugged Mahoosuc Range in the northeastern White Mountains of New Hampshire and Maine.*

ARMED WITH A lot more know-how for the start of this trip, my son,
Scott, and a friend of his drove me to Gorham, N.H. to get back on the
trail. They would stay with me for a couple of days and then return. Feel-

ing the familiar tug on my shoulders of a full pack, the three of us started out on a long uphill climb out of the notch. Two hours later we were perched high on a ledge overlooking us 2 snaking its way through the valley far below. To our right, the smoke plumes from Berlin and its mills curled high into the sky.

Our destination for today was Trident Col tentsite only a couple of miles ahead, and us being in no hurry, we enjoyed a long lunch with many trail stories passing back and forth. The trail from the ledges in was very mellow with knee-high ferns and white birches abundant. The tentsite was worth the little side trip to it as it offered the first good water since leaving the highway.

Each of us carefully chose his own space for the tents, making sure to kick out rocks, roots, and other objects which tend to make for a long night. Completing this task we checked out the water source via a blue blaze [trail] and came upon a nice spring which easily satisfied our needs. A little nap by all of us came next, falling asleep to the familiar sounds of the woods. There is something about the sighing of the wind through pine branches that tells you all is well.

Awaking to a setting sun found us scrambling to fire up our "Whisper-Lite" stoves in preparation for the evening meal. Scott had brought along home baked beans to be shared among us for a real treat. My stove developed a fuel leak over the year of non-use, but its repair would have to wait due to the failing light. Washing dishes on the trail is not my favorite pastime, and getting back into this familiar chore again brought back many memories. An evening campfire and two hours of conversation ended our day, having gone only seven miles, but a very good day.

Waking to a clear cool morning, we had breakfast, repacked our gear, and filled our water bottles for the coming day. After three miles of moderate ups and downs we came to Dream Lake, and just beyond the Peabody Brook Trail, by which Scott and Bob would descend back to the car. A bit of loneliness came over me as I watched them round the corner and out of sight, leaving me alone with the 278 miles of trail in Maine lying ahead. But I also knew that you were only alone on the AT if you chose, so getting under my heavy pack, I started my trek.

Around two in the afternoon I passed Moss Pond and came to Gentian Shelter. It was built not far from Moss Pond, in fact, within sight of its north shoreline. With huge thunderheads forming in the west and my stove still to repair, I decided to stop for the day where I had a roof. Checking the shelter roof for the telltale stains of a leak, I picked out my spot on the floor for the night.

In checking out my stove, I found a worn gasket to be the problem and soon had it replaced with a spare one from my stove kit. This was the only time it required any attention at all in the entire seven months of its use. It was and still is a very reliable friend, having helped me through many a hard time.

Finding myself with four hours of daylight left, I turned on my radio and used my repaired stove to make a cup of hot soup. I then explored the huge rocks surrounding the pond's north end, and amused myself for a time by throwing rocks at a piece of wood floating by. Tiring of this, I returned to the shelter and upon reading its log discovered that its caretaker was a friend of mine. "Mr. Worcester" was a thru-hiker companion of ours for two months in the spring of 1989. Leaving a note for him I returned the book to its shelf as the first drops of rain struck the shelter roof.

Feeling very cozy and wise, I prepared a meal of macaroni and cheese, which was made even more enjoyable having avoided this downpour! After dinner I washed the dishes in the torrent of water coming off the roof and was getting things ready for the night when I saw a person approaching from the north, soaked to the skin. As he changed into dry clothes I heated a cup of soup to drive the chill out of him. The ensuing evening conversation between us ran through a variety of subjects, finally settling on airplanes, a common interest to both of us. I thought I could match him in my knowledge of various aircraft, etc., but after two hours of conversation I had covered everything I knew, stretching from the Wright brothers to our modern-day astronauts, while he was still pushing on with facts and figures. An "uh-huh" every ten minutes or so was sufficient on my part for the continuing data flow, so I fell asleep with here a plane, there a plane, everywhere a plane. Thank god he was southbound!

Morning found the trees and bushes now dripping, but the rain had stopped and shafts of sunlight appearing over a nearby mountain promised a nice day. Two days now on the trail had seen me go only 12 miles, so I tried for an early start and better mileage. Fortified with oatmeal, coffee, and english muffins, I bid good-bye to my just-now-waking friend and started out raking the overhanging bushes with my walking stick to knock off the waiting water drops. Some time around noon I reached the Maine-N.H. state line and stopped for lunch, thinking, I'm finally in my last state!

While sitting there, two people from Massachusetts came by and stopped to visit. After passing on the latest news and some ball scores, they continued on southbound while I began the climb up to Carlo Col. A mile later I was I was taking a break on top, looking into the endless wilderness of Maine. Directly to my front, two abrupt peaks caught my eye and upon checking my map, it showed them to be the east and north peaks of Goose Eye Mountain, over which I was soon to pass. The trail up and down these two mountains was very steep but my plodding gait had me atop North Peak at 3 P.M., then I headed straight down to Full Goose Shelter, my planned haven for the night. Upon nearing the shelter, though, the sound of many voices told me there was more than likely a "no vacancy" sign out. Sure enough, an Outward Bound group had totally filled the shelter, so I looked around and found a nice piece of flat ground not too far away and when about finished setting up my tent agreed to an invitation to dinner with the leaders of the group.

The meal, which they served, consisted of a pasta dish spiced up with many stories about Outward Bound dealing with methods, etc., for breaking the spirits of the wayward youngsters. One of the more interesting facts to me was that for the two years records are kept on these kids after a session, 80 percent stayed out of trouble. To my way of thinking, it's money well spent. The many groups that I encountered use this particular section of the AT as their classroom as it ranks second in difficulty only to a section of trail between the Smokies and the Nantahala Range down south, which I remember so well. After dinner I drifted off to sleep feeling good about the 9.5 miles I made today.

With what I'm sure will be one of my hardest days on the entire trail, I'm off to an early start, racing the sun to the top of Fulling Mill Mountain. The sun won! Oh well, second is not that bad, I thought to myself, as I gazed down into Mahoosuc Notch. Here, I would be passing along a stretch of trail with the reputation as the hardest mile on the entire AT. First I had to deal with an 850-foot vertical drop in just two-fifths of a mile to reach the start of the actual Notch. This makes for a very steep downhill walk. With aching knees I picked my way over, under, and through caves with ice floors, through stretches of blowdowns, and finally through ice fog rising from the caves. This went on for two hours before I finally emerged at the east end of Mahoosuc Notch. Several times I had to remove my pack to accommodate the narrow caves. It was one of the few times on the trail that I really felt any danger. It would be a simple matter to get seriously hurt due to the very heavy pack, which can cause a hiker to lose their balance easily. It's one thing to slide down a steep gravel path and quite another to tumble 20 feet or so into a rocky pit.

After a short lunch break I struggled up Mahoosuc Arm, climbing 1,500 vertical feet upwards in 1.5 miles. About halfway to the top I encountered a series of ledge outcroppings that took innovative measures to traverse. I also came upon a beautiful dinner plate-sized piece of mica, which was re-

Buddy Newell, his daughter, Dianne, and his granddaughter, Nikki,
take a break along the Appalachian Trail in August 1989.

luctantly added to my pack for my grandsons back home. Upon reaching
the top of Mahoosuc Arm, I gazed back over the country I had traveled
the past few days and could see nothing but jagged peaks and deep valleys,
plus Old Speck Mountain looming high above me ahead on the trail.

My map verified that today's destination, Speck Pond Shelter, was less
than a mile away. My ears also verified this as I could hear wood being split
every now and then when the wind was just so. Soon after starting down
off the summit I could see the blue water of Speck Pond far below me. The
trail wound around the east end of the pond and then followed the shoreline to the shelter. It was now late afternoon, the 5.1 miles between Full
Goose and Speck Pond having taken me all day to traverse!

The shelter log had not been collected for two years, so I anxiously read
the 1989 entries and found perhaps 10 of my friends who had made it this
far. I also found where a friend from home—Roger Doucette—had
signed in the previous fall. After paying my fee to the caretaker I took up
residence in the shelter and was soon joined by three other northbound
thru-hikers. They were in a hurry to get to Katahdin and had been skip-

ping various sections of the trail to meet time commitments. After getting caught up on all the trail news, we all called it a day, though one of the guys continued his day for a while longer, reading by candlelight, a popular shelter pastime.

A good early start, with the coming day just breaking. I had breakfast on the rocks beside the pond so as not to wake my sleeping friends. A not-too-bad mile or so of climbing found me just about at the summit of Old Speck when voices behind me told me my young-legged friends had already caught up to me. They continued on down the three-mile-long descent into Grafton Notch, while I stopped to smell the roses on the summit. Looking across the seven-mile wide space between Baldpate Mountain, my next opponent, and myself, I tried to devise some way of not having to go down and then up the 2,300 feet vertical fall and rise that followed. Of course going straight across [to Baldpate] would have been so much easier, and imagine the look I would have gotten from the younger hikers as they approached Baldpate's summit only to find me waiting there for them.

Down I went, then finally, traffic noises, and in another 20 minutes I was walking through a parking lot put there for hikers. A thru-hiker I had met a few days earlier was sitting on a rock beside the highway trying to get a ride into Bethel, Maine. He also told me he was on his way home to Michigan as he was quitting the trail. I talked with him for a long time, trying to change his mind, but to no avail. He dumped out his food bag on the ground and told me to take what I wanted. Another attempt on my part to change his attitude was met by the old story I had heard so many times before, "I'm tired of being hungry, lonely, wet, and just plain tired." Wishing him luck, I crossed the highway and took the side trail to Grafton Notch Lean-To, where I stopped for lunch. Still, I couldn't get this guy off my mind; he'd been hiking six months and had covered almost 2000 miles, and now he was giving up with the end in sight.

After finishing my lunch I filled my water bottles with the icy water from a nearby stream, then started out on my five-mile march to Fry Notch Lean-To. Another equally hard up and down followed, with me dragging into the empty shelter around 5 P.M. The nine miles I had gone today had really taken it out of me and I was thankful for the vacant shelter, so after a quick supper I turned in, falling asleep while it was still twilight, with the birds singing their farewell to the passing day.

Selected Bibliography

Among the Clouds. Mount Washington, N.H.

Appalachia. Journal of the Appalachian Mountain Club, Boston.

Beals, Charles Edward, Jr. *Passaconaway in the White Mountains.* Boston: Richard G. Badger, 1916.

Belknap, Jeremy. *The History of New Hampshire, Vol. III.* Boston, 1792.

Bliss, L. C. *Alpine Zone of the Presidential Range.* Edmonton, Canada, 1963.

Bolles, Frank. *At the North of Bearcamp Water: Chronicles of a Stroller in New England From July to December.* Boston: Houghton Mifflin Company, 1983.

Burt, F. Allen. *The Story of Mount Washington.* Hanover, N.H.: Dartmouth Publications, 1960.

Burt, Frank H. *Mount Washington: A Handbook for Travellers.* Boston, 1904.

Crawford, Lucy. *The History of the White Mountains, From the First Settlement of Upper Coos and Pequaket.* Portland, Maine: B. Thurston & Company, 1886.

Cross, George N. *Dolly Copp and the Pioneers of the Glen.* 1927.

Daniell, Eugene S., III, ed. *AMC White Mountain Guide.* 26th edition. Boston: Appalachian Mountain Club, 1998.

Drake, Samuel A. *The Heart of the White Mountains, Their Legend and Scenery.* New York: Harper and Brothers, 1881.

Eastman, Samuel C. *The White Mountain Guidebook.* Seventh edition. Boston: Lee and Shepard, 1867.

Gove, Bill. *J. E. Henry's Logging Railroads: The History of the East Branch & Lincoln and Zealand Valley Railroads.* Littleton, N.H.: Bondcliff Books, 1998.

Granite Monthly (The). Concord, N.H.

Henry, James E., II. *An Account of the Life of James Everell Henry I and His Town of Lincoln, N.H.* Clearwater, Florida, 1962.

Hitchcock, C. H., and Huntington, Joshua. *The Geology of New Hampshire.* Concord, N.H.: Vol. I, 1874.

Julyan, Robert and Mary. *Places Names of the White Mountains.* Revised Edition. Hanover, N.H.: University Press of New England, 1993.

Kidder, Glenn M. *Railway to the Moon.* Littleton, N.H., 1969.

Kilbourne, Frederick W. *Chronicles of the White Mountains.* Boston: Houghton Mifflin Company, 1916.

King, Thomas Starr. *The White Hills: Their Legends, Landscape and Poetry.* Boston: Crosby and Ainsworth, 1859.

Little, William. *The History of Warren: A Mountain Hamlet Located Among the White Hills of New Hampshire.* Manchester, N.H., 1870.

Littleton Courier (The), Littleton, N.H.

McAvoy, George E. *And Then There Was One*. Littleton, N.H.: The Crawford Press, 1988.

Mount Washington Observatory News Bulletin. North Conway, N.H.

Mountain Ear (The). Conway, N.H.

Mudge, John T. B. *The White Mountains: Names, Places & Legends*. Etna, N.H.: The Durand Press, 1992.

New Hampshire Profiles, Portsmouth. N.H.

Putnam, William Lowell. *The Worst Weather on Earth*. Gorham, N.H.: Mount Washington Observatory, 1991.

Ramsey, Floyd W. *Shrouded Memories: True Stories from the White Mountains of New Hampshire*. Littleton, N.H., 1994.

Randall, Peter E. *Mount Washington: A Guide and Short History*. Third Edition. Woodstock, Vt.: Countryman Press, 1992.

Smith, Steven D. *Ponds and Lakes of the White Mountains: A Four-Season Guide for Hikers and Anglers*. Second Edition. Woodstock, Vt.: Backcountry Publications, 1998.

Spaulding, John H. *Historical Relics of the White Mountains, Also a Concise White Mountain Guide*. Boston, 1855.

Sweetser, Moses F. *The White Mountains: A Handbook for Travellers*. Fourth edition. Boston: James R. Osgood and Company, 1881.

Sweetser, Moses F. *Chisholm's White Mountain Guide*. Portland, Maine: Chisholm Brothers, 1902 edition.

Tolles, Bryant F., Jr. *The Grand Resort Hotels of the White Mountains: A Vanishing Architectural Legacy*. Boston: David R. Godine, 1998.

Torrey, Bradford. *Nature's Invitation: Notes of a Bird-Gazer, North and South*. Boston: Houghton, Mifflin and Company, 1904.

Ward, Julius H. *The White Mountains: A Guide to Their Interpretation*. New York: D. Appleton and Co., 1890.

Waterman, Laura and Guy. *Forest and Crag: A History of Hiking, Trail Blazing and Adventure in the Northeast Mountains*. Boston: Appalachian Mountain Club, 1989.

White Mountain Echo and Tourist's Register. Bethlehem, N.H.

Willey, Benjamin G. *Incidents in White Mountain History*. Boston: Nathaniel Noyes, 1856.